SENECA
MEDEA

SENECA

MEDEA

EDITED WITH INTRODUCTION

AND COMMENTARY

BY

C. D. N. COSTA

Senior Lecturer in Classics
University of Birmingham

OXFORD

AT THE CLARENDON PRESS

1973

Oxford University Press, Ely House, London W. 1

GLASGOW NEW YORK TORONTO MELBOURNE WELLINGTON
CAPE TOWN IBADAN NAIROBI DAR ES SALAAM LUSAKA ADDIS ABABA
DELHI BOMBAY CALCUTTA MADRAS KARACHI LAHORE DACCA
KUALA LUMPUR SINGAPORE HONG KONG TOKYO

*Printed in Great Britain
at the University Press, Oxford
by Vivian Ridler
Printer to the University*

TO

MY WIFE

PREFACE

THERE is no detailed commentary in English on a Senecan tragedy, and this edition of the *Medea* is an attempt both to present a relatively unknown play for study by schools and universities, and to stimulate wider interest in an unusual by-way of Latin literature. Because Seneca's plays, and this one in particular, are important for later literature I hope that the commentary will be found useful by students of English and French drama, though it is naturally focused on those with classical interests. Besides looking back to Greece and forward to England and France, I have tried throughout to make clear the Roman rhetorical background which gave the plays much of their special flavour.

It is a pleasure to offer my thanks to the people who have helped me. Mr. D. A. Russell and Professor R. G. M. Nisbet encouraged the project from the start and read drafts of the commentary: had I taken more of their advice the book would have fewer faults. I am very grateful, too, to many of my Birmingham colleagues who have guided me through numerous difficulties; to the Librarian of the University of Göttingen, who sent me a microfilm of part of the Hoffa–Düring *Materialien*, and the Librarian of Trinity College, Cambridge, who kindly allowed me access to C. E. Stuart's unpublished notebooks; to the staff of the Clarendon Press, who made many helpful suggestions; and to Miss Catharine Goulder, who compiled the indexes.

C. D. N. C.

Birmingham
May, 1973

CONTENTS

ABBREVIATIONS   xi

INTRODUCTION   1

BIBLIOGRAPHY   16

SIGLA   19

MEDEA   21

COMMENTARY   61

INDEX NOMINUM   161

INDEX VERBORUM   164

INDEX RERUM   167

ABBREVIATIONS
FOR WORKS OF REFERENCE

Abbreviated references to periodicals follow in general the system of
L'Année philologique.

D–S	C. Daremberg–E. Saglio, *Dictionnaire des antiquités grecques et romaines d'après les textes et les monuments*, Paris, 1877–1919.
E–M	A. Ernout–A. Meillet, *Dictionnaire étymologique de la langue latine*[4], Paris, 1959.
K–S	R. Kühner–C. Stegmann, *Ausführliche Grammatik der lateinischen Sprache*[4], Munich, 1962.
L–H–S	M. Leumann–J. B. Hofmann–A. Szantyr, *Lateinische Grammatik*, Munich, 1963–5.
L–S	Lewis–Short, *A Latin Dictionary*, Oxford, 1879 (often reprinted).
L–S–J	Liddell–Scott–Jones, *A Greek–English Lexicon*[9], Oxford, 1940–68.
OCD	*Oxford Classical Dictionary*[2], Oxford, 1970.
OLD	*Oxford Latin Dictionary*, Oxford, 1968– .
O–P–C	W. A. Oldfather–A. S. Pease–H. V. Canter, *Index verborum quae in Senecae fabulis necnon in Octavia praetexta reperiuntur*, Urbana, 1918 (reprinted Hildesheim, 1964).
Quicherat	L. Quicherat, *Thesaurus poeticus linguae Latinae*, Paris, 1922 (reprinted Hildesheim, 1967).
RE	A. Pauly–G. Wissowa–W. Kroll, *Realenzyklopädie der klassischen Altertumswissenschaft*, Stuttgart, 1893– .
Roscher	W. H. Roscher, *Ausführliches Lexikon der griechischen und römischen Mythologie*, Leipzig, 1884–1937.
TLL	*Thesaurus linguae Latinae*, Leipzig, 1900– .

INTRODUCTION

1. *Life and Works*

THE life of Lucius Annaeus Seneca the younger is well documented, at least during his later years. He was born two or three years before the beginning of the Christian era at Corduba in southern Spain, and was taken to Rome in the care of an aunt, where he received the standard education of the day, with its rhetorical bias, and acquired a taste for philosophy. His family was a literary one: his father was a historian and the author of the surviving collections of rhetorical exercises, the *Suasoriae* and *Controversiae*, and the poet Lucan was his nephew. He married at least once, achieved a quaestorship and some fame as a public speaker, and presumably moved in high circles, for in 41 on a charge of adultery with the emperor Gaius' sister, Julia Livilla, he was banished to exile in Corsica. His recall in 49, engineered by Agrippina, and his subsequent appointment as Nero's tutor led directly to the great powers and greater dangers of high political office when Nero became emperor in 54. For some years, in collaboration with the praetorian prefect Burrus, Seneca as imperial counsellor and speech-writer maintained an increasingly uncertain control over Nero's vicious tendencies; but by 62, when Burrus died, Seneca had had enough, and with some difficulty persuaded Nero to let him retire from public life. He did not long enjoy his respite, for in 65 he was improbably accused of favouring the conspiracy of Piso and, in the fashion of the time, died by a dictated suicide.

There is much in Seneca's life and his connection with Nero's activities which is distasteful to us, and a standard charge against him is that in acquiring great wealth and insufficiently opposing Nero he notably failed to follow the moral precepts he constantly offered to others. The charge must in part be admitted, but it should also be allowed that he lived in appallingly difficult times, that he certainly attempted to set his face against brutality and corruption, and that when he failed to curb it probably no one suffered more anguish than himself.

As a thinker Seneca was the most notable exponent in writing of the modified Roman Stoicism fashionable in his day, with its main emphasis on ethical teaching. Stoic ideas to a greater or less extent inform most of his prose works—the ten so-called dialogues (which include three *consolationes*), the *De Beneficiis*, *De Clementia*, and the *Epistulae Morales*, addressed to Lucilius, which have had the most lasting subsequent influence. His scientific interests are shown in the *Naturales Quaestiones*, and the tally of extant prose writings is completed by the *Apocolocyntosis*, a satire on the deification of Claudius, an interesting work, not least for its 'Menippean' form of mingled prose and verse.

Apart from a corpus of epigrams attributed to Seneca, most of which are almost certainly spurious, his poetic output consists of nine tragedies, entitled *Hercules Furens*, *Troades*, *Phoenissae*, *Medea*, *Phaedra*, *Oedipus*, *Agamemnon*, *Thyestes*, *Hercules Oetaeus*.[1] The *Hercules Oetaeus* is probably only partly by Seneca; another tragedy, *Octavia*, attributed to him and the only surviving *fabula praetexta*, or historical play, is for metrical and other reasons generally agreed to be by another hand. The themes of the plays derive, as the titles suggest, more or less closely from the Greek tragedians, but their characteristic features are explicable only by reference to the literary and educational background of the period which gave them birth.

2. *Seneca and Latin Tragedy*

Seneca's plays are the only surviving complete Latin tragedies, but in the third and second centuries B.C. there was considerable activity in this field. Tragedies are known to have been written by Livius Andronicus and Naevius, followed by

[1] This is the order of the plays in E. In the A group of manuscripts the order is different, and the titles of the *Troades*, *Phoenissae*, and *Phaedra* are given as *Troas*, *Thebais*, and *Hippolytus*. The *Octavia* is in A but not E.

Ennius and Pacuvius, and above all by Accius (170–*c.* 85 B.C.). The titles and surviving fragments of these poets indicate that they derived their themes largely from the Greek tragedians; it is harder to say what modifications they made in the structure of fifth-century Greek tragedy, but it is at least probable that they retained the chorus.[2]

Accius was the last great tragic playwright in Rome, and in the closing years of the Republic and the early Empire the Muse inspired few new tragic poets. The theatre did not die, though it had increasingly to contend with different and more garish forms of entertainment: there were revivals of earlier plays, and some notable new ones—Pollio was famous for his tragedies, Varius, the friend of Horace and Virgil, wrote a *Thyestes* (29 B.C.), and Ovid a *Medea*, both of which received lavish praise.[3] But the nature of play-performances was changing as public taste altered, and by the Neronian period the production of complete plays, though not entirely abandoned, seems to have been largely replaced by the presentation of scenes or extracts, and the art of acting had become the more restricted art of giving a solo virtuoso recital. Thus, in Tacitus' *Dialogus* (dramatic date 74–5) Curiatius Maternus had recently been reciting (*recitaverat*) his tragedy *Cato*, and under Nero he had acquired fame *recitatione tragoediarum* (*Dial.* 2 and 11). It should be stressed that this is a controversial matter and the evidence is inconclusive, but some such picture of dramatic literature in the mid first century A.D. fits the known facts fairly well, and helps to explain some of the formal features of Seneca's tragedies.

In order to understand these plays we must also bear in mind one dominant feature in the educational system of the time, and that was the concentration on rhetorical studies, on learning the art of declaiming. Schools of rhetoric had at least from the time of Cicero's youth begun to form the recognized third stage of a Roman boy's education, following his studies

---

[2] On this difficult point see H. D. Jocelyn, *The Tragedies of Ennius*, Cambridge, 1967, 18 ff., 30 ff.
[3] Tacitus, *Dialogus* 12, Quintilian x. 1. 98.

under a *litterator* and then a *grammaticus*; but by the early Empire this training under a *rhetor* had acquired a greatly increased complexity and importance, and its effect on literature was becoming much more strongly marked. We know a great deal about the teaching at these schools largely through Seneca's own father, whose interest in the subject led him to make the collections of *suasoriae* and *controversiae* which give us a clear idea of the nature of these exercises, the staple diet of the students of rhetoric. Briefly, *suasoriae* were speeches composed to be spoken in the person of historical characters debating with themselves how to deal with some great crisis in their lives; *controversiae* were speeches for both sides of a debate on some invented topic involving a legal or moral issue. The problem to be debated was often of an extraordinarily far-fetched, intricate, and contrived nature, which thus put to an extreme test the wit and verbal resource of the student: interest and merit lay not so much in deciding on the moral or legal rights of the case as in the linguistic inventiveness and subtlety displayed in marshalling one's own arguments or capping those of one's opponent. This fostered a taste for the clever use of language for its own sake, and it is easy to see that the literature as well as the oratory of the first century A.D. was deeply affected by the techniques of declamatory rhetoric. To some extent, of course, rhetoric had been endemic in Latin literature from its early days, but the 'Silver Age' of Latin prose and poetry shows in a greatly increased degree a love of rhetorical techniques: epigram, contrived balance and antithesis, striking verbal effects of all kinds, and above all the *sententia*—a pithy thought pithily expressed. Writers naturally varied in the extent to which they showed these characteristics, but Lucan may be taken as an extreme example in verse, and Seneca himself on almost any page of his treatises and letters illustrates the fashionable tricks in prose. It is likely that he inherited his father's particular interest as well as being a child of his age, and when he turned to writing tragedies it was inevitable that they should exemplify the popular literary tendencies.

The first essential for the appreciation of these tragedies is to come to terms with the rhetoric that informs them through and through. They illustrate all the declamatory elements outlined above, in particular the use of epigram and the *sententia*, and because of the static nature of their plots, their unsubtle characterization, their profusion of set-piece speeches, and their preoccupation with horror and blood, they have long since lost the wide appeal they once enjoyed (see below, section 4). Seneca followed the structure as well as the themes of Greek tragedy, using a chorus to divide episodes of dialogue or monologue, retaining stock figures like the nurse and the messenger, and using the iambic trimeter (as in Greek) as the standard metre for dialogue and a variety of lyric metres for the choruses. The old debate on whether the plays were acted or recited need raise little dust nowadays: in view of the known conditions of drama in the Neronian age discussed above and certain characteristics of the plays themselves, it is generally agreed that anything like a full-scale production is most unlikely, though of course the individual declaimer or actor in reciting the play, or extract from it, would have introduced whatever histrionic effects he liked of movement and gesticulation to enliven his own performance. Without analysing the controversy in detail, it is worth stressing that the old argument against staging of the plays, based on the grounds of the violence and bloodshed which would have been visible, will cut no ice with anyone who considers some of the effusions which were successfully performed on the Elizabethan stage,[4] and who recollects what the Romans were used to seeing in the arena. Rather we should note the basic lack of dramatic continuity in the action of some of the plays, the overriding importance of the individual scene, and some internal features, like the frequent uncertainty about the entrances and exits of characters, and the detailed circumstantial

---

[4] So the fact that Seneca ignores Horace's precept 'ne pueros coram populo Medea trucidet', *A.P.* 185, is not an argument against production, but if Seneca was in any case not writing for the stage he would not feel himself bound by the Greek convention of excluding violence from the visible stage.

descriptions by characters of events or activities on the stage
which would be visible to the audience of an acted play
(see note on 382 ff.). These points taken individually are not
conclusive, but they combine to banish almost all doubts on
the question.

It is more interesting to speculate on Seneca's reasons for
exploring this curious literary form, though the answer is not
easier to find. It has been suggested that Seneca was using
the dramatic form as a vehicle for Stoic moral teaching
similar to that of the prose works.[5] But while we certainly find
Stoic sentiments in profusion throughout the tragedies—and
Stoic resignation can appear a consoling and edifying reaction
to the blows of fate and overpowering moral dilemmas in
which they abound—it is arbitrary to force a system of teaching on the plays as a whole, and not everyone will agree that
Stoic lessons are to be derived from the treatments of individual plots. We should probably settle for a less august motive,
and, bearing in mind Seneca's preoccupation with language
and with the potential range of the declamatory style, consider
the possibility that he simply wanted to present the old tales
in a new dramatic form. From the schools he may have
derived the idea of the characters of legend, and human beings
generally, as type-figures—the tyrant, the loyal son, the
suffering wife, and so on—and by exaggerating characteristics
and polarizing contrasts he could both simplify and intensify
his picture of struggling, passionate humanity. His framework
was Greek legend, and his tools were mainly language and
the clash of arguments, whether between different characters
or in a self-debating monologue. At his worst he is extraordinarily turgid and bombastic; at his best he can show quite
movingly the pathos and futility of human suffering. He has
not on the whole a lyric bent, but occasionally there are
passages of great beauty, like the lovely *aubade* in the first
chorus of the *Hercules Furens*. For those who want a short-list
of the better plays it might be said that the *Troades, Medea,* and

[5] See articles by B. M. Marti in *TAPA* 76 (1945), 216 ff. and *REL* 27 (1949),
189 ff.

Phaedra have on the whole less of the Senecan extravagance, and are the most palatable to modern taste.

The plays are undatable, in spite of efforts based on various criteria to locate them at some point in his career.[6] Speculation is unprofitable, but one can bear in mind the years of exile, 41–9, when time hung heavy, and an experiment in literary drama might have satisfied a craving for mental stimulation.

3. *The* Medea *legend and Seneca's treatment of it*

The passion and violence associated with the story of Medea made it an obvious choice for the kind of dramatic treatment Seneca was attempting. The witch-princess, whose love and whose hatred equally drove her to appalling deeds, had a wide appeal, and the story was immensely popular with writers, dramatic and otherwise, before and after Seneca. It appears early, in Hesiod, *Theogony* 992 ff. and Pindar, *Pythian* iv, an extensive treatment of the Argonautic expedition. About six Greek and about six Latin *Medea* plays are known, but only fragments survive apart from Euripides' (431 B.C.) and Seneca's plays. The Latin playwrights include Ennius, Accius (a fair number of fragments each), and Ovid (two lines only). Ovid also treated the legend at length in his *Metamorphoses* vii. 1–424, and in the twelfth of the *Heroides*, an imagined letter to Jason from the deserted Medea. The only other version of much interest to the study of Seneca's play is the epic *Argonautica* of Apollonius Rhodius (third century B.C.), particularly the third and fourth books, where Medea plays a part in the story.[7]

One of the most familiar phases of the legend concerns the period when Medea and Jason were in exile at Corinth,

---

[6] See, for example, O. Herzog in *Rh. Mus.* 77 (1928), 51 ff., and M. Coffey's critique in *Lustrum* 2 (1957), 150.

[7] Other accounts of Medea include Apollodorus, i. 9. 23 ff.; Diodorus Siculus, iv. 46 ff.; Hyginus, *fabulae* 22–7; Valerius Flaccus, *Argonautica* vi et seq.; a tragedy *Medea* in the form of a Virgilian cento, possibly by Hosidius Geta (c. 200 A.D.), which survives in the Latin Anthology (Baehrens, *PLM* iv. 219 ff.); a hexameter poem *Medea* by Dracontius (fifth century A.D.; Baehrens, *PLM* v. 192 ff.).

and it is here that the action takes place in the plays of
Euripides and Seneca. After assisting Jason to obtain the
Golden Fleece at Colchis, Medea eloped with him and
accompanied him back to his native Iolcus; she there engineered the death of Jason's uncle Pelias, they were forced
to flee, and they took refuge with Creon in Corinth. Jason
here abandoned Medea for the king's daughter, and Medea
in revenge destroyed her and killed her own and Jason's
children.

So far as we can judge, Seneca's chief model was Euripides'
play, but he made substantial structural alterations, such as
eliminating the Aegeus scene and reducing the Jason/Medea
scenes, enlarging the nurse's role, and reversing the sympathies
of the chorus. (The more significant links with, and divergences
from, Euripides are noted in the commentary.) Of other
possible models Ovid's lost *Medea* has been a favourite source
of speculation. In his edition of the tragedies Leo (Vol. I,
163 ff.) pointed out that Seneca's Medea displays a high degree
of frenzy throughout the play compared with Euripides'
portrayal of her, and, arguing from Ovid's treatment of her
character in *Heroides* xii and from the two surviving lines of
his *Medea*, he suggested that this play was a major influence
on Seneca. Seneca must certainly have read Ovid's play, just
as he certainly knew *Metamorphoses* vii and *Heroides* xii, but
Ovid's habit of self-quotation and the evidence of two fragments cannot lead us to the firm conclusion that the Medea
of his surviving poems and the Medea of his lost play were
identical creations. No doubt Seneca's heroine is in many ways
unlike Euripides', and it is likely that Ovid's Medea was
nearer to Seneca's, but more than that we cannot safely say
(see note on 123). One other source should be stressed: Seneca
was evidently familiar with Apollonius Rhodius' *Argonautica*
(justly famous for its account of the birth of Medea's love for
Jason in the third book), as the commentary tries to indicate
where the links seem clear.

But discussion of sources must not obscure the fact that
Seneca's play is an original creation. The difficulty is to discuss

it as 'drama', for, as suggested above, it is only in a modified sense dramatic. Medea is a woman who has done much wrong and loved not wisely; but she has a claim to sympathy, and a case, and the play is fundamentally an exploration of this case, as it is put to the nurse, Creon, Jason, and above all to herself. This is what interests Seneca. In the course of the play her character does not 'develop' (this is probably true of most of Seneca's protagonists): she simply loses hope and becomes increasingly deranged, and, in the end, because of her extraordinary powers she destroys and ruins others as she has herself been ruined. The other characters are in effect foils to her passionate dialectic: she dominates the play totally. In addition Seneca has thrown in a long and brilliant incantation scene, and some quite pleasing choruses, which compare favourably with those of his other plays in variety of metre and theme. The play is of considerable interest, but it depends for its enjoyment on a suspension of the usual preconceptions with which we approach the reading of drama.

Since antiquity Medea and her troubles have continued to interest playwrights, and some of the subsequent versions derive, often quite closely, from Seneca. The following are worth mentioning: in England, Richard Glover's *Medea* (1761), of little interest except to students of the legend; in France, Corneille's *Médée* (1635: his first tragedy) and Longepierre's *Médée* (1694), both strongly indebted to Seneca; the Austrian poet Grillparzer wrote a *Medea* (1820), a powerful and effective play, as the third part of his trilogy *Das goldene Vlies*; and in our own day Anouilh's *Médée* (1946) is a testimony to the continued influence of Seneca, whose lines Anouilh virtually translates in several parts of the play.[8]

Traces of Seneca's *Medea* can also be found in later plays not on the same theme, e.g. Gregorio Corraro's *Progne* (in Latin: written *c.* 1429, printed 1558), and Fulke Greville's *Alaham* (*c.* 1600).[9]

---

[8] See J. C. Lapp in *Modern Language Notes* 69 (1954), 183 ff.
[9] For this play see *Poems and Dramas of Fulke Greville* Vol. II, ed. G. Bullough, Edinburgh, 1938.

Finally, one non-dramatic account of the legend worth mentioning is William Morris's *The Life and Death of Jason* (1867), a long poem, heavily overlaid with medieval trappings, but retaining still a kind of period charm.

In art too Medea was a favourite subject for representation in antiquity.[10] Numerous vases survive depicting scenes from her saga, and of the many known paintings the most celebrated was by Timomachus of Byzantium, who sold it to Julius Caesar for a handsome sum.[11]

Since antiquity, too, painters have continued to be fascinated by the legend, and there have been several operas, notably the *Médée* of Cherubini (1797). Few tragic figures have inspired artistic endeavour in so many fields.

4. *The influence of Seneca's tragedies*

The astonishing impact of the tragedies on later drama, especially French and English, is widely recognized and well documented, though the wrong emphasis has sometimes been placed on the elements of these works supposed to have most affected later writers. But enthusiastic acceptance was long in coming, and in the later first and the second centuries there was much criticism of Seneca's style—his prose style certainly, but many of the strictures would apply to his verse. Quintilian, who preached the gospel of Ciceronianism in style, condemns Seneca in measured and judicious terms (x. 1. 125 ff.). It is noteworthy too that Quintilian does not include Seneca in his list of Latin tragedians, though he quotes from the *Medea* as Seneca's (see note on 453), and refers to a discussion on tragic diction between Seneca and Pomponius Secundus (viii. 3. 31). Fronto, in a letter to his friend and former pupil Marcus Aurelius, and Aulus Gellius also speak slightingly of Seneca, not unnaturally in view of their archaizing literary practice.[12]

---

[10] See the excellent discussion on Medea in art in D. L. Page's edition of Euripides' *Medea*, lvii ff.

[11] There are several references to this famous painting: Pliny, *HN* xxxv. 136, 145, Plutarch, *Mor.* 18 a, *Anth. Pal.* xvi. 135, 136, 138, 139.

[12] Fronto in Loeb edn. ii. 102; Aulus Gellius xii. 2.

It should be noted that these three critics all concede that there is worthy ethical content to be found in Seneca.

By the end of the thirteenth century the tragedies were taking a first step towards fame through the activities of a group of Paduan humanists. Lovato Lovati wrote a brief note on Senecan metre, apparently based on a careful reading of the plays. The florilegist Geremia da Montagnone in compiling his *Compendium moralium notabilium* quoted extensively from them. Finally, in 1315 Mussato took the logical next step and wrote a successful Senecan tragedy in Latin, *Ecerinis*. At just this time, too, in England the Dominican Nicholas Trevet wrote his commentary on Seneca's tragedies, which has survived.[13] By the end of the fifteenth century the tragedies were in print, and in the course of the sixteenth they helped to change the nature of tragedy in France and England.

Full details cannot here be rehearsed, and the story is a familiar one.[14] In France the effect of Seneca was strong on Garnier's tragedies (1563–90), and Garnier influenced others. In England, starting with the schools and universities, with the writing of Latin imitations and the production of Latin plays, the Senecan model became all-pervasive. Important landmarks were: 1562, Norton and Sackville's *Gorboduc* produced, in a sense the prototype of the English Senecan play; 1581, Seneca's *Tenne Tragedies* (by various translators) collected and published by Thomas Newton (the *Medea* was done by John Studley in 1566); *c.* 1590, Kyd's *Spanish Tragedy* appeared, immensely successful and an important advance in the structure of English tragedies. Finally, the genius of Shakespeare which now appeared was also receptive to the Senecan manner, whether directly or through his own predecessors, and, more especially in some early plays (e.g. *Titus, Richard III*), he gave a kind of vicarious immortality to Seneca's achievement in tragedy.

[13] Trevet's commentary, which is largely a paraphrase, is of virtually no use to a modern editor: see E. Courtney in *CR* xi (1961), 166.

[14] See, for example, the useful account in F. L. Lucas, *Seneca and Elizabethan Tragedy*, Cambridge, 1922.

But critics have sometimes stressed the wrong elements in
Elizabethan tragedy as derivative from Seneca, and the crudest
excesses of the 'revenge' tragedy—the horrors of murders,
mutilations, ghosts, and so forth—are usually laid at his door.
Certainly the example of Seneca would not discourage these
features, but they are evident too in earlier vernacular drama,
which thus prepared fruitful ground for the arrival of the
Senecan seed.[15] The more important legacy of Seneca to
early English tragedy was the declamatory style, to which
the Elizabethan dramatists were particularly receptive—the
profusion of *sententiae*, epigram, and word-play, the use of
stichomythia (dialogue in alternating lines), the set speech
and the soul-searching monologue.[16] His influence is possible
too in some formal elements, e.g. the five-act structure (a
controversial point) and the use of a chorus. Some idea of
the impact of the Senecan style on Shakespeare can be gained
by a study of (to choose at random) *Richard III*, IV. iv, where the
rhetoric of Queen Margaret's speeches beginning 'If ancient
sorrow be most reverend', and the stichomythia in the exchanges between Elizabeth and Richard, starting at 'Infer fair
England's peace by this alliance', show the real debt to Seneca
of the Elizabethans.[17]

The attitude of the sixteenth century, then, can be represented by Giraldi Cinthio, who in his *Discorsi* on tragedy
(1543) praised Seneca above the Greeks (a view shared by
J. C. Scaliger). The seventeenth century continued to admire
him, and Dryden (himself, like Giraldi, a tragedian) can be
its spokesman in his *Essay of Dramatick Poesie* (1668), in which
he refers appreciatively to Seneca.[18] This century in England

[15] For arguments against over-stressing the Senecan influence see G. K.
Hunter in *Shakespeare Survey* 20 (1967), 17 ff.

[16] The delight of the Elizabethans in Senecan *sententiae* can be seen in Sir
William Cornwallis's *Discourses upon Seneca the Tragedian* (1601), the first
English book devoted entirely to Seneca, which consists of meditative com-
mentaries on eleven *sententiae* from the plays, and suggests that interest lay in
these rather than the plays as a whole.

[17] See T. S. Eliot's brilliant essay 'Seneca in Elizabethan Translation' (noted
in Bibliography).

[18] Amongst other comments Dryden praises the 'gravity and sententious-

showed no significant developments in Senecan influence, but in France the classical theatre reached its peak with Corneille and Racine, and to a large extent it was a Senecan peak. The debt here is clear and uncontroversial, and the commentary will refer to the more interesting links between the Medea plays of Seneca and Corneille.

By the eighteenth century, if the tragedies were looked at by critics, it was with a cooler eye. Thus Lessing in his *Laokoön* (1766) referred to the characters in Seneca's tragedies as 'prize-fighters in the cothurnus',[19] and expressed a low opinion of Roman tragedy.

The plays have never recovered their former reputation, and the epithets 'Senecan' and 'rhetorical' applied to literature are nowadays usually terms of abuse. No doubt the plays do not deserve the high praise they once received, but they do deserve to be understood, and when understood they can be enjoyed. They are a by-product of a most important phase in Roman education and literature, and they are a unique survival.

5. *Text and Manuscripts*

The manuscript tradition of the tragedies is divided into two branches. One is represented almost solely by E, the so-called 'Etruscus', of about the end of the eleventh century. The other is known as A, or the 'interpolated' tradition, of which there exist over three hundred manuscripts, the purest and most reliable being C, P (both first half of the thirteenth century), and S (fourteenth century). The two branches probably diverged before the end of the fourth century. The supreme authority once assigned by Leo to E has long since been demolished, and the tendency now is towards giving the A

'ness' of the *Medea*—though he thought it was ascribed to Ovid (Everyman edn., p. 41).

[19] *Laokoön* iv. 3: 'Klopffechter im Kothurne'. Lessing's point was that gladiatorial deaths in the arena, where a display of human nature and feeling was eschewed, affected Senecan tragedy, which under the influence of such 'artistic' death scenes descended to bombast.

tradition an equal hearing in difficult cruces. This change in attitude is the result of work on the manuscripts which started in the early years of this century with C. E. Stuart, W. Hoffa, and T. Düring, and has been continued by, among others, G. Carlsson, R. H. Philp, and G. C. Giardina. (See Bibliography for references. Philp's article (1968) is a valuable survey of the tradition and different scholars' approaches to it; Giardina's edition (1966) has the most reliable apparatus to date.) As a result of this work knowledge of the manuscripts has greatly advanced, and for the purposes of this edition I have not attempted a fresh recension. The apparatus offered is a select one, in which, it should be noted, the symbol A is abandoned as unspecific and misleading. The text of the *Medea* does not present many insoluble problems, and in general I have recorded only the more interesting or important variants and conjectures.

6. *Metre*

Dialogue. The metre of Senecan dialogue, as in the Greek tragedians, is regularly the iambic trimeter, a six-foot (or three-metra) line based on the iambus ∪ –. Several equivalents are allowed for the iambus, and the full scheme of the trimeter is as follows, the bracketed feet being rarely found:

1	2	3	4	5	6
∪ –	∪ –	∪ –	∪ –	(∪ –)	∪ ∪̲
– –		– –		– –	
∪ ∪ ∪	∪ ∪ ∪	∪ ∪ ∪	∪ ∪ ∪		
– ∪ ∪		– ∪ ∪		(– ∪ ∪)	
∪ ∪ –		(∪ ∪ –)		∪ ∪ –	
(∪ ∪ ∪ ∪)					

The trochaic tetrameter catalectic, a 7½-foot line based on the trochee – ∪, and also allowing equivalents for the trochee (spondee – –, anapaest ∪ ∪ –, tribrach ∪ ∪ ∪, dactyl – ∪ ∪), introduces the incantation:

cōmprĕcōr vūlgūs sĭlēntūm vōsquĕ fĕrālēs dĕōs   740

grăvĭŏr ūnī poenā sĕdĕāt cōnĭŭgĭs sŏcĕrō mĕī   746

Lyric. The lyric metres found in the choruses and incantation are:

anapaestic: ◡◡– allowing as equivalents the spondee ––
and dactyl –◡◡, but avoiding a run of four short syllables:

> aūdāx nĭmĭūm quī frĕtă prīmūs
> rătĕ tām frăgĭlī pērfĭdă rūpīt   301–2

glyconic: –––◡◡–◡–

> vīncĭt vīrgĭnĕūs dĕcōr   75

minor asclepiad: –––◡◡– –◡◡–◡◡

> ād rēgūm thălămōs nūmĭnĕ prōspĕrō   56

sapphic: the usual sapphic stanza is three hendecasyllables of the form –◡–– –◡◡– ◡– ◡ followed by the adonius –◡◡– ◡ (but see introductory note on 579 ff.):

> nūllă vīs flāmmāē tŭmĭdīvĕ vēntī
> tāntă, nēc tēlī mĕtŭēndă tōrtī,
> quāntă cūm cōniūnx vĭdŭātă tāēdīs
> ārdĕt ĕt ōdĭt.   579–82

Points of special interest or difficulty are discussed in the commentary.

BIBLIOGRAPHY

THE literature on Seneca's tragedies is enormous and I have merely tried to offer a realistic selection of the more useful works. More extensive lists may be found in Schanz–Hosius, *Geschichte der römischen Literatur* ii⁴, 1935, 456 ff.; Coffey, *Lustrum* 2 (1957), 113 ff.; Mette, *Lustrum* 9 (1964), 18 ff., 160 ff. Particularly important works are marked with an asterisk.

Editions of all the tragedies

(L) indicates a Latin commentary

Tragedies first printed by Andreas Gallicus at Ferrara, *c.* 1484.

*H. AVANTIUS, Venice, 1517.

J. LIPSIUS and H. COMMELINUS, Heidelberg, 1588–9 (L).

Jos. SCALIGER and D. HEINSIUS, Leiden, 1611 (L).

T. FARNABY, Leiden, 1623 (L).

*J. F. GRONOVIUS, Leiden, 1661 (L).

*J. C. SCHROEDER, Delft, 1728 (L, Variorum).

F. H. BOTHE, Leipzig, 1819 (L).

W. A. SWOBODA, Vienna, 1825–30 (German notes).

*F. LEO, Berlin, 1878–9.

*R. PEIPER and G. RICHTER, Leipzig (Teubner), 1902.

H. MORICCA, Turin (Paravia), 1917–23.

L. HERRMANN, Paris (Budé), 1924–6.

T. THOMANN, Zürich, 1961–9.

*G. C. GIARDINA, Bologna, 1966.

Commentaries on Medea

C. BECK, *Medea, Tragedy of Seneca*, Cambridge and Boston, 1834.

H. M. KINGERY, *Three Tragedies of Seneca* (*HF Tro Med*), New York, 1908.

Translations into English

J. STUDLEY, *Medea*, 1566 (published in the collected *Tenne Tragedies*, edited by Thomas Newton, 1581).

Sir E. Sherburne, *Medea*, 1648.

F. J. Miller, London, 1917 (Loeb Classical Library—all the plays).

E. F. Watling, *Seneca, Four Tragedies and Octavia* (Thy, Phae, Tro, Oed, Oct), Harmondsworth, 1966.

Influence

L. E. Kastner and H. B. Charlton, *The Poetical Works of Sir William Alexander*, London and Edinburgh, 1921, Vol. I: Introduction.

*F. L. Lucas, *Seneca and Elizabethan Tragedy*, Cambridge, 1922.

*T. S. Eliot, Introduction to the Tudor Translations edition of *Seneca His Tenne Tragedies*, 1927, reprinted as 'Seneca in Elizabethan Translation' in *Selected Essays*, London, 1948.

E. F. Watling, Introduction to his Penguin translation (above).

Manuscripts and text transmission

G. Richter, *Kritische Untersuchungen zu Senecas Tragödien*, Jena, 1899.

T. Düring, 'Die Überlieferung des interpolierten Textes von Senecas Tragödien', *Hermes* xlii (1907), 113 ff., 579 ff.

—— 'Zur Überlieferung von Senecas Tragödien', *Hermes* xlvii (1912), 183 ff.

W. Hoffa, 'Textkritische Untersuchungen zu Senecas Tragödien', *Hermes* xlix (1914), 464 ff.

C. E. Stuart, 'The MSS. of the interpolated (A) tradition of the tragedies of Seneca', *CQ* vi (1912), 1 ff.

*G. Carlsson, *Die Überlieferung der Seneca-Tragödien*, Lunds Universitets Årsskrift NF 1, 21, Nr. 5, 1925.

*—— *Zu Senecas Tragödien*, Bull. de la Société Royale des Lettres de Lund 1928–9, 39–72.

*R. H. Philp, 'The Manuscript Tradition of Seneca's Tragedies', *CQ* xviii (1968), 150 ff.

General

K. Anliker, *Prologe und Akteinteilung in Senecas Tragödien*, Bern, 1959.

B. Axelson, *Korruptelenkult. Studien zur Textkritik der unechten Seneca-Tragödie H.O.*, Lund, 1967.

*W. Beare, *The Roman Stage*[3], London, 1964.

M. Bieber, *The History of the Greek and Roman Theater*[2], Princeton, 1961.

⋆S. F. Bonner, *Roman Declamation*, Liverpool, 1949.

Mary V. Bragington, *The Supernatural in Seneca's Tragedies*, Wisconsin, 1933.

H. V. Canter, *Rhetorical Elements in the Tragedies of Seneca*, Univ. of Illinois Stud. in Lang. and Lit. 10, 1, 1925.

A. Cattin, *Les Thèmes lyriques dans les tragédies de Sénèque*, Fribourg, 1963.

H. L. Cleasby, 'The *Medea* of Seneca', *HSCP* xviii (1907), 39 ff.

⋆W.-H. Friedrich, *Untersuchungen zu Senecas dramatischer Technik*, Diss. Freiburg 1931, Leipzig, 1933.

A. Hempelmann, 'Senecas Medea als eigenständiges Kunstwerk', Diss. Kiel, 1960.

C. J. Herington, 'Senecan Tragedy', *Arion* 5 (1966) 422 ff.

L. Herrmann, *Le Théâtre de Sénèque*, Paris, 1924.

O. Herzog, 'Datierung der Tragödien des Seneca', *Rh. Mus.* 77 (1928), 51 ff.

H. D. Jocelyn, *The Tragedies of Ennius*, Cambridge, 1967.

⋆F. Leo, 'Die Composition der Chorlieder Senecas', *Rh. Mus.* 52 (1897), 509 ff.

J. E. Lowe, *Magic in Greek and Latin Literature*, Oxford, 1929.

B. M. Marti, 'Seneca's tragedies, a new interpretation', *TAPA* 76 (1945), 216 ff. (Criticized by N. T. Pratt, *TAPA* 79 (1948), 1 ff.)

M. Pohlenz, *Die Stoa*, Göttingen, 1948–9.

D. S. Raven, *Latin Metre*, London, 1965.

⋆O. Regenbogen, *Schmerz und Tod in den Tragödien Senecas*, Vortr. Bibl., Warburg, 1927–8, Leipzig–Berlin, 1930.

I. Spika, 'De imitatione Horatiana in Senecae canticis choris', *Jahresb.* 1889–90, Staatsgymn. Wien II, Vienna 1890, 3 ff.

⋆L. Strzelecki, *De Senecae trimetro iambico quaestiones selectae*, Cracow, 1938.

E. Tavenner, *Studies in Magic from Latin Literature*, New York, 1916.

T. Vente, 'Die Medea-Tragoedie Senecas: Eine Quellenstudie', *Beil. Jahresb. Bischoefl. Gymn. Strassburg* Progr. Nr. 713, 1909.

⋆O. Zwierlein, *Die Rezitationsdramen Senecas*, Meisenheim, 1966.

SIGLA

E   Laurentianus 37.13 ('Etruscus'), saec. XI
O   Oratorianus (Neapolis, Bibl. Gerolaminorum) CF. 4.5, saec. XIV
C   Cantabrigiensis Corpus Christi Coll. 406, saec. XIII
P   Parisinus Lat. 8260, saec. XIII
S   Escorialensis T. III 11, saec. XIV
R   Ambrosianus G. 82 sup., saec. V
l   Laurentianus 24 sin. 4, 1371
n   Neapolitanus Bibl. Nat. IV. D. 47, 1376
r   Vaticanus Reginensis 1500, 1389
d   Neapolitanus Bibl. Nat. IV. E. 1, saec. XIV
K   Cameracensis 555, saec. XIII–XIV
Q   Casinensis 392P, saec. XIV
G   Exoniensis Cath. Libr. 3549 (B), saec. XIII
e   Etonensis Bl. 2.9 (110), saec. XIII–XIV
L   Leidensis 191B, saec. XIII–XIV
B   Brussellensis 4791, saec. XII–XIII
τ   commentarius Nicolai Trevet, 1315–16
ϛ   codices recentiores
codd. consensus omnium codicum

DRAMATIS PERSONAE

MEDEA

NUTRIX

CREO

IASON

NUNTIUS

CHORUS

MEDEA

MEDEA

Di coniugales tuque genialis tori,
Lucina, custos quaeque domituram freta
Tiphyn novam frenare docuisti ratem,
et tu, profundi saeve dominator maris,
clarumque Titan dividens orbi diem,   5
tacitisque praebens conscium sacris iubar
Hecate triformis, quosque iuravit mihi
deos Iason, quosque Medeae magis
fas est precari: noctis aeternae chaos,
aversa superis regna manesque impios   10
dominumque regni tristis et dominam fide
meliore raptam, voce non fausta precor.
nunc, nunc adeste, sceleris ultrices deae,
crinem solutis squalidae serpentibus,
atram cruentis manibus amplexae facem,   15
adeste, thalamis horridae quondam meis
quales stetistis: coniugi letum novae
letumque socero et regiae stirpi date.
mihi peius aliquid, quod precer sponso malum:
vivat. per urbes erret ignotas egens   20
exul pavens invisus incerti laris,
iam notus hospes limen alienum expetat;
me coniugem optet, quoque non aliud queam
peius precari, liberos similes patri
similesque matri—parta iam, parta ultio est: 25
peperi. querelas verbaque in cassum sero?
non ibo in hostes? manibus excutiam faces

---

2 domituram freta E: domitorem freti CPS   6 tacitisque ECS: tacitumque P
10 aversa EP: adversa CSKQelnr   13 nunc nunc adeste Ee: adeste adeste
CPS   19 mihi peius aliquod Avantius: date peius aliud Richter, alii aliter
22a et 23a transposuit Leo   25 parta iam parta CPS: pariat iam parta E
ultio CPS: vitio E   26 sero E: fero CPS

caeloque lucem—spectat hoc nostri sator
Sol generis, et spectatur, et curru insidens
per solita puri spatia decurrit poli?   30
non redit in ortus et remetitur diem?
da, da per auras curribus patriis vehi,
committe habenas, genitor, et flagrantibus
ignifera loris tribue moderari iuga:
gemino Corinthos litore opponens moras   35
cremata flammis maria committat duo.
hoc restat unum, pronubam thalamo feram
ut ipsa pinum postque sacrificas preces
caedam dicatis victimas altaribus.
per viscera ipsa quaere supplicio viam,   40
si vivis, anime, si quid antiqui tibi
remanet vigoris; pelle femineos metus
et inhospitalem Caucasum mente indue.
quodcumque vidit Pontus aut Phasis nefas,
videbit Isthmos. effera ignota horrida   45
tremenda caelo pariter ac terris mala
mens intus agitat: vulnera et caedem et vagum
funus per artus—levia memoravi nimis:
haec virgo feci; gravior exurgat dolor:
maiora iam me scelera post partus decent.   50
accingere ira teque in exitium para
furore toto. paria narrentur tua
repudia thalamis: quo virum linques modo?
hoc quo secuta es. rumpe iam segnes moras:
quae scelere parta est, scelere linquenda est domus. 55

CHORUS

Ad regum thalamos numine prospero
qui caelum superi quique regunt fretum

29 spectatur *E*: spectator *CPSe²*   32 patriis *E*: patris *CPS*   35 corinthos
E: -thus *CPKQ*: -tho *S*   litori *codd.* (-tt- *P*): litore *Gronovius*   36 committat *ECPS*: committet *Lipsius*   44 pontus aut phasis *E*: phasis aut pontus
CPS   48 per artus *Ee²* *lnr*: peractus *CPS* (*corr. S²*, peractum *C mg.*)
52 narrentur *Eelr*: narrantur *CPSKQ*   53 linques *τ*: linquis *ECPS*
55 parta *EQl*: pacta *CPS* (*corr. S²*) *Kenr*   linquenda est *E*: linquetur *PSKQlnr*:
linquatur *Cτ*

adsint cum populis rite faventibus.
primum sceptriferis colla Tonantibus
taurus celsa ferat tergore candido;   60
Lucinam nivei femina corporis
intemptata iugo placet, et asperi
Martis sanguineas quae cohibet manus;
quae dat belligeris foedera gentibus
et cornu retinet divite copiam,   65
donetur tenera mitior hostia.
et tu, qui facibus legitimis ades,
noctem discutiens auspice dextera
huc incede gradu marcidus ebrio,
praecingens roseo tempora vinculo,   70
et tu quae, gemini praevia temporis,
tarde, stella, redis semper amantibus:
te matres, avide te cupiunt nurus
quamprimum radios spargere lucidos.

     Vincit virgineus decor   75
     longe Cecropias nurus,
     et quas Taygeti iugis
     exercet iuvenum modo
     muris quod caret oppidum,
     et quas Aonius latex   80
     Alpheosque sacer lavat.
     si forma velit aspici,
     cedent Aesonio duci
     proles fulminis improbi
     aptat qui iuga tigribus,   85
     nec non, qui tripodas movet,
     frater virginis asperae;
     cedet Castore cum suo
     Pollux caestibus aptior.
     sic, sic, caelicolae, precor,   90
     vincat femina coniuges,
     vir longe superet viros.

59 primum *E*: primus *CPS*   73 avide *CPS*: avidae *E*   75 vincit *Eer*:
vicit *CPSKQln*   82 *post* 83 *CPS*

Haec cum femineo constitit in choro,
unius facies praenitet omnibus.
sic cum sole perit sidereus decor,   95
et densi latitant Pleiadum greges
cum Phoebe solidum lumine non suo
orbem circuitis cornibus alligat.
ostro sic niveus puniceo color
perfusus rubuit, sic nitidum iubar   100
pastor luce nova roscidus aspicit.
ereptus thalamis Phasidis horridi,
effrenae solitus pectora coniugis
invita trepidus prendere dextera,
felix Aeoliam corripe virginem   105
nunc primum soceris sponse volentibus.
concesso, iuvenes, ludite iurgio;
hinc illinc iuvenes, mittite carmina:
rara est in dominos iusta licentia.

    Candida thyrsigeri proles generosa Lyaei,   110
multifidam iam tempus erat succendere pinum:
excute sollemnem digitis marcentibus ignem.
festa dicax fundat convicia Fescenninus,
solvat turba iocos—tacitis eat illa tenebris,
si qua peregrino nubit fugitiva marito.   115

MEDEA—NUTRIX

MEDEA

    Occidimus, aures pepulit hymenaeus meas.
vix ipsa tantum, vix adhuc credo malum.
hoc facere Iason potuit, erepto patre
patria atque regno sedibus solam exteris
deserere durus? merita contempsit mea   120

93 femineo *E*: virgineo *CPS*   94 praenitet *E*: preminet *CPS*: preeminet *eτ*
95 sydereus *E*: sideribus *CP*(sy-)*S*   97 solidum *E*: solitum *CPS*
102 horridi *E*: horridis *CPS*   105 aeoliam *E*: aoniam *CPS*   corripe *E*:
prendito *CPS*   106 soceris *CPS*: socero *E*   115 fugitiva *Ee*: fugitura
CPS   117 credo *Eeln*: condo *CPSKQd*

qui scelere flammas viderat vinci et mare?
adeone credit omne consumptum nefas?
incerta vecors mente vesana feror
partes in omnes; unde me ulcisci queam?
utinam esset illi frater! est coniunx: in hanc   125
ferrum exigatur. hoc meis satis est malis?
si quod Pelasgae, si quod urbes barbarae
novere facinus quod tuae ignorent manus,
nunc est parandum. scelera te hortentur tua
et cuncta redeant: inclitum regni decus   130
raptum et nefandae virginis parvus comes
divisus ense, funus ingestum patri
sparsumque ponto corpus et Peliae senis
decocta aeno membra. funestum impie
quam saepe fudi sanguinem—et nullum scelus   135
irata feci: saevit infelix amor.

    Quid tamen Iason potuit, alieni arbitri
iurisque factus? debuit ferro obvium
offerre pectus—melius, a melius, dolor
furiose, loquere. si potest, vivat meus,   140
ut fuit, Iason; si minus, vivat tamen
memorque nostri muneri parcat meo.
culpa est Creontis tota, qui sceptro impotens
coniugia solvit quique genetricem abstrahit
natis et arto pignore astrictam fidem   145
dirimit: petatur, solus hic poenas luat
quas debet. alto cinere cumulabo domum:
videbit atrum verticem flammis agi
Malea longas navibus flectens moras.

NUTRIX

Sile, obsecro, questusque secreto abditos   150
manda dolori. gravia quisquis vulnera

---

121 scelere *CPS*: scelera *E*   122 credit *CPS*: credet *E*   123 vesana *E*:
non sana *CPS*   128 ignorent *E*: ignorant *CPS*   132 ingestum *E*:
incestum *CPSen*: infestum *KQ*: incertum *r*   135 fudi *CPS*: vidi *E*
136 s(a)evit *codd.*: suasit *Peiper, alii aliter*   139 offerre *CPS*: afferre *E*   ha
CPS: ac *E*   142 muneri *CPS*: muneris *E*

patiente et aequo mutus animo pertulit,
referre potuit: ira quae tegitur nocet;
professa perdunt odia vindictae locum.

MEDEA

Levis est dolor qui capere consilium potest   155
et clepere sese; magna non latitant mala.
libet ire contra.

NUTRIX

        Siste furialem impetum,
alumna: vix te tacita defendit quies.

MEDEA

Fortuna fortes metuit, ignavos premit.

NUTRIX

Tunc est probanda, si locum virtus habet.   160

MEDEA

Numquam potest non esse virtuti locus.

NUTRIX

Spes nulla rebus monstrat afflictis viam.

MEDEA

Qui nil potest sperare, desperet nihil.

NUTRIX

Abiere Colchi, coniugis nulla est fides
nihilque superest opibus e tantis tibi.   165

MEDEA

Medea superest: hic mare et terras vides
ferrumque et ignes et deos et fulmina.

---

152 mutus *E*: motus *CPSp*   154 perdunt *ECPSG*: produnt *BLs*
156 *om. CPSKQln, habent Eer*

NUTRIX

Rex est timendus.

MEDEA

Rex meus fuerat pater.

NUTRIX

Non metuis arma?

MEDEA

Sint licet terra edita.

NUTRIX

Moriere.

MEDEA

Cupio.

NUTRIX

Profuge.

MEDEA

Paenituit fugae.   170

NUTRIX

Medea—

MEDEA

Fiam.

NUTRIX

Mater es.

MEDEA

Cui sim vides.

170 profuge *E*: fuge *CPS*   171 fiam *E*: fugiam *CPS*

NUTRIX

Profugere dubitas?

MEDEA

         Fugiam, at ulciscar prius.

NUTRIX

Vindex sequetur.

MEDEA

         Forsan inveniam moras.

NUTRIX

Compesce verba, parce iam, demens, minis
animosque minue: tempori aptari decet.   175

MEDEA

Fortuna opes auferre, non animum potest.
sed cuius ictu regius cardo strepit?
ipse est Pelasgo tumidus imperio Creo.

CREO—MEDEA

CREO

Medea, Colchi noxium Aeetae genus,
nondum meis exportat e regnis pedem?   180
molitur aliquid: nota fraus, nota est manus.
cui parcet illa quemve securum sinet?
abolere propere pessimam ferro luem
equidem parabam: precibus evicit gener.
concessa vita est, liberet fines metu   185
abeatque tuta. fert gradum contra ferox
minaxque nostros propius affatus petit.
arcete, famuli, tactu et accessu procul,

---

172 at *Avantius*: et *CPS*: sed *E*

iubete sileat. regium imperium pati
aliquando discat. vade veloci via   190
monstrumque saevum horribile iamdudum avehe.

MEDEA

Quod crimen aut quae culpa multatur fuga?

CREO

Quae causa pellat, innocens mulier rogat.

MEDEA

Si iudicas, cognosce; si regnas, iube.

CREO

Aequum atque iniquum regis imperium feras.   195

MEDEA

Iniqua numquam regna perpetuo manent.

CREO

I, querere Colchis.

MEDEA

Redeo: qui avexit, ferat.

CREO

Vox constituto sera decreto venit.

MEDEA

Qui statuit aliquid parte inaudita altera,
aequum licet statuerit, haud aequus fuit.   200

CREO

Auditus a te Pelia supplicium tulit?
sed fare, causae detur egregiae locus.

MEDEA

Difficile quam sit animum ab ira flectere
iam concitatum quamque regale hoc putet
sceptris superbas quisquis admovit manus,   205
qua coepit ire, regia didici mea.
quamvis enim sim clade miseranda obruta,
expulsa supplex sola deserta, undique
afflicta, quondam nobili fulsi patre
avoque clarum Sole deduxi genus.   210
quodcumque placidis flexibus Phasis rigat
Pontusque quidquid Scythicus a tergo videt,
palustribus qua maria dulcescunt aquis,
armata peltis quidquid exterret cohors
inclusa ripis vidua Thermodontiis,   215
hoc omne noster genitor imperio regit.
generosa, felix, decore regali potens
fulsi; petebant tunc meos thalamos proci,
qui nunc petuntur. rapida fortuna ac levis
praecepsque regno eripuit, exilio dedit.   220
confide regnis, cum levis magnas opes
huc ferat et illuc casus—hoc reges habent
magnificum et ingens, nulla quod rapiat dies:
prodesse miseris, supplices fido lare
protegere. solum hoc Colchico regno extuli,   225
decus illud ingens Graeciae et florem inclitum,
praesidia Achivae gentis et prolem deum
servasse memet. munus est Orpheus meum,
qui saxa cantu mulcet et silvas trahit,
geminumque munus Castor et Pollux meum est   230
satique Borea quique trans Pontum quoque
summota Lynceus lumine immisso videt,
omnesque Minyae; nam ducum taceo ducem,
pro quo nihil debetur: hunc nulli imputo;

204 putet E: caput CSKQR   213 dulcescunt CSKQelnr: durescunt EPR
214 exterret ECPSR: exercet KQ   218 proci ERe: viri CPS   219 rapida
CPS: rabida ER   220 exilio QR: et exilio ECPSKe   226 Graeciae
et Studemund: graeciae R: glorie ECPS   234 nulli imputo CPSR: nullum
puto E: nullum imputo e

vobis revexi ceteros, unum mihi.   235
incesse nunc et cuncta flagitia ingere:
fatebor; obici crimen hoc solum potest,
Argo reversa. virgini placeat pudor
paterque placeat: tota cum ducibus ruet
Pelasga tellus, hic tuus primum gener   240
tauri ferocis ore flagranti occidet.
fortuna causam quae volet nostram premat,
non paenitet servasse tot regum decus.
quodcumque culpa praemium ex omni tuli,
hoc est penes te. si placet, damna ream,   245
sed redde crimen. sum nocens, fateor, Creo;
talem sciebas esse, cum genua attigi
fidemque supplex praesidis dextrae peti.
terra hac miseriis angulum ac sedem rogo
latebrasque viles: urbe si pelli placet,   250
detur remotus aliquis in regnis locus.

CREO

Non esse me qui sceptra violentus geram
nec qui superbo miserias calcem pede,
testatus equidem videor haud clare parum
generum exulem legendo et afflictum et gravi   255
terrore pavidum, quippe quem poenae expetit
letoque Acastus regna Thessalica optinens.
senio trementem debili atque aevo gravem
patrem peremptum queritur et caesi senis
discissa membra, cum dolo captae tuo   260
piae sorores impium auderent nefas.
potest Iason, si tuam causam amoves,
suam tueri: nullus innocuum cruor
contaminavit, afuit ferro manus

---

241 flagranti *CPS*: fraglanti *R*: flammanti *E*   242 qu(a)e *ECPSR*: qua
Avantius   244 tuli *CPS*: tulit *E*   249 terra hac ⲥ: terram ac *CPSR*:
terram *E*: terra in hac *KQe*: terrae *Gronovius*   miseriis *EQ*: miseris *CSKeR*
ac *E*: et *CPSR*   252 violentus *EKQR*: violenter *CPS*   253 miserias
ECPSeR: miseras *KQ*   256 quippe quem *R*: quippe te *CPS*: quem (*om.*
quippe) *E*

proculque vestro purus a coetu stetit.   265
tu, tu malorum machinatrix facinorum,
cui feminae nequitia ad audenda omnia,
robur virile est, nulla famae memoria,
egredere, purga regna, letales simul
tecum aufer herbas, libera cives metu,   270
alia sedens tellure sollicita deos.

MEDEA

Profugere cogis? redde fugienti ratem
vel redde comitem—fugere cur solam iubes?
non sola veni. bella si metuis pati,
utrumque regno pelle. cur sontes duos   275
distinguis? illi Pelia, non nobis iacet;
fugam, rapinas adice, desertum patrem
lacerumque fratrem, quidquid etiam nunc novas
docet maritus coniuges, non est meum:
totiens nocens sum facta, sed numquam mihi.   280

CREO

Iam exisse decuit. quid seris fando moras?

MEDEA

Supplex recedens illud extremum precor,
ne culpa natos matris insontes trahat.

CREO

Vade: hos paterno ut genitor excipiam sinu.

MEDEA

Per ego auspicatos regii thalami toros,   285
per spes futuras perque regnorum status,
Fortuna varia dubia quos agitat vice,

---

266 tu tu ER: sed tu CPS   267 feminae nequitia R: feminea nequitia
ECPSr: nequitia cui feminea KQln   278 novas CPS: nota E   279 coniuges CPS: convoces E

precor, brevem largire fugienti moram,
dum extrema natis mater infigo oscula,
fortasse moriens.

CREO

     Fraudibus tempus petis.   290

MEDEA

Quae fraus timeri tempore exiguo potest?

CREO

Nullum ad nocendum tempus angustum est malis.

MEDEA

Parumne miserae temporis lacrimis negas?

CREO

Etsi repugnat precibus infixus timor,
unus parando dabitur exilio dies.   295

MEDEA

Nimis est, recidas aliquid ex isto licet:
et ipsa propero.

CREO

     Capite supplicium lues,
clarum priusquam Phoebus attollat diem
nisi cedis Isthmo. sacra me thalami vocant,
vocat precari festus Hymenaeo dies.   300

CHORUS

  Audax nimium qui freta primus
  rate tam fragili perfida rupit
  terrasque suas post terga videns
  animam levibus credidit auris,

---

294 infixus *E*: infelix *CPS* 296 recidas aliquid ex isto *E*: et ex hoc abscidas
aliquid *P*: et ex hoc aliquid abscidas *CSKQlnr* 297a *Creonti dant KQelnr*
297 propero *EP*: propera *CSKQelnr* 298 clarum *E*: clarus *CPS*

dubioque secans aequora cursu   305
potuit tenui fidere ligno
inter vitae mortisque vias
nimium gracili limite ducto.
nondum quisquam sidera norat,
stellisque quibus pingitur aether   310
non erat usus, nondum pluvias
Hyadas poterat vitare ratis,
non Oleniae lumina caprae,
nec quae sequitur flectitque senex
Arctica tardus plaustra Boötes,   315
nondum Boreas, nondum Zephyrus
    nomen habebant.
    Ausus Tiphys pandere vasto
carbasa ponto legesque novas
scribere ventis: nunc lina sinu   320
tendere toto, nunc prolato
pede transversos captare notos,
nunc antemnas medio tutas
ponere malo, nunc in summo
religare loco, cum iam totos   325
avidus nimium navita flatus
optat et alto rubicunda tremunt
    sipara velo.
    Candida nostri saecula patres
videre, procul fraude remota.   330
sua quisque piger litora tangens
patrioque senex factus in arvo,
parvo dives, nisi quas tulerat
natale solum, non norat opes.
bene dissaepti foedera mundi   335
traxit in unum Thessala pinus
iussitque pati verbera pontum,
partemque metus fieri nostri

---

312 ratis *E*: rates *CPS*   313 lumina *E*: sidera *CPS*   314 nec *E*: non
CPS   flectitque *ς*: defletque *ECPS*   315 arctica *P*: arcthica *S*: arethica *C*:
artica *KQl*: attica *E*   328 sipara *E*: suppara *CPS*

mare sepositum. dedit illa graves
improba poenas per tam longos   340
ducta timores, cum duo montes,
claustra profundi, hinc atque illinc
subito impulsu velut aetherio
gemerent sonitu, spargeret astra
nubesque ipsas mare deprensum.   345
palluit audax Tiphys et omnes
labente manu misit habenas,
Orpheus tacuit torpente lyra
ipsaque vocem perdidit Argo.
quid cum Siculi virgo Pelori,   350
rabidos utero succincta canes,
omnes pariter solvit hiatus?
quis non totos horruit artus
totiens uno latrante malo?
quid cum Ausonium dirae pestes   355
voce canora mare mulcerent,
cum Pieria resonans cithara
Thracius Orpheus solitam cantu
retinere rates paene coegit
Sirena sequi? quod fuit huius   360
pretium cursus? aurea pellis
maiusque mari Medea malum,
merces prima digna carina.
    Nunc iam cessit pontus et omnes
patitur leges: non Palladia   365
compacta manu regum referens
inclita remos quaeritur Argo—
quaelibet altum cumba pererrat;
terminus omnis motus et urbes
muros terra posuere nova;   370
nil qua fuerat sede reliquit
pervius orbis: Indus gelidum

344 astra CPS: astris Ee   345 deprensum eς: depressum ECPS   355 quid
E: quis CPSKQer   359 rates CPS: ratem E   369 motus CPS: metus E:
notus e   370 nova E: novos CPS

potat Araxen, Albin Persae
Rhenumque bibunt—venient annis
saecula seris, quibus Oceanus   375
vincula rerum laxet et ingens
pateat tellus Tethysque novos
detegat orbes nec sit terris
    ultima Thule.

NUTRIX—MEDEA

NUTRIX

Alumna, celerem quo rapis tectis pedem?   380
resiste et iras comprime ac retine impetum.
   Incerta qualis entheos gressus tulit
cum iam recepto maenas insanit deo
Pindi nivalis vertice aut Nysae iugis,
talis recursat huc et huc motu effero,   385
furoris ore signa lymphati gerens.
flammata facies, spiritum ex alto citat,
proclamat, oculos uberi fletu rigat,
renidet, omnis specimen affectus capit:
haeret minatur aestuat queritur gemit.   390
quo pondus animi verget? ubi ponet minas?
ubi se iste fluctus franget? exundat furor.
non facile secum versat aut medium scelus;
se vincet: irae novimus veteris notas.
magnum aliquid instat, efferum immane impium: 395
vultum Furoris cerno. di fallant metum!

MEDEA

Si quaeris odio, misera, quem statuas modum,
imitare amorem. regias egone ut faces
inulta patiar? segnis hic ibit dies,
tanto petitus ambitu, tanto datus?   400
dum terra caelum media libratum feret

---

382 entheos *PC* (*mg.*): pentheos *E*: ethneosi *CSKQ*: ethneos *lnr*   gressus *Ee*:
cursus *CPS*   384 nivalis *E*: iugalis *CPS*   391 animi *E*: istud *CPS*
verget *CPS*: vergat *E*   ponet *CPS*: ponat *E*   393 medium *ECPS*:
induit *K*   394 vincet *CPS*: iungit *E*   veteris *E*: veteres *CPS*

nitidusque certas mundus evolvet vices
numerusque harenis derit et solem dies,
noctem sequentur astra, dum siccas polus
versabit Arctos, flumina in pontum cadent, 405
numquam meus cessabit in poenas furor
crescetque semper—quae ferarum immanitas,
quae Scylla, quae Charybdis Ausonium mare
Siculumque sorbens quaeve anhelantem premens
Titana tantis Aetna fervebit minis? 410
non rapidus amnis, non procellosum mare
Pontusve coro saevus aut vis ignium
adiuta flatu possit inhibere impetum
irasque nostras: sternam et evertam omnia.

Timuit Creontem ac bella Thessalici ducis? 415
amor timere neminem verus potest.
sed cesserit coactus et dederit manus:
adire certe et coniugem extremo alloqui
sermone potuit—hoc quoque extimuit ferox;
laxare certe tempus immitis fugae 420
genero licebat—liberis unus dies
datus est duobus. non queror tempus breve:
multum patebit. faciet, hic faciet dies
quod nullus umquam taceat—invadam deos
et cuncta quatiam.

NUTRIX

Recipe turbatum malis, 425
era, pectus, animum mitiga.

MEDEA

Sola est quies,
mecum ruina cuncta si video obruta:
mecum omnia abeant. trahere, cum pereas, libet.

---

404 sequentur *ECS*: secuntur *P*
408 ausonium *E*: ionium *CPS*
412 pontusve *E*: pontusq; *CPS*
et *C*   coactus *E*: convictus *CPS*
442 est *Ee: om. CPS*

405 cadent *EPSe*: cadunt *CKQlnr*
409 quaeve *E*: qu(a)eq; *CPSQe*
417 cesserit *EQ²*: cessarit *PSKQ¹*: cessarit
418 et coniugem *CPS*: coniugem et *E*

NUTRIX

Quam multa sint timenda, si perstas, vide:
nemo potentes aggredi tutus potest.   430

IASON—MEDEA

IASON

O dura fata semper et sortem asperam,
cum saevit et cum parcit ex aequo malam!
remedia quotiens invenit nobis deus
periculis peiora: si vellem fidem
praestare meritis coniugis, leto fuit   435
caput offerendum; si mori nollem, fide
misero carendum. non timor vicit fidem,
sed trepida pietas: quippe sequeretur necem
proles parentum. sancta si caelum incolis
iustitia, numen invoco ac testor tuum: 440
nati patrem vicere. quin ipsam quoque,
etsi ferox est corde nec patiens iugi,
consulere natis malle quam thalamis reor.
constituit animus precibus iratam aggredi.
atque ecce, viso memet exiluit, furit,   445
fert odia prae se: totus in vultu est dolor.

MEDEA

Fugimus, Iason: fugimus—hoc non est novum,
mutare sedes; causa fugiendi nova est:
pro te solebam fugere. discedo, exeo,
penatibus profugere quam cogis tuis.   450
ad quos remittis? Phasin et Colchos petam
patriumque regnum quaeque fraternus cruor
perfudit arva? quas peti terras iubes?
quae maria monstras? Pontici fauces freti

---

430 potentes *CPSL*: potentem *E*   432 malam *CPSe*: mala *EKQl*
433 quotiens *E*: tociens *CPS*   436 nollem *E*: nolim *CPS*   437 carendum
E: carendum est *CPS*   non *EPSKQe*: nunc *C*   fidem *E*: virum *CPS*
438 necem *CPS*: neci *E*

per quas revexi nobilem regum manum   455
adulterum secuta per Symplegadas?
parvamne Iolcon, Thessala an Tempe petam?
quascumque aperui tibi vias, clausi mihi.
quo me remittis? exuli exilium imperas
nec das. eatur. regius iussit gener.   460
nihil recuso. dira supplicia ingere:
merui. cruentis paelicem poenis premat
regalis ira, vinculis oneret manus
clausamque saxo noctis aeternae obruat:
minora meritis patiar—ingratum caput,   465
revolvat animus igneos tauri halitus
interque saevos gentis indomitae metus
armifero in arvo flammeum Aeetae pecus,
hostisque subiti tela, cum iussu meo
terrigena miles mutua caede occidit;   470
adice expetita spolia Phrixei arietis
somnoque iussum lumina ignoto dare
insomne monstrum, traditum fratrem neci
et scelere in uno non semel factum scelus,
iussasque natas fraude deceptas mea   475
secare membra non revicturi senis.
aliena quaerens regna, deserui mea:
per spes tuorum liberum et certum larem,
per victa monstra, per manus, pro te quibus
numquam peperci, perque praeteritos metus,   480
per caelum et undas, coniugi testes mei,
miserere, redde supplici felix vicem.
ex opibus illis, quas procul raptas Scythae
usque a perustis Indiae populis agunt,
quas quia referta vix domus gazas capit,   485
ornamus auro nemora, nil exul tuli
nisi fratris artus: hos quoque impendi tibi;

455 nobilem *E*: nobiles *CPS*   manum *E*: manus *CPS*   459 exuli *CPS*:
exul *E*   465 ingratum *E*: o ingratum *CPS*   472 som(p)noque *CPS*:
summoque *E*   475 mea *EKQe*: meas *CPS*   477 querens *E*: sequens *CPS*
484 agunt *E*: petunt *CPS*   485 quas quia *E*: quasque *CPS*   gaza *vel* gazis
Bentley

tibi patria cessit, tibi pater frater pudor—
hac dote nupsi. redde fugienti sua.

IASON

Perimere cum te vellet infestus Creo,   490
lacrimis meis evictus exilium dedit.

MEDEA

Poenam putabam: munus, ut video, est fuga.

IASON

Dum licet abire, profuge teque hinc eripe;
gravis ira regum est semper.

MEDEA

                     Hoc suades mihi,
praestas Creusae: paelicem invisam amoves.   495

IASON

Medea amores obicit?

MEDEA

              Et caedem et dolos.

IASON

Obicere tandem quod potes crimen mihi?

MEDEA

Quodcumque feci.

IASON

           Restat hoc unum insuper,
tuis ut etiam sceleribus fiam nocens.

---

488 tibi pater frater *Avantius*: tibi pater tibi frater E: tibi frater pater *CSKQelnr*
492 munus *EKQe*[2]: minus *d*: mitis *P*: mitius *CS*   496 amores *CPS*: mores *E*
497 *et* 498b *Medeae*, 498a *Iasoni dant CPS*   497 potes *CPS*: potest *E*

MEDEA

Tua illa, tua sunt illa: cui prodest scelus   500
is fecit—omnes coniugem infamem arguant,
solus tuere, solus insontem voca:
tibi innocens sit quisquis est pro te nocens.

IASON

Ingrata vita est cuius acceptae pudet.

MEDEA

Retinenda non est cuius acceptae pudet.   505

IASON

Quin potius ira concitum pectus doma,
placare natis.

MEDEA

Abdico eiuro abnuo—
meis Creusa liberis fratres dabit?

IASON

Regina natis exulum, afflictis potens.

MEDEA

Ne veniat umquam tam malus miseris dies,   510
qui prole foeda misceat prolem inclitam,
Phoebi nepotes Sisyphi nepotibus.

IASON

Quid, misera, meque teque in exilium trahis?
abscede, quaeso.

MEDEA

Supplicem audivit Creo.

---

506 doma *EKQel*: domas *CPSn*   510 ne *EP*: non *C(corr. C²mg.)SQelnr*

IASON

Quid facere possim, loquere.

MEDEA

                                   Pro me vel scelus.   515

IASON

Hinc rex et illinc.

MEDEA

                        Est et his maior metus:
Medea. nos †confligere. certemus sine,
sit pretium Iason.

IASON

                        Cedo defessus malis:
et ipsa casus saepe iam expertos time.

MEDEA

Fortuna semper omnis infra me stetit.   520

IASON

Acastus instat.

MEDEA

                        Propior est hostis Creo:
utrumque profuge. non ut in socerum manus
armes nec ut te caede cognata inquines
Medea cogit: innocens mecum fuge.

IASON

Et quis resistet, gemina si bella ingruant,   525
Creo atque Acastus arma si iungant sua?

515 possim *ESKQe*: possum *CP*   516 his *E*: hiis *e²*: hic *CPSKQln*
517 confligere *ECPS*: confugere *K*: conflige *Avantius*: cum rege *Bücheler*:
conferre (certamen) *Gronovius*   certemus *codd.*: certamen *D. Heinsius*
520 infra *E*: intra *CPS*   522 non *E*: nolo *CPS*   525 quis *EQ²el*: quid
CPSKQ¹nr   ingruant *CPS*: ingravant *E*

MEDEA

His adice Colchos, adice et Aeeten ducem,
Scythas Pelasgis iunge: demersos dabo.

IASON

Alta extimesco sceptra.

MEDEA

Ne cupias vide.

IASON

Suspecta ne sint, longa colloquia amputa.   530

MEDEA

Nunc summe toto Iuppiter caelo tona,
intende dextram, vindices flammas para
omnemque ruptis nubibus mundum quate.
nec deligenti tela librentur manu
vel me vel istum: quisquis e nobis cadet   535
nocens peribit, non potest in nos tuum
errare fulmen.

IASON

Sana meditari incipe,
et placida fare. si quod ex soceri domo
potest fugam levare solamen, pete.

MEDEA

Contemnere animus regias, ut scis, opes   540
potest soletque; liberos tantum fugae
habere comites liceat in quorum sinu
lacrimas profundam. te novi nati manent.

---

534 diligenti *codd. corr. Bothe ex ed. Ascensiana*   manu *CPS*: manum *E*
535 vel me *E*: in me *CPS*   538 quod *Er*: quid *CPSeln*: quis *KQ*¹ (*corr.* Q²)

IASON

Parere precibus cupere me fateor tuis;
pietas vetat: namque istud ut possim pati,   545
non ipse memet cogat et rex et socer.
haec causa vitae est, hoc perusti pectoris
curis levamen. spiritu citius queam
carere, membris, luce.

MEDEA

                Sic natos amat?
bene est, tenetur, vulneri patuit locus.—   550
suprema certe liceat abeuntem loqui
mandata, liceat ultimum amplexum dare:
gratum est et illud. voce iam extrema peto,
ne, si qua noster dubius effudit dolor,
maneant in animo verba; melioris tibi   555
memoria nostri sedeat; haec irae data
oblitterentur.

IASON

             Omnia ex animo expuli
precorque et ipse, fervidam ut mentem regas
placideque tractes: miserias lenit quies.

MEDEA

Discessit. itane est? vadis oblitus mei   560
et tot meorum facinorum? excidimus tibi?
numquam excidemus. hoc age, omnes advoca
vires et artes. fructus est scelerum tibi
nullum scelus putare. vix fraudi est locus:
timemur. hac aggredere, qua nemo potest   565
quicquam timere. perge nunc, aude, incipe
quidquid potest Medea, quidquid non potest.

---

545 ut possim *E*: non possim *CPS*: non possum *KQe*   549 signatos *E*: si
hic natos *CPSKQ²ln*: sic hic natos *er*: sic gnatos *Peiper*   555 melioris *E*:
melior *CPS*: sed melior *ϛ*   556 sedeat *E*: subeat *CPS*   562 excidemus
CPS: excides *E*   567 potest . . . potest *Ee*: potes . . . potes *CPS*   medea
CPS: om. E

Tu, fida nutrix, socia maeroris mei
variique casus, misera consilia adiuva.
est palla nobis, munus aetherium, domus   570
decusque regni, pignus Aeetae datum
a Sole generis, est et auro textili
monile fulgens quodque gemmarum nitor
distinguit aurum, quo solent cingi comae.
haec nostra nati dona nubenti ferant,   575
sed ante diris inlita ac tincta artibus.
vocetur Hecate. sacra letifica appara,
statuantur arae, flamma iam tectis sonet.

CHORUS

Nulla vis flammae tumidive venti
tanta, nec teli metuenda torti,   580
quanta cum coniunx viduata taedis
    ardet et odit;
non ubi hibernos nebulosus imbres
Auster advexit properatque torrens
Hister et iunctos vetat esse pontes   585
    ac vagus errat;
non ubi impellit Rhodanus profundum,
aut ubi in rivos nivibus solutis
sole iam forti medioque vere
    tabuit Haemus.   590
caecus est ignis stimulatus ira
nec regi curat patiturve frenos
aut timet mortem: cupit ire in ipsos
    obvius enses.
parcite, o divi, veniam precamur,   595
vivat ut tutus mare qui subegit.
sed furit vinci dominus profundi
    regna secunda.
ausus aeternos agitare currus

---

570 aetherium *E*: etereum *e*: etheree *CPS*   577 loetifica *E*: luctifica
CPSKQ: luctifera *e*   578 statuantur *E*: struantur *CPS*: sternantur *O*
579 tumidive venti *E*: tumidiq; venti *CPSKeL*   585 iunctos *ES*: vinctos
CPe   587 impellit *CSKQe*: pellit *EP*

immemor metae iuvenis paternae 600
quos polo sparsit furiosus ignes
    ipse recepit.
constitit nulli via nota magno:
vade qua tutum populo priori,
rumpe nec sacro violente sancta 605
    foedera mundi.
Quisquis audacis tetigit carinae
nobiles remos nemorisque sacri
Pelion densa spoliavit umbra,
quisquis intravit scopulos vagantes 610
et tot emensus pelagi labores
barbara funem religavit ora
raptor externi rediturus auri,
exitu diro temerata ponti
    iura piavit. 615
exigit poenas mare provocatum:
Tiphys in primis, domitor profundi,
liquit indocto regimen magistro;
litore externo, procul a paternis
occidens regnis tumuloque vili 620
tectus ignotas iacet inter umbras.
Aulis amissi memor inde regis
portibus lentis retinet carinas
    stare querentes.
ille vocali genitus Camena, 625
cuius ad chordas modulante plectro
restitit torrens, siluere venti,
cum suo cantu volucris relicto
adfuit tota comitante silva,
Thracios sparsus iacuit per agros, 630
at caput tristi fluitavit Hebro:

605 sacro *E*: sancti *CPS*: sancta *E*: mundi *CPS*   606 mundi *E*: sacra *CPS*
608 remos *E*: ramos *CPS*   612 funem *EQe*: finem *CPS*   religavit *EPe*:
relegavit *CSKQl²*   614 diro *ECPKQe*: duro *S*   628 cum *CPS*; tum *E*
volucris *CPS*: volucres *E*   631 at *Gronovius*: ad *ECPS*   tristi fluitavit
Hebro *Gronovius*: tristis fluitavit hebri *e*: tristis fluvitavit hebri *E*: tractus fluvialis
ebri *CPS*

contigit notam Styga Tartarumque,
    non rediturus.
stravit Alcides Aquilone natos,
patre Neptuno genitum necavit   635
sumere innumeras solitum figuras;
ipse post terrae pelagique pacem,
post feri Ditis patefacta regna,
vivus ardenti recubans in Oeta
praebuit saevis sua membra flammis,   640
tabe consumptus gemini cruoris
    munere nuptae.
stravit Ancaeum violentus ictu
saetiger; fratrem, Meleagre, matris
impius mactas morerisque dextra   645
matris iratae. meruere cuncti
morte quod crimen tener expiavit
Herculi magno puer inrepertus,
raptus, heu, tutas puer inter undas.
ite nunc, fortes, perarate pontum   650
    fonte timendo.
Idmonem, quamvis bene fata nosset,
condidit serpens Libycis harenis;
omnibus verax, sibi falsus uni
concidit Mopsus caruitque Thebis.   655
ille si vere cecinit futura,
exul errabit Thetidis maritus;
igne fallaci nociturus Argis
Nauplius praeceps cadet in profundum
†patrioque pendet crimine poenas†   660
fulmine et ponto moriens Oileus;
coniugis fatum redimens Pheraei,

---

641 cruoris *CPS*: prioris *E*   644 fratrem *ECSKQe*: fremit *P*: fratres ς
647 morte *ECPSK*: mortem *Qer*   quod *ECPKQe*: qui *S*   649 heu *E*:
est *CPS*   651 fonte timendo *Gronovius*: ponte timendo *E*: sorte timenda
CPS   657 errabit *Gruter*: erravit *ex* errabit *Q*: erravit *ECPSKe*   658 igne
CPS: ille *E*   659 cadet *Gruter*: cadet *ex* cadit *Q*: cadit *ECSKe*: eadē *P*
660 pendet *EPS*: pendit *CKQelnr*   crimine *ECPSQe*: criminum *K*   *varie*
suppleverunt viri docti   661 fulmine *ECPS*: flumine *e*

uxor, impendes animam marito.
ipse qui praedam spoliumque iussit
aureum prima revehi carina,   665
ustus accenso Pelias aeno
arsit angustas vagus inter undas.
iam satis, divi, mare vindicastis:
        parcite iusso.

NUTRIX—MEDEA

NUTRIX

Pavet animus, horret: magna pernicies adest.   670
immane quantum augescit et semet dolor
accendit ipse vimque praeteritam integrat.
vidi furentem saepe et aggressam deos,
caelum trahentem: maius his, maius parat
Medea monstrum. namque ut attonito gradu   675
evasit et penetrale funestum attigit,
totas opes effudit et quidquid diu
etiam ipsa timuit promit atque omnem explicat
turbam malorum, arcana secreta abdita,
et triste laeva †comprecans sacrum manu   680
pestes vocat quascumque ferventis creat
harena Libyae quasque perpetua nive
Taurus coercet frigore Arctoo rigens,
et omne monstrum. tracta magicis cantibus
squamifera latebris turba desertis adest.   685
hic saeva serpens corpus immensum trahit
trifidamque linguam exertat et quaerit quibus
mortifera veniat; carmine audito stupet
tumidumque nodis corpus aggestis plicat
cogitque in orbes. 'parva sunt' inquit 'mala   690

663 impendes *Gronovius*: impendens *E*: impendit *CPS*   678 promit *Ee*:
premit *CPSKQn*   680 comprecans *E*: complicans *CPSQ²e*: complicant
KQ¹: complicat *l*   sacrum *ECSKQelnr*: sacra *P*   681 ferventis *nrτ*: ferventi
ECPSKQel   683 arctoo rigens *CSKQe*: arcto rigens *P*: arcto oriens *E*
685 squamifera *E*: squamea *CPSe²*   686 s(a)eva *Ee*: sera *CPS*   687 quęrit
E: querens *CPS*

et vile telum est, ima quod tellus creat:
caelo petam venena. iam iam tempus est
aliquid movere fraude vulgari altius.
huc ille vasti more torrentis iacens
descendat anguis, cuius immensos duae,   695
maior minorque, sentiunt nodos ferae
(maior Pelasgis apta, Sidoniis minor)
pressasque tandem solvat Ophiuchus manus
virusque fundat; adsit ad cantus meos
lacessere ausus gemina Python numina,   700
et Hydra et omnis redeat Herculea manu
succisa serpens, caede se reparans sua.
tu quoque relictis pervigil Colchis ades,
sopite primum cantibus, serpens, meis.'

    Postquam evocavit omne serpentum genus,   705
congerit in unum frugis infaustae mala:
quaecumque generat invius saxis Eryx,
quae fert opertis hieme perpetua iugis
sparsus cruore Caucasus Promethei,
pharetraque pugnax Medus aut Parthi leves,   710
et quis sagittas divites Arabes linunt,
aut quos sub axe frigido sucos legunt
lucis Suebae nobiles Hyrcaniis;
quodcumque tellus vere nidifico creat
aut rigida cum iam bruma discussit decus   715
nemorum et nivali cuncta constrinxit gelu,
quodcumque gramen flore mortifero viret,
dirusve tortis sucus in radicibus
causas nocendi gignit, attrectat manu.
Haemonius illas contulit pestes Athos,   720
has Pindus ingens, illa Pangaei iugis

691 ima *ESKQe*: una *C*   692 iam iam *Gronovius*: iam *E*: iam nunc *CPS*
693 movere *E*: moveri *CPSKQer*   701 manu *CPS*: manus *ER*   706 congerit *ERKQe*: contigit *CPSτ*: contingit *l*   709 sparsus *CPS*: sparsas *E*
710 parthi leves *E*: parthus levis *CPS*   711 quis *Avantius*: qui *ECPS*
712 quos *CPS*: quo *E*   713 suebae *E*: suevi *CPS*   hyrcaniis *E*: (h)yrcaneis
CPS: hercyniis *Avantius*   714 quodcumque *CPS*: quotcumque *E*
718 dirusve *CPS*: durusque *O*: virusque *E*   721 illa *CPS*: illas *EKQ¹e*

teneram cruenta falce deposuit comam;
has aluit altum gurgitem Tigris premens,
Danuvius illas, has per arentes plagas
tepidis Hydaspes gemmifer currens aquis,   725
nomenque terris qui dedit Baetis suis
Hesperia pulsans maria languenti vado.
haec passa ferrum est, dum parat Phoebus diem,
illius alta nocte succisus frutex,
at huius ungue secta cantato seges.   730

    Mortifera carpit gramina ac serpentium
saniem exprimit miscetque et obscenas aves:
maestique cor bubonis et raucae strigis
exsecta vivae viscera. haec scelerum artifex
discreta ponit; his rapax vis ignium,   735
his gelida pigri frigoris glacies inest.
addit venenis verba non illis minus
metuenda. sonuit ecce vesano gradu
canitque. mundus vocibus primis tremit.

MEDEA

Comprecor vulgus silentum vosque ferales deos   740
et Chaos caecum atque opacam Ditis umbrosi domum,
Tartari †ripis ligatos squalidae Mortis specus.
supplicis, animae, remissis currite ad thalamos novos:
rota resistat membra torquens, tangat Ixion humum,
Tantalus securus undas hauriat Pirenidas.   745
gravior uni poena sedeat coniugis socero mei:
lubricus per saxa retro Sisyphum volvat lapis.
vos quoque, urnis quas foratis inritus ludit labor,
Danaides, coite: vestras hic dies quaerit manus.—
nunc meis vocata sacris, noctium sidus, veni   750
pessimos induta vultus, fronte non una minax.

730 at *ECPKQ*: ad *RS*: ac *e*   740 comprecor *E*: vos precor *CPSKQ*
741 atque *ECPS*: adque *R*   742 *sic codd.*: specu *Haase*: ligatae squalido . . .
specu (743) supplicis, animae *Peiper, alii aliter*   743 suppliciis *codd.*
746 gravior uni *E*: graviorum *CPSl²rd*: gravior *KQe¹ln*   748 vos quoque
EP: vosque *CSKQelnr*

Tibi more gentis vinculo solvens comam
secreta nudo nemora lustravi pede
et evocavi nubibus siccis aquas
egique ad imum maria, et Oceanus graves   755
interius undas aestibus victis dedit;
pariterque mundus lege confusa aetheris
et solem et astra vidit et vetitum mare
tetigistis, ursae. temporum flexi vices:
aestiva tellus floruit cantu meo,   760
coacta messem vidit hibernam Ceres;
violenta Phasis vertit in fontem vada
et Hister, in tot ora divisus, truces
compressit undas omnibus ripis piger.
sonuere fluctus, tumuit insanum mare   765
tacente vento, nemoris antiqui domus
amisit umbras, vocis imperio meae.
die relicto Phoebus in medio stetit,
Hyadesque nostris cantibus motae labant.
adesse sacris tempus est, Phoebe, tuis.   770

Tibi haec cruenta serta texuntur manu,
    novena quae serpens ligat,
tibi haec Typhoeus membra quae discors tulit,
    qui regna concussit Iovis.
vectoris istic perfidi sanguis inest,   775
    quem Nessus expirans dedit.
Oetaeus isto cinere defecit rogus,
    qui virus Herculeum bibit.
piae sororis, impiae matris, facem
    ultricis Althaeae vides.   780
reliquit istas invio plumas specu
    Harpyia, dum Zeten fugit.
his adice pinnas sauciae Stymphalidos
    Lernaea passae spicula.
sonuistis, arae, tripodas agnosco meos   785
    favente commotos dea.

753 nemora ECS: littora P   766 domus CPS: decus domus E   767 umbras
E: umbram CPS   775 vectoris Er: victoris CPS   785 are CPSKe: á. é. E

Video Triviae currus agiles,
non quos pleno lucida vultu
pernox agitat, sed quos facie
lurida maesta, cum Thessalicis   790
vexata minis caelum freno
propiore legit. sic face tristem
pallida lucem funde per auras,
horrore novo terre populos
inque auxilium, Dictynna, tuum   795
pretiosa sonent aera Corinthi.
tibi sanguineo caespite sacrum
sollemne damus, tibi de medio
rapta sepulcro fax nocturnos
sustulit ignes, tibi mota caput   800
flexa voces cervice dedi,
tibi funereo de more iacens
passos cingit vitta capillos,
tibi iactatur tristis Stygia
ramus ab unda, tibi nudato   805
pectore maenas sacro feriam
bracchia cultro. manet noster
sanguis ad aras: assuesce, manus,
stringere ferrum carosque pati
posse cruores—sacrum laticem   810
percussa dedi.
quodsi nimium saepe vocari
quereris votis, ignosce, precor:
causa vocandi, Persei, tuos
saepius arcus una atque eadem est   815
semper, Iason.
tu nunc vestes tinge Creusae,
quas cum primum sumpserit, imas
urat serpens flamma medullas.
ignis fulvo clusus in auro   820
latet obscurus, quem mihi caeli

---

790 mesta *CPS*: metat *E*   803 cingit *E*: vincit *CPS*   819 serpens *E*:
repens *CPS*   821 obscurus *CPS*: obscura *E*

qui furta luit viscere feto
dedit et docuit condere vires
arte, Prometheus. dedit et tenui
sulphure tectos Mulciber ignes,   825
et vivacis fulgura flammae
de cognato Phaëthonte tuli.
habeo mediae dona Chimaerae,
habeo flammas usto tauri
gutture raptas, quas permixto   830
felle Medusae tacitum iussi
servare malum. adde venenis
stimulos, Hecate, donisque meis
semina flammae condita serva.
fallant visus tactusque ferant,   835
meet in pectus venasque calor,
stillent artus ossaque fument
vincatque suas flagrante coma
nova nupta faces.
    Vota tenentur: ter latratus   840
audax Hecate dedit et sacros
edidit ignes face lucifera.

Peracta vis est omnis: huc natos voca,
pretiosa per quos dona nubenti feras.
ite, ite, nati, matris infaustae genus,   845
placate vobis munere et multa prece
dominam ac novercam. vadite et celeres domum
referte gressus, ultimo amplexu ut fruar.

CHORUS

Quonam cruenta maenas
praeceps amore saevo   850
rapitur? quod impotenti

824 arte *E*: artem *CPS*   tenui *E*: tenuit *CPQe*: timuit *S*   836 meet *ECS*:
manet *P*   837 stillent *CPS*: stillet *E*   841 sacros *Ee*: sacro *CPS*
842 lucifera *ECPS*: luctifera *ς recte?*   847 ac *E*: et *CPS*

facinus parat furore?
vultus citatus ira
riget et caput feroci
quatiens superba motu   855
regi minatur ultro.
quis credat exulem?
flagrant genae rubentes,
pallor fugat ruborem.
nullum vagante forma   860
servat diu colorem.
huc fert pedes et illuc,
ut tigris orba natis
cursu furente lustrat
Gangeticum nemus.   865
frenare nescit iras
Medea, non amores;
nunc ira amorque causam
iunxere: quid sequetur?
quando efferet Pelasgis   870
nefanda Colchis arvis
gressum metuque solvet
regnum simulque reges?
nunc, Phoebe, mitte currus
nullo morante loro,   875
nox condat alma lucem,
mergat diem timendum
dux noctis Hesperus.

NUNTIUS—CHORUS—NUTRIX—MEDEA—IASON

NUNTIUS

Periere cuncta, concidit regni status.
nata atque genitor cinere permixto iacent.   880

CHORUS

Qua fraude capti?

NUNTIUS

       Qua solent reges capi:

donis.

CHORUS

In illis esse quis potuit dolus?

NUNTIUS

Et ipse miror vixque iam facto malo
potuisse fieri credo.

CHORUS

       Quis cladis modus?

NUNTIUS

Avidus per omnem regiae partem furit   885
ut iussus ignis: iam domus tota occidit,
urbi timetur.

CHORUS

Unda flammas opprimat.

NUNTIUS

Et hoc in ista clade mirandum accidit:
alit unda flammas, quoque prohibetur magis,
magis ardet ignis; ipsa praesidia occupat.   890

NUTRIX

Effer citatum sede Pelopea gradum,
Medea, praeceps quaslibet terras pete.

MEDEA

Egone ut recedam? si profugissem prius,
ad hoc redirem, nuptias specto novas.
quid, anime, cessas? sequere felicem impetum.   895

---

882 *sic CPS, totum versum choro dat E*   891-2 *nutrici dant CPS, nuntio E*

pars ultionis ista, qua gaudes, quota est?
amas adhuc, furiose, si satis est tibi
caelebs Iason. quaere poenarum genus
haut usitatum iamque sic temet para:
fas omne cedat, abeat expulsus pudor;   900
vindicta levis est quam ferunt purae manus.
incumbe in iras teque languentem excita
penitusque veteres pectore ex imo impetus
violentus hauri. quidquid admissum est adhuc,
pietas vocetur. hoc age et faxo sciant   905
quam levia fuerint quamque vulgaris notae
quae commodavi scelera. prolusit dolor
per ista noster: quid manus poterant rudes
audere magnum? quid puellaris furor?
Medea nunc sum; crevit ingenium malis.   910
   Iuvat, iuvat rapuisse fraternum caput;
artus iuvat secuisse et arcano patrem
spoliasse sacro, iuvat in exitium senis
armasse natas. quaere materiam, dolor:
ad omne facinus non rudem dextram afferes.   915
   Quo te igitur, ira, mittis, aut quae perfido
intendis hosti tela? nescio quid ferox
decrevit animus intus et nondum sibi
audet fateri. stulta properavi nimis:
ex paelice utinam liberos hostis meus   920
aliquos haberet—quidquid ex illo tuum est,
Creusa peperit. placuit hoc poenae genus,
meritoque placuit: ultimum, agnosco, scelus
animo parandum est—liberi quondam mei,
vos pro paternis sceleribus poenas date.   925
   Cor pepulit horror, membra torpescunt gelu
pectusque tremuit. ira discessit loco
materque tota coniuge expulsa redit.

897 furiose *Bentley*: furiosa *codd.*   901 purę *E*: parve *CPSL*   904 violentus *E*: violentius *CPS*   913 spoliasse *EKQe*: spoliare *CPSr*   923 ultimum *EKQelnr*: ultimo *CPS*   agnosco *E*: magno *CPSKQ*   924 parandum *CPS*: parendum *E*   927 discessit *EPSQe*: discedit *C*

egone ut meorum liberum ac prolis meae
fundam cruorem? melius, a, demens furor!   930
incognitum istud facinus ac dirum nefas
a me quoque absit; quod scelus miseri luent?
scelus est Iason genitor et maius scelus
Medea mater—occidant, non sunt mei;
pereant, mei sunt. crimine et culpa carent,   935
sunt innocentes: fateor, et frater fuit.
quid, anime, titubas? ora quid lacrimae rigant
variamque nunc huc ira, nunc illuc amor
diducit? anceps aestus incertam rapit,
ut saeva rapidi bella cum venti gerunt   940
utrimque fluctus maria discordes agunt
dubiumque fervet pelagus, haut aliter meum
cor fluctuatur. ira pietatem fugat
iramque pietas—cede pietati, dolor.

  Huc, cara proles, unicum afflictae domus   945
solamen, huc vos ferte et infusos mihi
coniungite artus. habeat incolumes pater,
dum et mater habeat—urguet exilium ac fuga.
iam iam meo rapientur avulsi e sinu,
flentes, gementes: osculis pereant patris,   950
periere matri. rursus increscit dolor
et fervet odium, repetit invitam manum
antiqua Erinys—ira, qua ducis, sequor.
utinam superbae turba Tantalidos meo
exisset utero bisque septenos parens   955
natos tulissem! sterilis in poenas fui—
fratri patrique quod sat est, peperi duos.

  Quonam ista tendit turba Furiarum impotens?
quem quaerit aut quo flammeos ictus parat,
aut cui cruentas agmen infernum faces   960

---

939 diducit $CPSKQ^1eln$: deducit EQ^2r 940 rapidi E: rabidi $CPSKQe$
942 meum Ee: metu CPS: mecu Q 950 osculis E: oculis $CPSQ$: occulis
K: o scelus $Gronovius$ patris CPS: patri E 952 invitam $Gronovius$:
invisam $codd.$ 953 erinis E: mentis CPS 958 furiarum E: funerum
$CPSKQ$ (corr. $Q^2mg.$)

intentat? ingens anguis excusso sonat
tortus flagello. quem trabe infesta petit
Megaera? cuius umbra dispersis venit
incerta membris? frater est, poenas petit—
dabimus, sed omnes. fige luminibus faces,   965
lania, perure, pectus en Furiis patet.
   Discedere a me, frater, ultrices deas
manesque ad imos ire securas iube:
mihi me relinque et utere hac, frater, manu
quae strinxit ensem—victima manes tuos   970
placamus ista. quid repens affert sonus?
parantur arma meque in exitium petunt.
excelsa nostrae tecta conscendam domus
caede incohata. perge tu mecum comes.
tuum quoque ipsa corpus hinc mecum aveham.   975
nunc hoc age, anime: non in occulto tibi est
perdenda virtus; approba populo manum.

IASON

   Quicumque regum cladibus fidus doles,
concurre, ut ipsam sceleris auctorem horridi
capiamus. huc, huc, fortis armiferi cohors,   980
conferte tela, vertite ex imo domum.

MEDEA

Iam iam recepi sceptra germanum patrem,
spoliumque Colchi pecudis auratae tenent;
rediere regna, rapta virginitas redit.
o placida tandem numina, o festum diem,   985
o nuptialem! vade, perfectum est scelus,
vindicta nondum: perage, dum faciunt manus.
quid nunc moraris, anime? quid dubitas potens?

961 intentat CPS: intendat E   ingens anguis CPS: igne sanguis E
965 omnes. sic interpunxit Bothe   975 ipsa Ee[1]: ipse CPS   aveham E:
avehe CPS   977 approba Ee: approbo CPSKQ   978 regum E: regum
es CPSQe   doles ex –et E: dolens CPS   980 armiferi EP: armigeri
CSKQeln   985 numina CPS: nomina E   987 om. CPSKln, habent
EeQ(in mg.)   988 potens E: potes CPSKe

iam cecidit ira. paenitet facti, pudet.
quid, misera, feci? misera? paeniteat licet,   990
feci. voluptas magna me invitam subit,
et ecce crescit. derat hoc unum mihi,
spectator iste. nil adhuc facti reor:
quidquid sine isto fecimus sceleris perit.

IASON

En ipsa tecti parte praecipiti imminet.   995
huc rapiat ignes aliquis, ut flammis cadat
suis perusta.

MEDEA

    Congere extremum tuis
natis, Iason, funus, ac tumulum strue:
coniunx socerque iusta iam functis habent,
a me sepulti; natus hic fatum tulit,   1000
hic te vidente dabitur exitio pari.

IASON

Per numen omne perque communes fugas
torosque, quos non nostra violavit fides,
iam parce nato. si quod est crimen, meum est:
me dedo morti; noxium macta caput.   1005

MEDEA

Hac qua recusas, qua doles, ferrum exigam.
i nunc, superbe, virginum thalamos pete,
relinque matres.

IASON

Unus est poenae satis.

991 invitam P: et invitam E: invisam CSKQln   993 iste E: ipse CPS
996 cadat Ee: cedat CPSKQl   1005 dedo E: dede CPS   1006 doles
EKQel: dolet CPS(corr. S²mg.)n

MEDEA

Si posset una caede satiari manus,
nullam petisset. ut duos perimam, tamen   1010
nimium est dolori numerus angustus meo.
in matre si quod pignus etiamnunc latet,
scrutabor ense viscera et ferro extraham.

IASON

Iam perage coeptum facinus, haut ultra precor,
moramque saltem supplicis dona meis.   1015

MEDEA

Perfruere lento scelere, ne propera, dolor:
meus dies est; tempore accepto utimur.

IASON

Infesta, memet perime.

MEDEA

.   Misereri iubes.
bene est, peractum est. plura non habui, dolor,
quae tibi litarem. lumina huc tumida alleva,   1020
ingrate Iason. coniugem agnoscis tuam?
sic fugere soleo. patuit in caelum via:
squamosa gemini colla serpentes iugo
summissa praebent. recipe iam natos, parens;
ego inter auras aliti curru vehar.   1025

IASON

Per alta vade spatia sublimi aetheris,
testare nullos esse, qua veheris, deos.

1009–27 *desunt CPSK, extant Eeς*   1009 satiari manus *Qeς*: satiariamanus *E*:
satiari haec manus *Gronovius*   1014 perage ς: perge *Ee*   haut ς: haud *Q²e*:
aut *E*   1015 supplitiis *E*   1025 vehar *EQ²*: vehor *e*   1026 sublimi
Ee: sublimis *Q²*   etheris *eς*: aetheri *E*: aethere *Farnaby*

COMMENTARY

Six of the opening passages in the nine Senecan plays ('prologue' would be a misleading term in some) are spoken by characters in the plays, two by ghosts, and one by a goddess. The metre of all except *Phaedra* (anapaests) is iambic. The *Octavia* starts with a speech by Octavia in anapaests.

The play opens with a spirited and bitter monologue by Medea (1–55). She has been deserted by Jason, and she now invokes gods and infernal powers to bring destruction on his new wife and her family, and homeless exile to Jason himself. From line 26 her thoughts turn to personal vengeance and deeds of witchcraft more terrible than any she has yet performed: the close of her life with Jason is to be marked by crimes as dreadful as those at its start. Throughout the speech there is an emphasis on her state as a wronged *wife*: 'di coniugales, genialis tori' 1, 'thalamis meis' 16, 'me coniugem' 23, 'paria repudia thalamis' 52–3.

Seneca's opening owes nothing to Euripides' nurse, who gives a sorrowful and leisurely exposition of the situation. (Ennius followed Euripides fairly closely: fr. 246–54V; we know nothing of the openings of Accius' and Ovid's *Medea*s.) Hatred and frenzy infuse our play from the start, and we are at once struck by Medea's strength of mind and passion. Again in contrast with Euripides, Seneca's Medea already has strong if incoherent ideas about her revenge on Jason—possibly including the killing of her children (see note on 23 ff.)—whereas in Euripides these ideas grow gradually in her mind. In this sense Euripides' Medea develops where Seneca's is static—a comment which is generally true of Seneca's protagonists.

The extended speech and soliloquy are a feature of Senecan tragedy, and point to the roots of his art in declamation and the schools of rhetoric. They allow elbow room for the formal amplification of a situation or theme, with more or less subtle vacillations of mood, the development of ancillary ideas, building up of internal climaxes, and other rhetorical devices. The drawback of this technique is that it makes for static drama, but against this should be set the numerous scenes of quick cut-and-thrust argument, with single lines or half-lines only given to each speaker—another rhetorical trick aimed at a different sort of effect (see 157 n.).

1. di coniugales: mainly Jupiter, Juno, Hymenaeus, Venus (γαμήλιον Ἀφροδίταν, Eur. fr. 781. 17N): for the phrase see *Thy* 1102–3, Tac. *Germ.* 18 'hos coniugales deos arbitrantur'.

genialis tori: 'marriage-bed', so called because as part of the marriage ceremony the bridal bed was dedicated to the *genius* or tutelary spirit of the bridegroom ('genialis lectus, qui nuptiis sternitur in honorem genii', Festus 83. 23L): see Rose in *OCD*, s.v. 'Genius'.

2. Lucina: Juno in her role of attendant on women in labour ('she who brings to the light of day') is singled out as the most important of the *di coniugales*.

quaeque: i.e. *tuque quae*: Pallas, under whose guidance the Argo was built by Argus: cf. 365–7 'Palladia compacta manu . . . Argo'; Ap. Rhod. i. 18–19 νῆα μὲν οὖν οἱ πρόσθεν ἔτι κλείουσιν ἀοιδοὶ / Ἄργον Ἀθηναίης καμέειν ὑποθημοσύνῃσι. Thus M. invokes Pallas because she had played a leading part in the destiny which had linked herself with Jason.

domituram freta: the reading of *E* is preferable to *domitorem freti CPS* (i.e. Tiphys), in view of *dominator maris* 4, referring to Neptune, though Tiphys is called *domitor profundi* at 617. Neptune is also *dominus profundi* 597, and *dominator freti Phae* 1159. Here Tiphys tames the ship and the ship tames the sea—or we could read *domiturum freta*. So too Val. Fl. i. 600 of the Argo '(Graia iuventus) ingenti gaudens domat aequora velo'.

3. Tiphyn: the helmsman of the Argo, whose fate is described 617 ff.

novam ratem: the Argo was not merely 'new' but 'strange', because it was traditionally the first boat to defy the high seas: below 318 ff., 364 ff., Ovid, *Her.* xvi. 345 'Phasida puppe nova vexit Pagasaeus Iason', *Tr.* iii. 9. 7–8. There were other claimants to the title of the first navigator, e.g. Minos, Danaus: see the Elder Pliny's discussion, *HN* vii. 206 ff., *RE* ii. 722–3, Pease on Cic. *ND* ii. 89.

frenare: used of controlling a ship also by Manilius iv. 283 'et frenare ratem fluctusque effundere rector', Sil. It. xiv. 489; cf. the similar metaphor with *habenae*, Virg. *Aen.* vi. 1 'classique immittit habenas'.

4–5. Neptune and the Sun are invoked because the former allowed Jason to sail over his waters to Colchis and the latter was M.'s grandfather (28–9).

dominator: Seneca's fondness for this word is notable—five times in the tragedies and in *Ep.* 107. 11 (translating Cleanthes into iambics)—in view of its rarity elsewhere in classical Latin (Cic. *ND.* ii. 4, Sil. It. xiv. 79, *Eleg. Maec.* 87). Later it was common in Christian writers.

dividens orbi (sc. *terrarum*) **diem:** 'apportioning daylight to the world'.

6. 'showing forth your beams to witness silent rites': Apuleius has the phrase 'nullo lumine conscio' (*Met.* viii. 10).

6–7. Hecate was a primitive goddess possessing heavenly, earthly, and chthonic powers, being associated with the Moon, Diana, and

Proserpina. Hence descriptions of her as *triformis* (here and *Phae* 412, Hor. *C.* iii. 22. 4, Ovid, *M.* vii. 94); *triceps* (Ovid, ibid. 194); *tergemina* (Virg. *Aen.* iv. 511). She is here addressed in her guise of Luna, but with her underworld connections she is a fitting power to be invoked by the witch Medea, and summoned to aid her magic poisons at 577, 750, 833, as at Ovid, *M.* vii. 194-5 'tuque triceps Hecate, quae coeptis conscia nostris / adiutrixque venis'.

tacitis sacris: secret and sinister rites of witchcraft, as at 577 (no specific mysteries are meant). Silence is a regular feature of ancient magic: cf. Hor. *Epode* v. 51-2, the witch Canidia invokes 'Nox et Diana, quae silentium regis / arcana cum fiunt sacra', and for further details Gow on Theocr. ii. 38.

7-8. quosque . . . deos: in fact Jason swears by the same gods as M. in two passages of Ovid: *Her.* xii. 78 ff. 'per genus et numen cuncta videntis avi, / per triplicis vultus arcanaque sacra Dianae / et si forte aliquos gens habet ista deos', *M.* vii. 94 ff.; cf. Ap. Rhod. iv. 95-6 Ζεὺς . . . Ἥρη τε Ζυγίη (watching over marriage); but tact may have dictated his reference to Diana and the Sun in his appeal to M. See also Apollod. i. 9. 28 (of Medea) ἡ δέ, οὕς τε ὤμοσεν Ἰάσων θεοὺς ἐπικαλεσαμένη . . .

quosque Medeae . . .: the underworld spirits and places enumerated in the following lines.

9. noctis aeternae chaos: the same phrase *HF* 610. Probably the underworld region (cf. 741) rather than the personified spirit of it, but the distinction is often not precise. There are similar invocations by Orpheus in Ovid, *M.* x. 29 ff., and Dido's priestess in Virg. *Aen.* iv. 510 ff.

10. manes impios: spirits of the unholy dead who would be sympathetic to unholy designs.

11-12. fide meliore: Pluto had carried off Proserpine to rule with him (*dominam*) in Hades, but had shown 'better faith' than Jason by not subsequently repudiating her.

12. fausta: her prayer is *voce non fausta* because addressed to the underworld powers. The expression is hard to parallel but cf. Ammianus xvi. 10. 9 'faustis vocibus appellatus'; Tac. *A.* iv. 9 'precationibus faustis'. (The word occurs only here in the tragedies, *infaustus* several times.)

13 ff. ultrices deae: cf. 967, *Oct* 263 and 619 ('ultrix Erinys'), 966 ('deas scelerum ultrices'), Virg. *Aen.* iv. 473, 610 (another passionate appeal by a wronged woman). M. invokes to her aid the Furies or Erinyes, who are primarily avengers of wrong done to a close relation: e.g. they pursued Orestes for the murder of his mother, and later in this play M.'s frenzy pictures them pursuing her for her brother's murder (958 ff.). The physical details of the snaky hair and the firebrands are conventional: see below on 960 ff.

14. 'your hair foul with bristling serpents': *crinem* is acc. with *squalidae*.

16 ff.: the idea of the Furies standing in as *pronubae* at an ill-starred marriage occurs several times in Ovid, e.g. *M.* vi. 428 ff. (Tereus and Procne), and as a repeated lament of the deserted ladies in the *Heroides* (ii. 117 ff., vi. 45 ff., vii. 96); cf. also Lucan, viii. 90 'me pronuba ducit Erinys' (Cornelia, the wife of Pompey), Virg. *Aen.* vii. 319 'et Bellona manet te pronuba'. Elsewhere in the tragedies at *Oed* 644, *Oct* 23–4; cf. below, 37 ff. (M. herself as *pronuba*), and see further Leo, I. 165–6.

17. coniugi novae: Creon's daughter is not named in Euripides' play, and the later tradition varies between Creusa and Glauce: see *RE* vii. 1395, s.v. 'Glauke' (5). Seneca follows Ovid in calling her Creusa.

18. socero: Creon.

19 ff. Creusa and her family being mentally disposed of, M. says 'I have something worse to call down as a curse upon Jason—let him live on'. This is the reading of all manuscripts, in which *est* would be understood with *mihi . . . aliquid*, and *quod . . . malum* is appositional. But the reading is unsatisfactory: (1) *mihi* is by position unnecessarily emphatic; (2) *peius/malum* is a strained verbal effect even for Sen. *mihi* may have replaced a verb, and Richter's *date peius aliud* is probably on the right lines.

   sponso stresses Jason's hateful position as bridegroom of Creusa. The emphatic *vivat* illustrates a rhetorical trick of which Sen. is very fond, the unexpected climax producing a strongly ironic effect: very similar are *HF* 1316–17, 'eat ad labores hic quoque Herculeos labor: / vivamus', *Phoe* 318–19 'iubente te praebebit alitibus iecur, / iubente te vel vivet', and other examples are *Thy* 293–4, *HF* 1260–1, *Phoe* 297.

20 ff. ignotas egens . . .: Accius, fr. 415R 'exul inter hostes exspes expers desertus vagus', Ap. Rhod. iv. 385–6 ἐκ δέ σε πάτρης / αὐτίκ' ἐμαὶ ἐλάσειαν Ἐρινύες (Medea to Jason), fr. adesp. 284N ἄπολις ἄοικος πατρίδος ἐστερημένος, / πτωχὸς πλανήτης, βίον ἔχων τοὐφ' ἡμέραν, Virg. *Aen.* iv. 615–16 (Dido's curse) 'bello . . . vexatus et armis, / finibus extorris'; perhaps too a verbal recollection of *Aen.* i. 384 'ipse ignotus, egens . . .'. The plight of the expatriate was regarded with peculiar horror in the ancient world.

   incerti laris: 'without a fixed home': gen. of quality equivalent to an adjective. The force and urgency of M.'s bitter curse are reflected in the extended asyndeton.

22–3: the text follows Leo's transposition of 22a and 23a ('iam notus hospes / me coniugem optet'), which offers a more natural sequence of thought. (The tradition is defended by C. Knapp, *CR* xvii (1903), 44, Damsté, *Mnem.* 46 (1918), 404–5.)

   iam notus hospes: a notorious wanderer, always seeking hospitality.

me coniugem optet: Ap. Rhod. iv. 383–4 μνήσαιο δὲ καί ποτ' ἐμεῖο / στρευγόμενος καμάτοισι. (And is there another Virgilian echo— nomine Dido / saepe vocaturum' (*Aen.* iv. 383–4)?)

quō-que: with *peius.*

23 ff.: 'let him long for me as his wife, let him—I cannot pray for anything worse for him—long for children who are like their father and their mother.' *matri* apparently refers to Creusa, but the words *liberos . . . matri* suddenly suggest to M., however vaguely, that through her own and Jason's children lies the means of her revenge: her train of thought alters after *matri*, and this is reflected in the disjointed syntax.

Other ways of taking this rather obscure passage are:

(1) *matri* means Medea, and Jason in the bitterness of exile is to long again for the wife and children he has given up—though the children are destined to be like their father and mother ('id est proditores ac desertores: ut ille coniugis, haec patris', Gronovius). (2) *matri* means Creusa and *similes . . .* 'looking like father and mother', i.e. resembling both parents and thus proving legitimacy and faithful parents (cf. *Ag.* 196, Cat. 61. 214 ff.). This gives a weaker force to the words *quoque . . . precari*, which must then mean 'my worst curse is that he should long for children of an honourable marriage (and not have them)'. In any case we have here the first hint of the fate of M.'s children: cf. note on 37–40, and contrast Euripides' Medea who decides only at a later stage to kill her children (Eur. *Med.* 792). Gronovius has an interesting note: 'At ars est Poetae iubentis eam adhuc ignaram imprudentemque et necdum intelligentem, quid ominetur, praesagire et turbatam dictitare, quod futuris eius consiliis congruit, etsi nondum ipsa verbis hos sensus imponat.'

For further discussion see K. Anliker, *Prologe und Akteinteilung in Senecas Tragödien* 36, W.-H. Friedrich, *Untersuchungen zu Senecas dramatischer Technik* 20.

26. querelas verbaque . . . sero: cf. 281, 'quid seris fando moras?' *serere* is commonly used, e.g. with *sermonem*, to mean 'talk, speak together'. M. tires of imprecations, and in the second half of her monologue she considers personal intervention and revenge. She works herself up to a climax of passion and fury, resolving to unleash a horror of crime and witchcraft that shall surpass all her past record (48–50).

27. manibus faces: the hands are those of the members of the wedding-procession for Jason and Creusa, which M. knows will soon appear, carrying the conventional torches: cf. 67, 111; Cat. 61. 77–8 'faces splendidae quatiunt comas', 114, 'tollite . . . faces'. (That she has not yet actually heard the sounds of the procession is shown by 116.) In Ovid, *Her.* xii. 155–6 M. debates whether to rush into the procession and snatch the garland from Jason's head.

28 ff. caeloque lucem: M.'s catalogue of her magical powers in Ovid includes 'te quoque Luna traho . . . currus quoque carmine nostro / pallet avi, pallet nostris Aurora venenis' (*M.* vii. 207–9); below, 768 (in a similar list) 'Phoebus in medio stetit'. In the present passage she probably refers to the sun, in view of the following words: *lucem* prompts the bitter question *spectat hoc . . . Sol*, which leads in turn to the request *da da* 32. (Farnaby connected *caeloque lucem* with *faces*, and interpreted 'inducamque extinctis facibus tenebras?'—which gives little point to *caelo*.)

    spectat . . . spectatur: can the sun bear to see this wickedness, and be seen pursuing his normal course through the heavens? Does he not feel like retracing his steps in revulsion? Cf. the sun's retreat before the horror of Thyestes' meal, *Thy* 789 ff., and Hippolytus' appeal, 'tuque, sidereum caput, / radiate Titan, tu nefas stirpis tuae / speculare? lucem merge et in tenebras fuge' *Phae* 677–9.

    nostri sator generis: M.'s father Aeetes was the son of Sol and Persa: thus too *patriis, genitor* 32–3.

    puri: there is not even a cloud to obstruct the sun's view of M.'s injury.

    spatia: regularly used of a race-course and appropriate with *curru*.

    remetitur diem: 'retrace his journey through the sky': Virg. *Aen.* ii. 181 'pelago remenso', Stat. *Theb.* iii. 324 'remensus iter'. For *dies* in the sense of 'sky' see *Thy* 263, 'tonat dies serenus', *HO* 1632, Lucan, vii. 189, viii. 217.

32 ff. da, da: with these and the following imperatives supply *mihi*. This request to borrow the sun's chariot and set fire to Corinth is suggested by the disastrous exploit of Phaethon, who, taking the sun's place in his chariot for a day, lost control of the horses and started to set the world on fire until destroyed by Jupiter: below, 599 ff., Ovid, *M.* ii. 1–328.

    M.'s extravagant and passionate address to the sun appealed to subsequent playwrights. Richard Glover's *Medea* v. ii. 3 ff.:

> Now to complete my vengeance will I mount
> The burning chariot of my bright forefather;
> The rapid steeds o'er Corinth will I drive,
> And with the scatter'd lightnings from their manes
> Consume its walls, its battlements and tow'rs,
> Its princes, people, palaces and temples.

Corneille, *Médée* 261 ff.:

> Soleil, qui vois l'affront qu'on va faire à ta race,
> Donne-moi tes chevaux à conduire en ta place:
> Accorde cette grâce à mon désir bouillant.
> Je veux choir sur Corinthe avec ton char brûlant.

Longepierre, *Médée* ii. 1:

> Ou plutôt donne-moi tes chevaux à conduire,
> En poudre dans ces lieux je saurai tout réduire,
> Je tomberai sur l'isthme avec ton char brûlant,
> J'abymerai Corinthe et son peuple insolent,
> J'écraserai ses rois, et ma fureur barbare
> Unira les deux mers que Corinthe sépare.

habenae and *lora* are synonymous, so that *et flagrantibus . . . iuga* is merely an expansion of *committe habenas*.

ignifera iuga: the 'fiery steeds' of the sun ('ignem vomentes', Ovid, *M.* ii. 119) are named and vigorously described in Ovid's account of Phaethon's adventure. For *iuga* meaning 'team of horses' cf. Virg. *Aen.* v. 147.

35. Corinthos: here and *Thy* 629 *E* gives the Greek form where *CP* and *CPS* respectively give *Corinthus*. Similarly with *Alpheos* 81 and elsewhere: see O–P–C, and on Seneca's spelling of Greek names generally see the Index Orthographicus in Peiper–Richter, 498–9.

opponens moras: sc. *navibus*: cf. 149 'Malea longas navibus flectens moras'. The Isthmus of Corinth prevented ships sailing between the Aegean and Ionian Seas (*maria duo*): *Thy* 112–13 'Isthmos . . . vicina gracili dividens terra vada'. Thus *bimaris* is a standard epithet of Corinth or its Isthmus: Hor. *C.* i. 7. 2, and several times in Ovid.

litore: Gronovius' correction of *litori* (*codd.*: the tradition is defended by C. E. Stuart in *CQ* v (1911), 36): instrumental abl., like 'gracili terra' in *Thy* 113.

36. committat: 'join, unite' the seas on either side of the isthmus: so *HO* 83 'committat undas Isthmos'. Pliny lists some attempts to cut through the isthmus: 'perfodere navigabili alveo angustias eas tentavere Demetrius rex, dictator Caesar, Gaius princeps, Domitius Nero . . .' (*HN* iv. 10). Success was finally achieved in 1893.

(Lipsius' *committet* is attractive, making 35–6 the apodosis of a conditional in which 32–4 are the protasis.)

37–40. An enigmatic and sinister suggestion which has been variously interpreted. After her flight of fancy in the last few lines, and wishful recollection of Phaethon, M. says suddenly that the only remaining course for her ('hoc restat unum ut feram') is to attend the wedding ceremony as one of the *pronubae* (attendant matrons) and slaughter 'victims' on the altar. Who or what are the victims?

(1) Jason and Creusa (or just Creusa: so Leo (I. 166), comparing Deianira in *HO* 348 'me nuptiali victimam feriat die', and Octavia in *Oct* 663–4 'hos ad thalamos servata diu / victima tandem funesta cades'). This is the most likely solution: *viscera* is then a horrible

double entendre, and M. pictures herself as an avenging Fury at the ceremony, whose firebrand is identified with the processional torch (note on 16 ff.).

(2) M.'s own children: a veiled reference to what later follows (cf. note on 23 ff.). In this case *viscera* will have the meaning 'children', as at *Ag* 27, but it is not clear what sort of *supplicium* (40), and for whom, she will be devising. The motivation for killing her children does not appear until 549–50.

(3) The normal victims at marriage ceremonial sacrifices (so Thomann and, apparently, Miller in his Loeb translation). But why should these particular victims reveal to M. a *supplicio via*?

(4) M. herself: 'peri dum perdas' Gronovius.
Kingery takes *victimas* as in (3), but refers *viscera ipsa* to M.'s children. This sudden switch of thought is too abrupt even for M.'s distraught condition, and it is surely impossible not to link *victimas* and *viscera*. Whatever the meaning, the lines probably owe something to Eur. *Med.* 887–8 καὶ παρεστάναι λέχει / νύμφην τε κηδεύουσαν ἥδεσθαι σέθεν. See further Anliker, *Prologe* 37.

hoc restat unum: cf. 498.

pronubam pinum: the torches (cf. on 27) were of pinewood: below, 111, Catullus 61. 15 'pineam quate taedam'. *pronubam* is adjectival: *Ciris* 439 'pronuba nec castos accendet pinus odores', Claudian, *Rapt. Pros.* 1. 131 'pronuba flamma'.

thalamo: dat. of end of motion with *feram*.

41. si vivis: M. addresses herself harshly; cf. the Comic use of *si vivo* in threats: Plautus, *Pseud.* 1325 'erit ubi te ulciscar, si vivo', Terence, *Eun.* 990, *Andr.* 866. For the self-apostrophe see 895 'quid, anime, cessas?', 937, 976, 988; *Othello* v. ii. 1 'It is the cause, it is the cause, my soul': this is a marked feature of the declamatory style.

43. inhospitalem: ἄξενον, the name originally applied to the Black Sea, later altered to the euphemistic εὔξεινος, Euxine (Strabo vii. 3. 6, Pliny, *HN* vi. 1). It became a stock epithet too for the harsh bleakness of this mountain range between the Black Sea and Caspian Sea, and bordering on M.'s own country, Colchis: *Thy* 1048–9 'quis inhospitalis Caucasi rupem asperam / Heniochus habitans', Hor. *C.* i. 22. 6–7, *Epode* i. 12. The physical qualities of the region were thought to be reflected in the nature of its inhabitants, so that by 'clothing her mind with the inhospitable Caucasus' M. means reverting to her wild native character. Cf. Virg. *Aen.* iv. 366–7 'duris genuit te cautibus horrens / Caucasus', *Phae* 906–7. The abl. *mente* of the thing covered or clothed is unusual, but can be paralleled in Claudian *de tert. cons. Hon.* 157, 'indue mente patrem' ('assume a father's thoughts'). The normal constructions with *induo* are *aliquem induere aliquo* and *alicui induere aliquid*: here the (local) abl. *mente* replaces the dat. and is virtually adverbial, 'mentally assume harsh Caucasus'.

44-5: 'all the crimes I committed at home I will repeat in Corinth': she presumably refers in particular to the murder and mutilation of her brother Absyrtus (131 n.).

   Pontus (Euxinus: 43 n.): the Black Sea, on the eastern shore of which lay Colchis, and into which flowed the river Phasis.

   Isthmos: sc. *Corinthius*: *Thy* 124. The Greek forms of second declension names predominate in the tragedies.

45 ff. effera ignota horrida: 395 'efferum immane impium', *Phoe* 264-5 'facinus ignotum efferum / inusitatum': strings of epithets in asyndeton are rife in the tragedies. Probably *eff. ign. horr.* are adjectival, like *tremenda* qualifying substantival *mala*, but they may themselves be substantival.

   caelo, terris: i.e. *dis, hominibus.*

   The *mala* are further defined by *vulnera, caedem, vagum funus*, which are then contemptuously dismissed as too trivial (*levia nimis*) for her present purposes. (Cf. 906-7 'quam levia fuerint quamque vulgaris notae / quae commodavi scelera'.)

   vagum funus per artus: probably lingering disease that kills limb by limb, which M. can induce, not a reference to the scattering of Absyrtus' dismembered body, as most editors take it: cf. *HO* 706 'vagus per artus errat excussos tremor'.

49. haec virgo feci: 908 ff. 'quid manus poterant rudes / audere magnum? quid puellaris furor? / Medea nunc sum'. *virgo* contrasts with *post partus* 50.

   gravior . . . : 'more sternly let my wrath rise up'. *exurgat* for *exsurgat* as often with verbs in *s-* compounded with *ex*: *exiluit* 445, *expirans* 776.

51. Again she dramatically addresses herself: *accingere* is passive imperative in 'middle' sense, 'gird (i.e. arm) yourself with wrath' (*Ag* 192 'accingere, anime').

   exitium: sc. *hostium tuorum.*

52. furore toto: 'with no feeling but of passionate rage'. For *totus* qualifying the word for the emotion felt see 446, *Phoe* 155-6 'toto impetu / toto dolore': the commoner idiom is shown in Ter. *Ad.* 589 'in amore est totus'.

52 ff. paria . . . thalamis: 'let the story of thy rejection match the story of thy marriage' (Miller). A double rhetorical amplification of this theme leads M. to the climax of her monologue: (1) *quo . . . modo? hoc* (*modo*) *quo . . .*: the crimes she committed (fratricide, disloyalty to Aeetes) when she first came to Jason will now be equalled by fresh ones when she leaves him; (2) *quae scelere . . . domus*: the same idea repeated. Notice the triple antithesis: *repudia/thalamis, linques/secuta es, scelere parta est/scelere linquenda est.* For the double tribrach in 53 (*rĕpŭdĭă thălămis*) cf. *Ag* 959, *Tro* 642, 908.

   repudia: *repudium* was technically the breaking off of betrothal or marriage by one partner (opposed to *divortium*, mutual dissolution of marriage): *Ag* 283, *HO* 432.

rumpe segnes moras: cf. Virg. *G.* iii. 42–3 *segnes / rumpe moras.*

quae scelere . . .: with her life now in ruins M. freely admits her past guilt: cf. 121, 129, 135, 500, and *nefas* 44.

56–115. M.'s outburst is followed by the entry of a chorus of Corinthians whose parodos, or opening song, takes the form of a processional chant or wedding-hymn for the nuptials of Jason and Creusa. It is not clear whether both Jason and Creusa are present in the procession: at Greek marriages the new husband took part in the troupe which accompanied his bride to his house; at Rome she was escorted by relatives and friends, including the matrons or *pronubae* who later attended her in the bridal chamber. In both countries the religious ceremony and wedding-feast took place at the bride's home in the evening; then followed the *deductio* of the bride to her new husband's house, during which torches were carried and the singing was accompanied by flute-playing.

The wedding-song (ἐπιθαλάμιον, ὑμέναιος) as an institution goes back to Homer, in a scene on the shield of Achilles, *Il.* xviii. 493, a passage imitated in ps.-Hesiod, *Sc.* 273 ff. It was not part of the Roman wedding ritual, though of course Roman writers took it over as a literary form, fusing with it the conventional *Fescennina iocatio* (see below, and G. Williams in *JRS* xlviii (1958), 16 ff.). As a literary genre it can be traced back at least to Alcman in the seventh century B.C., and Sappho eclipsed her contemporaries with the fame of her own book of epithalamia. The genre continued to be popular, though the only surviving independent Greek specimen is Theocritus xviii, on the marriage of Helen and Menelaus. Greek tragedy supplies examples in Euripides, *Tro.* 307–40, and fr. 781. 14 ff.N (from his lost *Phaethon*); there are comic burlesques in Aristophanes, *Av.* 1731 ff., *Pax* 1332 ff., and Plautus, *Cas.* 800 ff. The most important surviving Latin examples are Catullus 61 and 62, but his contemporaries Calvus and Ticidas also wrote them. Philodemus (died *c.* 40 B.C.) remarks that wedding-songs in his day were practically obsolete (*de mus.* p. 68 Kemke—he may mean songs for actual performance, not literary exercises), but Ovid mentions having written one (*Pont.* i. 2. 131–2). So it is difficult to say whether *Medea* 56 ff. represents a modest revival of the genre: at any rate the epithalamium, in one form or another, survived throughout the classical period and long after, and we have specimens by Statius, Ausonius, Claudian, and Sidonius, among others. Erasmus included one, *Epithalamium Petri Aegidii*, in his *Colloquia* (1524). In English literature some of our greatest poets have turned their hand to the wedding-song, and conventional elements of the classical epithalamium are to be found in those, for example, of Spenser, Ben Jonson, and Herrick. Anyone interested will find a useful anthology in R. H. Case, *English Epithalamies*, London, 1896.

From Catullus 61 and from late Greek rhetoricians, who discussed the epithalamium as a literary form (e.g. Menander Rhetor (third cent. A.D.) who wrote treatises περὶ ἐπιθαλαμίου and περὶ κατευναστικοῦ (Spengel, *Rhet.* iii. 399 ff. and 405 ff.)), we get a good idea of the traditional themes of the wedding-song, some of which appear in the present example. They include an invocation to Hymen or Hymenaeus, the god of marriage (67 ff., 110 ff.), praise of the bride's and bridegroom's beauty (75–101), prayers for happiness and children for the married couple, and a certain amount of good-natured ribaldry (see notes to 107 ff., 113).

There is some uncertainty about the correct terms to apply to the three songs associated with marriages—the song at the wedding-feast, the processional song, and the song outside the θάλαμος. The commonest terms are ἐπιθαλάμιον (sc. μέλος) and ὑμέναιος (sc. ὕμνος), and it is usually thought that the former, as the name indicates, referred specifically to the song outside the wedding-chamber, while ὑμέναιος meant primarily the processional song, but could be applied to the other songs as well. (At line 116 M. calls this song *hymenaeus*, but at Ap. Rhod. iv. 1160 and Stat. *S.* ii. 7. 87 ff. the term is applied to an epithalamium proper.) For further discussion of this subject see Maas, *Philol.* 66 (1907), 590 ff., and 69 (1910), 447–8; Muth, *Wien. St.* 67 (1954), 5–45 (who thinks *Med* 56 ff. is 'ein Gesang vor dem θάλαμος'). Fuller accounts of the wedding-song in classical literature may be found in Weir Smyth, *Greek Melic Poets*, cxii–cxx, and A. L. Wheeler, 'Tradition in the Epithalamium', *AJP* 51 (1930), 205 ff.

There is no wedding-song in Euripides' play, where Jason's new marriage has already taken place (Eur. *Med.* 18–19), but M.'s suddenly hearing the sounds of Jason's wedding-cortège is the dramatic climax of Ovid, *Her.* xii (135–58), and Seneca may well have taken over the idea from this passage. (There are verbal reminiscences between 116–17 and *Her.* xii. 137 ff., and between 118 ff. and *Her.* xii. 161, and the whole epistle should be read in conjunction with our play.) It is also quite likely that Ovid introduced a wedding-song into his *Medea*, which might have been a more immediate model for Seneca: see Leo, I. 168–9. In any case Seneca has written a dramatically effective incident, which thrusts the knife further into M.'s wounded heart, and gives an unusually organic role to the chorus, which here at least is by no means the conventional passive commentator. (Cf. Leo, *Rh. Mus.* 52 (1897), 511.) Note that the chorus throughout is hostile to M. and friendly to Jason (102 ff., 362, 596): in Eur. the chorus is friendly to M. (e.g. 267–8).

The content of this chorus so offended the translator Studley (1566) that he replaced it by a chorus of his own composition, remarking in his 'Preface to the Reader': '. . . bycause that all thynge myght be to the better understandyng and commodytye of the unlearned, as in some places I do expound at large the darke sense of the Poet: so have I chaunged the fyrste *Chorus*, because in it I sawe nothyng but an heape of prophane storyes, and names of prophane Idoles: therfore I have altered the whole matter of it, begynnynge thus: Who hath not wist . . .'.

The song may be considered in three sections: (*a*) 56–74: The chorus calls upon the gods of the heavens and the sea to favour the royal marriage: the invocation includes Hymen and the Evening Star. (*b*) 75–101: Praise for the beauty of the bride and bridegroom. (*c*) 102–15: Let Jason forget Medea in the joy of his new marriage; let Hymen light his torch; and let all enjoy the jests permitted on the occasion.

	Metres:	56–74	Minor asclepiadean
		75–92	Glyconic
		93–109	Minor asclepiadean
		110–15	Dactylic hexameter

There is no strict sequence in the formal elements of the song: praise of Creusa is in two parts with Jason in between; the reference to *licentia* is interrupted by a second address to Hymen; and there are separate slighting references to M. Similarly, the different metres are not tied to particular themes: the bride's beauty is discussed in glyconics and asclepiadeans, and the invitation to ritual ribaldry is made in asclepiadeans and hexameters; see note on 75 ff.

56. regum thalamos: 'royal marriage'.

numine prospero: cf. *Ag* 172 'prospero deo'. Best translated by inverting adjective and noun in English, 'divine favour'.

58. rite faventibus: 'preserving due religious silence'. The strict protocol of Greek and Roman sacrificial procedure enjoined that no inauspicious words should be uttered by those present which might vitiate the ceremony: as the safest way to achieve this was not to speak at all, *favere*, like εὐφημεῖν, came to mean 'be silent'. Sen. himself explains (*vit. beat.* 26. 7) '. . . favete linguis. hoc verbum non, ut plerique existimant, a favore trahitur, sed imperatur silentium, ut rite peragi possit sacrum nulla voce mala obstrepente'. *favere* is usually with *ore* or *linguis* (Virg. *Aen.* v. 71, Hor. *C.* iii. 1. 2, Ovid, *M.* xv. 677), but cf. Tib. iii. 1. 1 'quisquis ades, faveas'.

59 ff. If, as seems clear, this is a processional wedding-song, the reference to sacrifice at this stage is not to be taken literally: the religious part of the ceremony normally took place earlier.

sceptriferis: a rare word: cf. 685 n. and Ovid, *F.* vi. 480.

Tonantibus: the singular being an epithet of Jupiter, the plural is usually taken to include Juno, though she is mentioned in 61 (*Lucinam*, cf. 2). (At *HF* 1 she calls herself bitterly 'soror Tonantis . . . solum mihi / nomen relictum est'.) The dative is governed by *ferat*: 'let a bull offer his neck (to be cut in sacrifice) to . . .'. The bull and his mate (*femina*) must be white, as offerings to *di superi* (cf. Virg. *Aen.* iii. 20–1 and see Frazer on Ovid, *F.* i. 720), and the heifer at least must not have been used for work (*intemptata iugo*)—a very ancient and widespread religious idea, e.g. Numbers 19 : 2 'Speak unto the children of Israel, that they bring thee a red heifer without spot, wherein is no blemish, and upon which never came yoke.' For the content and phraseology of this passage cf. *Ag* 364 ff. 'ad tua coniunx candida tauri / delubra cadet, / nescia aratri, nullo collum / signata iugo' (a sacrifice to Juno); *Oed* 299 ff. 'appellite aris candidum tergo bovem / curvoque numquam colla depressum iugo'.

61. femina: often used of animals, and of a heifer also by Ovid, *M.* ii. 701.

62. Note **plācet** from *placare*.

62-3: et (sc. *illam placet*) **quae cohibet:** probably Venus who restrains Mars, as at Lucr. i. 31 ff. But the clause may belong with what follows and refer to Pax, with whom Venus is here in any case virtually identified.

64 ff. This divinity must be Pax, who is associated with the cornucopia, 65. Significantly, the personification of peace is almost unknown in pre-Augustan Latin literature, but the Greek poets regularly associate Εἰρήνη with wealth, Πλοῦτος (e.g. Pindar, *O.* xvi. 7, Eur. *Suppl.* 491), and an Athenian coin of the second century A.D. depicts her holding the child Plutos who carries the cornucopia (illustrated in G. M. A. Richter, *Sculpture and Sculptors of the Greeks*, Fig. 661). Pax and the cornucopia are linked by Horace, *CS* 57 ff. 'Fides et Pax et Honos Pudorque . . . apparetque beata pleno / copia cornu', and in our passage too she 'holds plenty in her rich horn' to symbolize the prosperity that comes in time of peace. Spenser remembered the imagery when he wrote his *Prothalamion* (102–3): 'Let endlesse Peace your steadfast hearts accord, / And blessed Plentie wait upon your bord.'

The well-known symbol of the *cornu copiae* is given a varied origin: either the horn was broken off the river-god Achelous during his fight with Hercules, filled with fruit and flowers by the Naiads, and given to Bona Copia (Ovid, *M.* ix. 85–8); or it broke off Amalthea, the nymph (or goat) who nursed Jupiter, was covered with herbs and filled with fruit and given to Jupiter, who placed Amalthea and her horn among the stars (Ovid, *F.* v. 121–8). From this horn flowed nectar and ambrosia, so that it became proverbial (e.g. Hor. *C.* i. 17. 14–16).

Pax is not usually a marriage goddess, but cf. Aristoph. *Pax* 975–6 πότνι' Εἰρήνη, δέσποινα χορῶν, δέσποινα γάμων, Eur. *Suppl.* 490 (Εἰρήνη) τέρπεται δ' εὐπαιδίᾳ, Tib. i. 10. 53 ff. (Pax brings time for love-making).

66. donetur: jussive subj. and parallel with *ferat* and *placet*. The understood subject Pax picks up the preceding relatives and is qualified by *mitior*: 'let Peace, who . . . , be given a tender victim, and so become more gentle.' Translation must bring out the force of *tenera, mitior* juxtaposed: Peace is *mitior* because of the tender offering, and the line recalls Hor. *C.* i. 19. 16 'mactata veniet lenior hostia'. For *mitis* applied to Peace cf. Ovid, *F.* i. 712 'Pax, ades, et toto mitis in orbe mane'.

hostia: apparently a sheep: Aristoph. *Pax* 1018 σφάξεις τὸν οἶν.

67–70. Invocation to Hymen: like Pax he is not named, but the description of his attributes is unmistakable. The address to the marriage-god was conventional in the epithalamium, and in Cat. 61 the invocation and encomium of Hymen account for nearly one-third of the poem. The repeated refrain in Cat. 62 is 'Hymen o Hymenaee, Hymen ades o Hymenaee'. Originally, ὑμήν was probably a ritual cry from which derived the personified Hymenaeus, who does not appear until Ovid, *Her.* vi. 44 'sertis tempora vinctus Hymen'. (See further the articles of Maas cited in introduction to 56–115.) *Hymenaeus* occurs twice in the *Medea*, 116 ('song'), 300 ('god'); elsewhere in the tragedies (except *Tro* 202 'song') *hymen* and *hymenaeus* mean 'marriage' (see O–P–C).

67. facibus: *faces* alone for 'wedding', as 398: cf. Prop. iv. 11. 46 'viximus insignes inter utramque facem', 'between marriage and death'. The torchlight procession was a picturesque and memorable feature of the marriage ceremony, and so the words *fax* and, more frequently, *taeda* (581) came themselves to mean 'marriage' in the poets (*taeda* first in this sense Cat. 64. 25).

68. Cf. Cat. 61. 14–15 'manu / pineam quate taedam'.

auspice: probably adjectival, 'favouring, auspicious' (cf. 285 'auspicatos toros'), but it may be an appositional noun with *dextera*, with reference to the *auspices*, official witnesses, at Roman weddings: cf. *Tro* 863 'auspice Helena'.

69. gradu marcidus ebrio: *ebrio* is suggested by Hymen's connection with Dionysus (110 n.). (Delrius' suggestion is more practical: 'temulentum Hymenaeum fingebant: an quia sine Cerere et Baccho friget Venus?') But *marcidus* itself probably does not mean 'reeling' (Miller), but 'languid, effete'. The long description of Hymen in Cat. 61 contains certain bisexual features which may be reflected here in *marcidus* and in *marcentibus* 112. See Wheeler, op. cit. 210 ff., and cf. the use of *marcidus* in a picture of docile effeminacy, *HO* 376 'hirtam Sabaea marcidus myrrha comam'; also *de prov.* 3. 10 'voluptatibus marcidum'.

70: Hymen conventionally wears garlands: Cat. 61. 6 'cinge tempora floribus . . .', Ovid, *Her.* vi. 44 (quoted on 67-70).

71 ff. et tu: sc. *incede*. Hesperus, the evening star, has its place in earlier and later epithalamia: Cat. 62. 1-2 'Vesper adest, iuvenes, consurgite: Vesper Olympo / exspectata diu vix tandem lumina tollit', Sappho, fr. 104 L-P *Ἔσπερε πάντα φέρων ὅσα φαίνολις ἐσκέδασ' αὔως*, 'Shine, Hesperus, shine forth, thou wished star!' (refrain of Ben Jonson's *Epithalamion* for Lord Ramsey, 1608). The anaphora *tu . . . te . . . te* is a traditional technique in hymns (cf. 797 ff.), where the god's attributes or powers are enumerated. For Latin examples cf. Lucr. i. 6 ff. (Venus), Cat. 34. 13 ff. (Diana), Hor. *C.* ii. 19. 17 ff. (Bacchus), and see Norden, *Agnostos Theos* 149 ff., Nisbet-Hubbard on Hor. *C.* i. 10. 9.

gemini praevia temporis: 'bringing on the twilight', lit. 'double time', half day, half night; or *gemini temporis* means 'both times', night and morning, which the same star introduces: below, 878 'dux noctis Hesperus', Ovid, *M.* xv. 190-1 'praevia lucis . . . Pallantias', *Her.* xviii. 112.

matres . . . nurus: *nurus* has the general sense 'young wives': cf. Ovid, *M.* xii. 215-16 'ecce canunt Hymenaeon, et ignibus atria fumant; / cinctaque adest virgo matrum nuruumque caterva'.

75 ff. The chorus now praises the beauty of bride and bridegroom, and the metre changes to glyconics. (Cat. 61 is written in glyconics and pherecrateans.) The topic is conventional in the epithalamium: Sappho, fr. 115 L-P *τίῳ σ' ὦ φίλε γάμβρε κάλως εἰκάσδω; | ὄρπακι βραδίνῳ σε μάλιστ' εἰκάσδω*, Cat. 61. 82 ff., 185 ff. In true choral manner there is a wealth of geographical and mythological references to underline the points which are made. The function of a Greek and Senecan chorus is often to generalize, or to highlight a particular situation or person by setting it against a background of similar situations drawn from history or legend. The present passage should be compared with the choral eulogy to Hippolytus' beauty in *Phae* 741-60. (There have been attempts to break down the rest of this chorus into a strophic pattern on Greek lines, with alternate passages sung by groups of girls and young men such as we find in Cat. 62. Thus Bentley suggested giving 75-81 and 93 ff. to a chorus of girls, and 82-92 to one of young men (A. Stachelscheid, *Neue Jahrbücher für Philologie und Paedagogik* 125 (1882), 488). But there is very little evidence for strophic construction in Seneca's choruses, and certainly anything like the complex responsions of Greek tragic choruses is out of the question: see Leo, I. 135 ff., and note on 579 ff.)

75-81. Creusa's beauty is supreme throughout Greece.

75. virgineus: i.e. Creusae. Neither Creusa nor Jason is named in the song, but they are referred to allusively, e.g. 'Aesonio duci' 83, 'Aeoliam virginem' 105: contrast Cat. 61. 16.

76. Cecropias: 'Athenian', from the traditionally first king of Athens, Cecrops: a touch of mythological elevation, though the word is common in Latin poetry (*Phae* 2, *Thy* 1049).

77 ff.: 'and the brides whom the unwalled town (Sparta) trains like young men on the heights of Taygetus'. The freedom of association between the sexes at Sparta, particularly in physical exercise, was the cause of shocked surprise to many writers, and of envy to Propertius: 'multa tuae, Sparte, miramur iura palaestrae, / sed mage virginei tot bona gymnasii; / quod non infames exercet corpore ludos / inter luctantes nuda puella viros' (iii. 14. 1–4: he goes on to contrast the difficulty of getting to know one's girl friend at Rome. For a different point of view on the Spartan practice see Eur. *Andr.* 595 ff.). For the association with the near-by range of Taygetus cf. Prop. ibid. 13–14 (the Spartan girl) 'et modo Taygeti crines adspersa pruina / sectatur patrios per iuga longa canes', Virg. *G.* ii. 487–8. See too frag. inc. (Accius?) 206–8 R 'nihil horum similest apud Lacaenas virgines, / quibus magis palaestra Eurota sol pulvis labor / militia studio est quam fertilitas barbara'.

   muris caret: Ovid, *M.* x. 169–70 'immunitamque . . . Sparten', Livy xxxiv. 38 'fuerat quondam sine muro Sparta'. Protected by its natural position Sparta remained without defensive walls until the time of Nabis at the end of the third century B.C.: Livy xxxix. 37. 2, Paus. vii. 8. 5.

80 ff.: 'the maidens whom Boeotian waters and (those whom) the holy Alpheus bathe'.

   Aonius: 'Boeotian', from Aon, a legendary local hero.

   lavat: cf. *Oed* 714 'lavitque Dirce', Stat. *S.* ii. 7. 18 'quas Dirce lavat'. For identification of peoples by local springs or rivers see on 372–4.

81. sacer. The worship of rivers and their gods was a very primitive element in Greek folk-lore, so that 'sacred' is a common description of springs and rivers in the Greek and Latin poets: see *OCD*, s.v. 'River-Gods'. The Alpheus, the longest river in the Peloponnese, was honoured by Zeus, according to Pindar (*O.* v. 17–18) and Pausanias (v. 13. 11). So also *Thy* 116–17 'sacer Alpheos', Milton, *Arcades* 29–30 'that renowned flood, so often sung, / Divine Alpheus'.

82–9. Jason's beauty is unmatched by Bacchus, Apollo, Castor, or Pollux.

82. velit: sc. *Iason*.

   formā aspici: 'regarded, considered as to his beauty'; cf. Sil. It. iii. 114 'sin solo adspicimur sexu'. (Gronovius: '*si velit*, inquit, quasi dubitans: nam fortes pulcritudinis laudem dedignantur.')

83. cedent: with *proles* and *frater* 87. Jason's father was Aeson.

84. Bacchus was the son of Jupiter and the Theban princess Semele, who was tricked by Juno into making Jupiter promise to appear to

her in his true form. She was consumed by the thunderbolts with
which Jupiter had then to visit her, but the unborn Bacchus was
rescued (Eur. *Bacchae* 2–3, Ovid, *M.* iii. 259 ff., *HF* 457 'e matris utero
fulmine eiectus puer'). There is a long dithyrambic chorus in *Oed*
403–508 in praise of Bacchus and his achievements; but just as even
his beauty yields here to that of Jason, so he is unfavourably compared
with Hippolytus, *Phae* 753–60, and the idea recurs in late Greek epic
in Colluthus, *Rape of Helen* 251 (Paris is superior to Bacchus in
beauty).

85. Cf. *Phae* 755 '(Liber) tigres pampinea cuspide territans', Virg. *Aen.*
vi. 805–6 'nec qui pampineis victor iuga flectit habenis, / Liber agens
celso Nysae de vertice tigres', Hor. *C.* iii. 3. 13–15. Bacchus-Dionysus
is all-powerful over man and nature, and the tigers reflect his association with the east and India (*Phae* 753, *Oed* 424 ff., Eur. *Bacchae*
13 ff., Ovid, *M.* iv. 20–1).

86 ff. qui . . . frater: Apollo, whose oracles (the most important
being at Delphi) are referred to by *tripodas movet*. These words
describe the physical, though unseen, presence of the god as he
delivers his oracle: he shakes the tripod on which sits the priestess
who is his mouthpiece. See below, 785–6 'sonuistis, arae, tripodas
agnosco meos / favente commotos dea', Ovid, *M.* ix. 782 'visa dea
est movisse suas (et moverat) aras', Lucan v. 120 ff. 'sic tempore
longo / immotos tripodas . . . sollicitat'. The 'stern (almost 'tough')
maiden' is Diana, the epithet referring to her masculine interest in
hunting and her inviolate virginity. Apollonius too likened Jason to
Apollo (iii. 1283).

88–9. Castor and Pollux were sons of Zeus or Tyndareus, and brothers
of Helen of Troy. Castor was a famous horseman and Pollux a boxer
(*caestibus*): Hom. *Il.* iii. 237 Κάστορά θ' ἱππόδαμον καὶ πὺξ ἀγαθὸν
Πολυδεύκεα, Hor. *C.* i. 12. 25–7, *Sat.* ii. 1. 26–7. Both took part in the
expedition of the Argo.

    suo: sc. *fratre.* For *aptior* in this sense cf. *HF* 906 'soror sagittis
aptior'.

90–2. The statements by the chorus of the supremacy of the bride's
beauty over maidens or brides, and of the bridegroom's even over
gods, are supplemented by a prayer that she may continue to outshine
all wives and he all husbands. Thus we are brought back from the
level of mythology (84–9) to the present time and occasion, and
reminded that it is a newly-wedded pair who are being lauded. For
sic sic with jussive subjunctive cf. *Thy* 102 'sic sic ferantur'.

93–101. After praising Jason the chorus returns to Creusa and dwells
again upon her beauty. There is, however, no corresponding second
description of Jason to follow: instead, the chorus urges him to seize
his opportunity and exchange a disastrous marriage for a happy one
(102–6).

93 ff. Creusa's beauty outshines all her maiden attendants, just as the sun eclipses the stars and the Pleiades fade beside the full moon.

    choro: in a general sense 'troop, retinue'.

94. praenitet: 'outshine': of physical beauty, as at Hor. *C.* i. 33. 3–4 'cur tibi iunior / laesa praeniteat fide'.

95. cum sole: 'at dawn', as Virg. *Aen.* iii. 568 'ventus cum sole reliquit'. The phrase and several variants are common in this sense: see *OLD*, s.v. 'cum' 6a.

96–8. The thought goes back to Sappho, fr. 34 L–P ἄστερες μὲν ἀμφὶ κάλαν σελάνναν / ἂψ ἀποκρύπτοισι φάεννον εἶδος / ὅπποτα πλήθοισα μάλιστα λάμπῃ / γᾶν . . . Cf. Hor. *C.* i. 12. 46–8 'micat inter omnes / Iulium sidus, velut inter ignes / Luna minores' (Nisbet–Hubbard ad loc. give many other parallels), and a similar passage at *Phae* 743–8 (the beauty of Hippolytus) 'pulchrior tanto tua forma lucet, / clarior quanto micat orbe pleno / cum suos ignes coeunte cornu / iunxit et curru properante pernox / exerit vultus rubicunda Phoebe / nec tenent stellae faciem minores'.

    densi Pleiadum greges: the familiar constellation of the seven daughters of Atlas. The description (*greges* is a loose poetic plural) refers to the close clustering of the group: Prop. iii. 5. 36 'Pleiadum spisso cur coit igne chorus'.

    cum Phoebe . . . : 'when the Moon with borrowed light binds a full circle with (or 'to') her surrounding horns': as the Moon waxes to become full, her horns are supposed to meet and enclose a complete circle of light. It is a rather odd use of *alligare*—the linked horns enclose the orb as though tying it up—found also in Martial, viii. 50. 7 'sic alligat orbem, / plurima cum tota lampade luna nitet'. Other passages with *alligare* suggest that *cornibus* is abl. (e.g. *Thy* 161 'inclusisque famem dentibus alligat'), but it may be dat. in view of the abl. *lumine*. For *circuitis cornibus* cf. *Phae* 745 'coeunte cornu', Lucan, i. 537–8 'cornuque coacto / iam Phoebe toto fratrem cum redderet orbe'. That the moon merely reflects the sun's light (*lumine non suo*) was first taught by Thales, according to Aëtius (ii. 28. 5, Diels, *Dox. Gr.* 358): see also Parmenides, fr. 14 D–K νυκτιφαὲς περὶ γαῖαν ἀλώμενον, ἀλλότριον φῶς, Cat. 34. 15 ff. 'et notho es / dicta lumine Luna', Lucr. v. 575–6, 705 ff. (a discussion of theories on the subject), Lucan, loc. cit., Virg. *G.* i. 396.

    circuitis is active—the horns surround, are not themselves surrounded. Passive participles of transitive verbs are not common in an active sense, but, apart from forms like *osus* and its compounds, cf. Petronius, 48. 4 'ne me putes studia fastiditum' (K–S i. 99).

99 ff. Leo thought that there was a lacuna before *ostro sic . . .* and suggested as a stop-gap 'talem dum iuvenis conspicit, en rubor / perfudit subito purpureus genas'. The sequence of thought is a little abrupt, but if the text is sound the words pick up and further describe the bride's features: the clauses *sic . . . rubuit* and *sic . . . aspicit* have the same, if slightly looser, connection with *facies praenitet* as does *sic . . . latitant*. Her beauty glows as 'the snow-white colour (of cloth or ivory) blushes red when dyed in Phoenician purple' etc. For the stock description of a pink-and-white complexion cf. Cat. 61. 186–8 (the bride) 'ore floridulo nitens, / alba parthenice velut / luteumve papaver', and Fordyce ad loc. Sen. might be recalling Ligurinus' cheeks: Hor. *C.* iv. 10. 4 'qui color est puniceae flore prior rosae'. Tyre was celebrated for producing the finest known purple dye, so that its use was a hall-mark of elegance and luxury: *Thy* 955–6 'Tyrio saturas ostro / . . . vestes', *HO* 644 'caespes Tyrio mollior ostro', Virg. *Aen.* v. 111–12 'ostro perfusae vestes' (as prizes). (The parent passage for similes with Phoenician purple is Hom. *Il.* iv. 141 ὡς δ' ὅτε τίς τ' ἐλέφαντα γυνὴ φοίνικι μιήνῃ.) Mayor on Juv. i. 27 has an exhaustive note on Tyre and its dyeing industry.

100. nitidum iubar: the same phrase is used of the setting sun at *Ag* 463: here of its first rays at dawn—glowing like Creusa's cheeks.

101. roscidus: 'wet with dew': the epithet applied to a human being is unusual.

102 ff. The chorus's first clear statement of hostility to M., but she is referred to obliquely and not by name (*Phasidis, effrenae coniugis*): cf. 75 n.

  ereptus . . . solitus . . . trepidus . . . felix corripe . . . sponse: The address to Jason builds up to a climax in *felix*: 'happy (at last), clasp the Aeolian maiden'. The chorus suggests that Jason has never enjoyed his marriage with M.

  thalamis Phasidis: *HO* 950 'Phasiaca coniunx'. *Phasidis* here by metonymy for *Medeae* (44–5 n.); epithets for the river reflect the feelings of other peoples about Medea or the Colchians (*horridi* here, *cruentum* Stat. *Th.* v. 457).

105. Aeoliam: 'Corinthian': Ephyre or Corinth was said to have been founded by Sisyphus, son of Aeolus (son of Hellen, not the wind-god): Apollod. i. 9. 3.

106. soceris volentibus: abl. abs. The goodwill of Creusa's parents contrasts with Aeetes' open hostility to Jason. *soceri* occurs several times for 'parents-in-law', e.g. *Tro* 1002.

  sponse: for the vocative 'attraction' see 605 n.

107 ff. The references here and in lines 113 'dicax Fescennimus', 114 'iocos', are to the cheerful ribaldry which was a conventional element in both Greek and Roman epithalamia: see Aristoph. *Pax* 1336 ff., Theocr. xviii. 9 ff. with Gow's note, Page, *Sappho and Alcaeus* 120, and in particular Cat. 61. 119 ff., where the *Fescennina iocatio* includes uninhibited banter addressed to the bridegroom's erstwhile *concubinus*. At Rome this ribald chanting was customary at generals' triumphs as well as at weddings, and the purpose in both cases seems to have been to counteract by ritual abuse any effect of the 'evil eye' on persons thought to be too fortunate.

concesso: 'permitted': cf. 'iusta licentia' 109.

hinc illinc: 'responsively, in answer to each other', giving an amoebean performance, like Cat. 62.

109: 'seldom are we allowed to act as we like towards our masters' (*dominos* here being Jason and the Corinthian royal family). Apart from the licensed abuse at triumphs and weddings, Seneca may be thinkinga nachronistically (see on *Fescenninus* 113) of the Roman Saturnalia (beginning 17 December), during which slaves were allowed to do as they liked. So Horace tells his slave Davus to speak his mind freely at this time: 'age, libertate Decembri / (quando ita maiores voluerunt) utere: narra' (*Sat.* ii. 7. 4–5).

licentia: Hor. *Ep.* ii. 1. 145 'Fescennina licentia'.

110–15. Dactylic hexameters are very rare in the tragedies, and are used elsewhere only at *Oed* 233–8 (an oracle, traditionally given in this metre), and at intervals during the long dithyramb in the same play (403–4, 429–31, 445–8, 446–71, 504–8). (It is probably coincidental that the present lines also contain a reference to Bacchus.) It is also noticeable that 110–15 contain several words which occur nowhere else in the tragedies (*multifidam, dicax, convicia, fescenninus, peregrino, fugitiva*), and this cluster may be partly explained by the use of the rare hexameter. (On hexameters in Greek tragedy see Wilamowitz, *Griechische Verskunst* 347 ff., A. M. Dale, *Lyric Metres of Greek Drama* 25 ff.)

110. proles Lyaei: Hymen, of whose parentage there were varied accounts (see *RE* ix. 127 ff.): one version, here followed by Seneca, made him the son of Dionysus and Aphrodite (Servius on Virg. *Aen.* iv. 127; Donatus on Terence, *Ad.* 905; Martianus Cap. i. 1).

thyrsigeri: θυρσοφόρου (cf. Eur. *Cycl.* 64). *Phae* 753 'thyrsigera Liber ab India': the familiar picture of Dionysus carrying the thyrsus, or staff wreathed in ivy and vine-leaves.

Lyaei: *Oed* 508 'candida formosi venerabimur ora Lyaei', *HO* 244. Lyaeus ('loosener' from λύειν) is a common name for Bacchus in Latin writers.

111. multifidam: 'well-split, frayed' ('in modum spicarum incisam, quo facilius flammam concipiat' Farnaby). Used of *faces* at Ovid, *M.* vii. 259, viii. 644, and cf. Stat. *Th.* iii. 142 'multifida attollens antiqua lumina cedro'.

pinum: 38 n.

iam tempus erat: for the idiom *tempus erat* referring to present time, and expressing an impatient desire for something which is overdue, cf. Hor. *C.* i. 37. 2–4 'nunc Saliaribus / ornare pulvinar deorum / tempus erat dapibus', Ovid, *Am.* iii. 1. 23–4 'tempus erat thyrso pulsum graviore moveri; / cessatum satis est: incipe maius opus', *Tr.* iv. 8. 24 ff.

112. excute: 'shake or toss out' the flames, by vigorously waving the torch: Lucr. vi. 688 '(aer) excussit calidum flammis velocibus ignem', *Oed* 500 'geminus Cupido concutit taedas', Cat. 61. 77–8, Pliny, *Ep.* iv. 9. 11. Contrast the sense of 'excutiam faces' 27 ('snatch away').

sollemnem: 'ritual': the word has close ceremonial and religious associations; e.g. 797–8 'sacrum sollemne', *Phae* 424.

marcentibus: 'languid': cf. *marcidus* 69 n. The word is rather oddly linked with the vigorous *excute*. (There is an echo of the line in Stat. *S.* i. 2. 4–5 'quatiuntque novena / lampade sollemnem thalamis coeuntibus ignem'.)

113. Fescenninus: Festus 76L 'Fescennini versus, qui canebantur in nuptiis, ex urbe Fescennina dicuntur allati, sive ideo dicti, quia fascinum ('witchcraft') putabantur arcere'. Cf. 107 n., Fordyce on Cat. 61. 120. Fescennine banter was said to have had a place in early times at Italian harvest festivals (Hor. *Ep.* ii. 1. 145–6, Livy vii. 2), and literary Fescennines for marriages survived until the time of Claudian (*flor.* 400 A.D.), who wrote them for the wedding of Honorius and Maria. Seneca was no doubt unconcerned at his anachronistic use of the word in the heroic age. For other possible anachronisms in the tragedies (e.g. *HF* 48 'opima', *Phae* 351 'Lucaeque boves') see Herrmann, *Le Théâtre de Sénèque* 330.

dicax: 'sharp, witty': Cat. 61. 119–20 'procax Fescennina iocatio'.

festa convicia: cf. Lucan, ii. 368–9 'non soliti lusere sales nec more Sabino / excepit tristis convicia festa maritus'.

This is an example of a so-called 'golden line' i.e. a hexameter with a verb in the centre, followed by two nouns and preceded by two adjectives agreeing respectively with them. There are many examples in Catullus and Virgil, and they are more common still in Ovid and Lucan: see Williams on *Aen.* v. 46.

114. solvat: 'release' i.e. 'utter freely': *Oed* 292 (*responsa*), *Thy* 682 (*vocem*)—a mainly Silver sense of the verb.

tacitis eat illa … : 'let her depart in silent darkness—whoever runs away and weds a foreign husband'. The chorus breaks off at a half-line to end its song with an insulting reference to M.—another sign of informal construction in the lyric. Both *peregrino* and *fugitiva* are of course contemptuous, and both are applied to Helen of Troy, by Horace (*C.* iii. 3. 20 'mulier peregrina') and Ovid (*Her.* v. 91 'Tyndaris infestis fugitiva reposcitur armis'). Notice the emphatic *illa* picked up by the indefinite *si qua*, almost as though the chorus suddenly catches sight of M. and tactfully generalizes the rest of the sentence.

115. nubit: 481 n.

116–78. At the sound of the wedding-song M.'s horror and frenzy are redoubled, and she pours forth a further torrent of bitter and sometimes incoherent words, as her rage at Jason's conduct battles with the love she still feels for him. Her old nurse tries in vain to calm this *furialis impetus*, and to show the hopelessness of her position.

116–17. Ovid, *Her.* xii. 137–41 'ut subito nostras Hymen cantatus ad aures / venit . . . pertimui, nec adhuc tantum scelus esse putabam'.

    hymenaeus: see intr. note to 56–115 and on 67–70.

    ipsa: 'myself' opposed to *aures*: my ears have heard but my mind cannot believe.

118–19. hoc: picked up by *deserere* 120: 'could Jason do this . . . cruelly desert me?'

    erepto patre . . . : Ovid, ibid. 109 'proditus est genitor, regnum patriamque reliqui', 161 'deseror amissis regno patriaque domoque'.

    solam: sc. *me*.

121. scelere: sc. *meo*: 52 ff. n.

    flammas: 466 'igneos tauri halitus': the breath of the bulls which Jason yoked with the help of M.'s magic drugs.

    mare: presumably means their escape from Aeetes by sea, made possible by M.'s murder of her brother.

122. adeo: goes with *consumptum*: 'does he believe that my resources of evil are so exhausted?' Cf. a line of Ovid's *Medea* (quoted by Quintilian viii. 5–6) 'servare potui; perdere an possim rogas?' (perhaps M. addressing Jason); 560–1 below.

123. Seneca the Elder preserves (*Suas.* iii. 7) the other surviving verse of Ovid's *Medea*: 'feror huc illuc ut plena deo'. Leo (I. 167) uses this fragment as evidence that Seneca followed Ovid rather than Euripides in his portrayal of M.'s character (see too Vente, *Die Medea-Tragoedie Senecas* 28–9): while we should beware of extensive inferences about Ovid's play, it is certainly true that, as Leo says, we see Seneca's M. 'furere ab initio paene per totam fabulam'. He compares 382 ff., 675, 738, 805 ff., 849 ff., 862 ff. For the possible influence of Ovid see also introductory notes to 137 ff. and 179–300. Apollonius' Medea too had her violent moments: ὣς φάτ', ἀναζείουσα βαρὺν χόλον· ἵετο δ' ἥγε / νῆα καταφλέξαι . . . iv. 391 ff.

    ve- (*vae-*) in **vecors, vesanus** is a negativing prefix, and the words are virtually synonymous, 'insane, wild, deranged': cf. 738 'vesano gradu'. Note the scansion *incertă . . . vesană*.

124. queam: this verb is more common in negative or virtually negative sentences: cf. 23, 548.

125. utinam . . . frater: sc. 'so that I might treat him as I treated my own'.

126. ferrum exigatur: M. uses nearly the same words at 1006, 'ferrum exigam'—but there the blow is against her own child.

    sătĭs ēst malis: a rare example of a fifth-foot anapaest where the two short syllables are in a separate word: cf. *HO* 406 'cărĕt Hērcule'. Much more common are the types 'dŏmĭnām fide' 11, and (with elision) 'flagĭtĭa ingere' 236.

127 ff. si quod . . . parandum: M. resolves to extend her repertoire of crimes in order to do justice to her vengeance.

Pelasgae (urbes): 'Greek': a name originally referring to a pre-Hellenic tribe of uncertain origin, and later to Greeks in general. It is opposed to *barbarae*, i.e. non-Greek, not the derived sense of 'wild, savage'. (Thus M. refers to her own country in Eur. *Med.* 256 ἐκ γῆς βαρβάρου λελησμένη.)

tuae . . . tua: in her distraught condition M. slips from *meis* 126 to the hortatory second-person adjectives here, then to the third person reference to herself, *nefandae virginis* 131. This is probably a deliberate rhetorical touch: cf. 41 n.

129–30. scelera . . . cuncta redeant: 'let all your (past) crimes return', i.e. 'be repeated'.

inclitum decus: the Golden Fleece. This and the following phrases down to *membra* 134 expand and define *scelera* 129: her record since meeting Jason is a succession of sins, and all were prompted by love for him, *amor* 136.

131 ff. Seneca here follows the version of the legend according to which M., in her flight with Jason from Colchis, took her brother with her, killed and dismembered him, and scattered his fragments on the sea. Thus they escaped from Aeetes, who stopped in his pursuit to pick up the pieces. (So Pherecydes, Jacoby, *FGH* 3 F 32b, Apollod. 1. 9. 23–4, Cic. *Leg. Man.* 22, and a variant in Ovid, *Tr.* iii. 9). Other accounts were: (*a*) Absyrtus pursued them and was ambushed and killed by Jason (Ap. Rhod. iv. 303 ff., Hyg. *fab.* 23); (*b*) M. murdered him in the palace of Aeetes (Sophocles in his *Colchian Women*, according to Schol. on Ap. Rhod. iv. 228; Eur. *Med.* 1334, cf. below, 452–3). The brother (not named by Seneca) is usually called Absyrtus. (Cic. *ND* iii. 48 says that Pacuvius called him Aegialeus, as did Diodorus iv. 45: so Milton, *Sylvarum liber* i. 20, 'Aegiali soror usa virga'). This act above all preys on M.'s conscience: 473, 963 ff. (In Euripides she herself does not allude to it.)

132. funus ingestum patri: 'his murder forced upon his father's sight' (Miller). *ingerere* is used of forcing a (usually unpleasant) sight on someone: *Thy* 282–3 'ingesta orbitas / in ora patris', Lucan, vii. 798–9 'caeloque nocenti / ingerit Emathiam'; cf. *de ira* i. 18. 2. 'etiam si ingeritur oculis veritas', Stat. *S.* ii. 2. 84–5.

133. Peliae senis: Pelias was Jason's uncle, who had usurped his father's throne and sent him to find the Golden Fleece. When Jason and M. returned to Iolcos, M. restored Jason's father Aeson to youth, and induced the daughters of Pelias to believe that she could similarly rejuvenate their father. Following her instructions they cut up Pelias' body, and she threw it into a cauldron in which she had deliberately placed powerless herbs. Thus she engineered his death at their hands, and it was to escape the ensuing wrath of his son Acastus that she and Jason fled from Iolcos and arrived in Corinth (below, 256 ff.). The incident is an early element in the Medea legend (Pindar, *P.* iv. 250, lost plays by Soph. and Eur.; and see further Ovid, *Her.* xii. 129–30, *M.* vii. 297 ff., Apollod. i. 9. 27 with Frazer's Loeb note). A 'rationalist' variant of the legend appears in Diodorus (iv. 51–2), where, Aeson being already dead, M. wins the trust of Pelias' daughters by disguising herself as an old woman and then apparently restoring her own youth. Then (as in other versions) she does her cauldron act with the ram, but here we are explicitly told that she works it by means of a dummy lamb (ἀρνὸς εἴδωλον).

134–5. aeno: 'bronze vessel, cauldron': local abl. Cf. 666 'ustus accenso Pelias aeno'.

   funestum fudi sanguinem: 'caused fatal bloodshed'.

   et: 'and yet', as often in Sen.: see Summers on *Ep.* 56. 11.

136. irata … amor: yet now that her wrath is aroused it does not completely dispel her love, and the interplay of the two feelings is a root cause of her mental turmoil and subsequent actions: cf. 397–8, 866 ff.

   saevit: this has troubled editors (*movit* Leo, *suasit* Peiper, *fecit* Garrod, *CQ* v (1911), 216), but it can stand. The present tense is significant: M.'s passion for Jason raged when she committed crimes in the past—and still it rages (like Dido's, *Aen.* iv. 532 *saevit amor*).

137 ff. The word *amor* and a resurgence of her old feelings for Jason prompt a sudden change to a more tender mood, and M. now makes excuses for his conduct. 'But what could he do when under the control of another (Creon)?' Then a return to resentment: 'He should have resisted at the risk of his life'. Then tenderness again: 'No, no, may he at all costs live on—whether mine or another's'. She then goes on to blame Creon for the situation that has arisen and to plot her vengeance against him. This un-Euripidean tenderness may owe something to Ovid—his M. clearly retains her love for Jason in *Her.* xii. 185 ff.; at any rate, in portraying these vacillations of mood Seneca is exploiting the resources of declamatory rhetoric, and behind M.'s shifting arguments can be heard the popular exercises of the debating schools.

137–8. alieni … factus: 'subject to the will and control of another'. For this type of genitive used as a predicate (commonly with *esse* and *facere*) cf. Livy, i. 25. 13 'alteri dicionis alienae facti', *de ben.* v. 19. 1 'mei mancipii res est', and the phrase *sui iuris*, 'one's own master'.

139. melius … dolor: cf. 930 'melius, a, demens furor'.

140. vivat: this tender wish is very different from the earlier *vivat* 20.

   meus: predicative, and emphatic by position (like ἐμόν at Eur. *Med.* 375 πατέρα τε καὶ κόρην πόσιν τ' ἐμόν).

141. si minus: sc. *vivere potest meus*—if he becomes Creusa's.

142. nostri: probably singular, as often (e.g. Juv. iii. 318 'vale, nostri memor'), but possibly plural and including her children.

muneri: i.e. *vitae suae*, continuing the theme of *vivat*: he owed his life to M. For the same idea cf. Ovid, *Her.* xii. 203 'dos mea tu sospes', 205–6 'quod vivis . . . meum est'. But the expression is strained and Richter's *muneris parcat mihi* is persuasive.

143. impotens: 'violent, ungovernable', with abl. as *Tro* 266–7 *impotens regno*.

144 ff. genetricem abstrahit natis: this must be a generalization, or an accurate prophecy of her own fate, as M. has not yet learnt of her banishment and forced parting from her children (190, 284). In Eur. Creon orders her to take her children with her into exile (272–3).

145. arto . . . fidem: 'faith, promise bound by strict pledge': cf. *Oed* 804 'liberi astringunt fidem'. If there is a particular reference it must be to M.'s share in Creon's promise to protect them when they came as exiles to Corinth.

147. alto . . . domum: 'I shall make the palace a towering heap of ashes'. The burning of the palace is reported 885 ff. Euripides' M. debates whether to burn Creon's palace (πότερον ὑφάψω δῶμα νυμφικὸν πυρί 378) but abandons the idea.

148. verticem flammis agi: either 'the roof harried, attacked by the flames', or 'a column of (smoke and) flames driven upwards', which shall be visible right across the Peloponnese at Malea.

149. Mălĕă: the south-east promontory of the Peloponnese, which 'delays ships by its long curving coastline': cf. 35, Lucan, vi. 58 'et ratibus longae flexus donare Maleae', Ovid, *Am.* ii. 16. 24.

150 ff. As often with Seneca's characters, the Nurse's arrival on the scene is unheralded. *ECPS* record her presence at the head of this scene (116), and we may imagine that she arrives in the wake of the wedding-procession, and listens with growing alarm to M.'s passionate reaction to it. She urges M. to conceal her frenzy, and opens with a string of Senecan *sententiae*: cf. the philosophical nurses in Eur. (e.g. *Hipp.* 186 ff., *Med.* 190 ff.), and the scenes between other Senecan nurses and their mistresses (Phaedra, *Phae* 129 ff., Deianira, *HO* 256 ff., Clytaemnestra, *Ag* 108 ff.). In our play the Nurse's part is much more developed than in Euripides' *Medea*, where she disappears after line 203, and Seneca's Nurse in effect takes over the sympathetic role which the chorus has in Eur. but not here.

As a faithful foil and confidante to the heroine the nurse descends virtually unchanged from Greek drama through Seneca to English and French tragedy. Oenone in *Phèdre* and Juliet's nurse differ in no essentials from their classical forerunners, and the loyal, gossipy, querulous old lady has offered playwrights much scope for pathos, humour, and good sense. (In Corneille, Médée's Nérine is called a 'suivante', but belongs clearly to the nurse tradition.) Pease on *Aen.* iv. 632 has a long list of nurses in classical literature.

This scene between M. and the Nurse is a good example of a Senecan dramatic debate, and well illustrates both the virtues and the weaknesses of the declamatory style: neatness, economy of phrase, epigrammatic balance on the one hand; on the other, artificiality, remoteness from flesh-and-blood discussion, and the impression we receive of a rhetorical show-piece emanating from the schools. As Senecan tragedy can fairly be considered to a large extent a dramatic extension of rhetorical debate, it is not surprising that we find features which seem stilted and grotesque to modern taste, and criticism, while recognizing what is dramatically implausible and unintentionally funny in the plays, should also try to understand them as a unique literary development.

There is a good adaptation of the scene in Corneille (*Médée* i. 5), with less of the Senecan extravagance, and a comparison of the two passages is instructive.

150–1. questusque . . . dolori: so Deianira's nurse *HO* 276–7 'questus comprime et flammas doma; / frena dolorem'.

152–3. pertulit, potuit: 'gnomic' perfects, equivalent to presents, indicating what has been found to be true in the past, and can be taken as a general rule. Seneca is fond of the idiom in his prose works: K–S i. 133.

referre: 'repay', return wound for wound. *referre* (*gratiam*) more commonly expresses gratitude.

nocet: i.e. avenges itself, balancing *vindictae* 154. The thought is a commonplace: Creon to Medea in Eur. *Med.* 319–20 γυνὴ γὰρ ὀξύθυμος, ὡς δ' αὔτως ἀνήρ, / ῥᾴων φυλάσσειν ἢ σιωπηλὸς σοφός, Seneca the Elder, *Contr.* i. praef. 21 'magis nocent insidiae quae latent', Tac. *H.* iv. 24. 9.

154. professa: passive, 'proclaimed'.

156. clepere: (cf. κλέπτειν) 'steal away, i.e. hide, itself': an old and rare verb which Seneca would have found in early Latin tragedy, as we see from surviving examples of its use by Accius (frs. 212, 292R) and Pacuvius (fr. 185R). Elsewhere in Seneca's plays it occurs only as a variant at *HF* 799, and the only near-contemporary example cited in *TLL* is Manilius i. 27. Perhaps Seneca deliberately archaizes— *tegere* would have done as well. (156 is omitted in *CPS* and others.)

157. ire contra: sc. *hostes meos.*

siste furialem impetum: *Ag* 203 *siste impetus.*

Division of a verse between more than one speaker (ἀντιλαβή) in excited or argumentative dialogue is quite common in Soph. and Eur., and frequent in Seneca's tragedies, e.g. the present exchange between M. and the Nurse, below, 493 ff. (M. and Jason), *Thy* 204 ff. (Atreus and servant). The technique clearly lends itself to rhetorical drama: like stichomythia, but sharper in its impact, it accelerates the cut-and-thrust of opposing arguments and the capping of point by point, and is ideally suited to Seneca's epigrammatic style. The present passage illustrates the most obvious feature of the technique: the swift rebuttal of a point by another which picks up and repeats key words—*locum virtus/virtuti locus*; *spes/sperare*; *superest/superest*; *rex/rex*.

158. alumna: the regular form of address by nurse to mistress in the tragedies: below, 380.

    vix ... quies: i.e. even if you keep quiet you may not be safe (to say nothing of what would happen if you showed open hostility).

159. fortuna fortes metuit: M. gives a scornful turn to a common proverb (Virg. *Aen.* x. 284 'audentes fortuna iuvat', Terence, *Ph.* 203 'fortes fortuna adiuvat'; other examples in Otto, *Sprichwörter* 144): a good rhetorical touch which underlines her defiance.

160: 'then (only) should courage be approved when it finds a fitting occasion'. *si* virtually = *cum*, 'if and when'.

163: 'who can hope for nothing may despair of nothing': the thought and its formulation are a typical Senecan epigram. Cf. *Ep.* 5. 7 (quoting Hecato) 'desines timere si sperare desieris'.

164. abiere: 'have departed' from you, i.e. have nothing more to do with you. The word suggests M.'s both physical and spiritual isolation from her own people.

166. Medea superest: (cf. below, 517) imitated and improved by Corneille:

> Nérine. Dans un si grand revers que vous reste-t-il?
> Médée.   Moi,
>
>   Moi, dis-je, et c'est assez.
>
>   (*Médée* 320-1)

Cf. Shakespeare, *Ant. and Cleop.* iii. xiii. 92-3 'Have you no ears? I am Antony yet'.

    hic ... fulmina: here (i.e. in me) you see all the forces which I can control and bring to my aid.

168. rex ... rex: Creon, Aeetes. M. means that the fact that her father was a king did not prevent her opposing him.

    fuerat either loosely for *erat*, or literally means 'my father had kingly power until I proved him powerless against me'.

169. sint ... edita: '(no) even if they sprang from the earth'—like the *terrigena miles* (470) which Jason conquered by her help.

171. *CPS* give *Medea fugiam* (M. continuing from 170 with a deliberative rhetorical question, 'Shall M. fly?'). The text follows *E*: the Nurse begins a remark which is curtly interrupted by M.: 'I shall become (Medea)', i.e. I shall fight back and show my old powers, cf. 910 'Medea nunc sum'. The latter reading is now usually accepted, and *fugiam* could have been introduced from the following line. It is worth noting too that with this division lines 170 and 171 are similar in form, having four speeches each which divide the lines in roughly the same metrical pattern. (Fourfold division of lines in the tragedies occurs elsewhere only at *Thy* 257 and *HO* 438: Strzelecki, 10–11.)

cui . . . : 'you see for, or by, whom I am (a mother)', not 'to whom', as the reference must be to Jason, not her children. The Nurse appeals to M. to have a care for her children's sake, but M.'s tortured thoughts at once fasten on the unworthiness of the agent of her motherhood.

172. The Nurse, running out of arguments, repeats her appeal to flee: M. grimly promises to do so—after exacting vengeance.

173. vindex: the 'avenger' is not specified, as the Nurse does not know M.'s plans; but M.'s reply recalls her ghastly method of delaying her own father's pursuit by dismembering his son—and both Jason and Creon, who might now pursue her, were fathers.

175. animos: 'passion, violent feelings' or 'pride': the plural is frequent in both senses.

   minuere occurs only here in the tragedies.

   tempori . . . decet: 'you must fit yourself to the time', act as the situation demands: 'middle' use of passive *aptari*.

176. That Fortune could rob the *sapiens* of his wealth and leave him unimpaired was a characteristic Stoic doctrine, argued at length in *de vita beata* (e.g. 'sapientis quisquis abstulerit divitias omnia illi sua relinquet . . .' 26. 4). See also *de ben.* iv. 10. 5, *Ep.* 36. 6, and for similar lines in tragedy Accius, fr. 619–20R 'nam si a me regnum Fortuna atque opes / eripere quivit, at virtutem non quiit', Eur. fr. 1066N ἢ τοῖς ἐν οἴκῳ χρήμασιν λελείμμεθα, / ἢ δ' εὐγένεια καὶ τὸ γενναῖον μένει.

177: 'but who pushes the palace door so that its hinges creak?' though *cardo* is not the modern hinge. The ancient door was hung on two pivots or pins which fitted into sockets in the lintel and the sill of the doorway, the word *cardo* being used of either pivot or socket. (See Page on *Aen.* ii. 493 and illustrations in D–S s.v. *cardo*.) As the door opened the pivots squeaked in their sockets, and in Roman Comedy a reference to this noise regularly introduces the arrival of a character out of a house on to the stage: Plautus, *Curc.* 94 ('num muttit cardo?'), *Amph.* 496, *M.G.* 154, Terence, *Ad.* 264 (cf. Menander, *Perik.* 126K, *Samia* 222K).

178. tumidus: 'haughty, arrogant': *HF* 384 'dominare tumidus, spiritus altos gere'. (Studley: 'puft up with pouncing pryde'.)

179–300. Creon enters with attendants (*famuli* 188) and, apparently surprised to find M. still around, forthwith pronounces banishment upon her. She appeals against the sentence and defends her actions at length, pointing out that she has rescued not only Jason but all the

Argonauts. Creon is unmoved, but as a concession allows her one day's grace before her departure.

This encounter between M. and Creon is somewhat longer than the corresponding scene in Euripides (271–356: the disproportion is even more in view of the greater length of Eur.'s play), and there are differences of detail: (a) in Sen. Creon himself says that he has commuted sentence of death to exile in response to Jason's appeal (183–5), but it is Jason himself who reports this later in Eur. (455–8); (b) M.'s children are included in her banishment in Eur. (273, 353) but not in Seneca (cf. 282 ff.). Moreover, the characters of M. and Creon show differences of treatment in the two playwrights. In Eur., after Creon's opening speech with its curt command to depart, M. indulges in wordy lamentation (αἰαῖ· πανώλης ἡ τάλαιν᾽ ἀπόλλυμαι. . . . 277 ff.) before asking the reason for her banishment: Seneca's M. is made of sterner stuff and comes to the point at once ('quod crimen...multatur fuga?' 192). Again, in Eur. Creon is a not wholly unsympathetic figure: his dominant feeling in the situation seems to be love for his daughter, and fear for her dictates his banishment of M. (283, 329), and M. plays on these feelings (344 ff.). In Sen. Creon is the harsh *tyrannus* of the *controversiae* (like Lycus in *HF* and Aegisthus in *Ag*), a stock type of arrogance and the misuse of power, who does not even refer to Creusa. This difference is further underlined by the contrasting accounts of Creon's death as he flings himself on his daughter's corpse: in Eur. this occupies eighteen lines (1204–21), in Sen. it is dismissed in one ('nata atque genitor cinere permixto iacent' 880).

M.'s long speech (203–51) is a rhetorical set piece in which she passes from commonplace reflections on the precariousness of royal power, which she herself exemplifies, to her main point, that she has aided Jason and the other Argonauts ('decus illud ingens Graeciae et florem inclitum' 226) and brought them safely away from her country. This action is the only *crimen* which can be laid against her (237), and she glories in admitting it; furthermore, Creon knew she was guilty when he received her into his country, and should at least allow her to live there in obscurity.

M.'s plea that she has saved Jason is a natural and obvious feature of other treatments of the legend: Eur. *Med.* 476 ff., 515, Ovid, *Medea* fr. quoted on 122, *Her.* xii. 173. The boast that all the Argonauts owe their lives to her is stressed also by Ovid (*M.* vii. 56, 'magna sequar: titulum servatae pubis Achivae', *Her.* xii. 203 'dos est mea Graia iuventus', and very probably in his *Medea*), and developed by Sen. in this speech 225 ff., and below, 455 'revexi nobilem regum manum'.

179. Medea . . . genus: *genus* in apposition, as 845 'nati, matris infaustae genus'.

180. There has been no mention hitherto of a decree of exile, so Creon must simply be surprised that M. has not heard rumours of his intentions and anticipated them. As in Eur., he now tells her she must go.

181. molitur: used of plotting something sinister or disastrous, as at *Oed* 28 'iam iam aliquid in nos fata moliri parant', *Ag* 230.

    nota fraus . . . : sc. *mihi* or *omnibus*: Eur. *M*. 285 σοφὴ πέφυκας καὶ κακῶν πολλῶν ἴδρις.

    manus: 'power'.

182. cui parcet: 'quae non patri pepercit, non fratri' Farnaby.

183–4. Jason corroborates this at 490–1.

    luem: 'pest, plague', used abusively of an individual as at *HF* 358 (Lycus), *Tro* 892 (Helen).

185. liberet . . . metu: the dread which the Corinthians feel for M. is stressed again at 270, 872: Creon is afraid even to be near her (*accessu procul* 188).

186. fert gradum . . . : during Creon's speech so far M. has been getting herself under control after the rebellious rage she showed in the previous scene. She now advances towards him and is able to argue her case fervently but coherently. (Damsté, op. cit. 406, would insert *en* or *at* before *fert*, but a pause by the declaimer would be sufficient.)

    ferox: σκυθρωπόν Eur. *M*. 271: a characterizing epithet of M. in Hor. *A.P.* 123 'sit Medea ferox'.

189. iubete sileat: *iubere* with the plain (paratactic) subj. is common in poetry and post-Augustan prose.

190. aliquando: 'at last'.

190–1. vade . . . avehe: Creon finally addresses M. directly. (Farnaby and Beck took the words as spoken to one of the *famuli*, but this would be dramatically much more tame, and the singular imperative would be odd after the previous plurals.) 'Begone in haste, and take hence at last a barbarous and fearful horror' (slightly elliptical for *te, monstrum . . . horribile, avehe*).

    veloci via: cf. *HF* 66 'lenta veniet ut Bacchus via', *Oed* 908 'audacis viae'. For the alliteration see 362 n.

191. In **iamdudum** the sense of 'immediately' sometimes shades into 'at last', and it is so used with an imperative or jussive subjunctive, the implication being that what is ordered is overdue: cf. *Tro* 65–6 'iamdudum sonet / fatalis Ide', Virg. *Aen.* ii. 103 'iamdudum sumite poenas' (with Austin's note), Cat. 64. 374, Ovid, *M.* xiii. 457, and in prose Sen. *Ep.* 75. 7, 84. 11; see Hand, *Tursellinus* s.v.

192. Eur. *M*. 281 τίνος μ' ἔκατι γῆς ἀποστέλλεις, Κρέον;

193: generally taken as ironic (like *egregiae* 202), but perhaps merely sententious: '(only) an innocent woman asks . . .'.

194: 'if you are my judge, examine my case (before pronouncing sentence); if you are a tyrant, just order (me to go)'. Leo quite

needlessly gave *si regnas iube* to Creon and deleted 195: M. is offering
Creon the choice of showing whether he is reasonable or arbitrary,
and Creon, brushing this aside, asserts the duty of a subject to obey
all royal commands.

195. A proverbial expression found in various forms in Greek: δοῦλε,
δεσποτῶν ἄκουε καὶ δίκαια κἄδικα Leutsch and Schneidewin, ii. 157
(Macarius) = trag. adesp. 436N; cf. Leutsch and Schneidewin, i. 213
(Diogenianus); Soph. *El*. 340 τῶν κρατούντων ἐστὶ πάντ' ἀκουστέα. 195
is quoted from the *Medea* by Geremia da Montagnone in his flori-
legium (see Introd. p. 11).

196. Cf. *Thy* 215 ff. 'ubi non est pudor . . . instabile regnum est'.

197. Colchis: dat.

> **qui avexit . . . :** '(but) let him (i.e. Jason) who brought me away
> take me back': 273 'redde comitem'.

198: 'my resolution is firm: your plea comes too late'.

199 ff. statuit, fuit: 152-3 n.

> **inauditus** is commonly used in Silver and later prose of an 'un-
> heard' defendant (Tac. *A*. ii. 77, *Dial*. 16. 4, Pliny, *Ep*. iv. 11. 6, Apul.
> *Met*. x. 6).

200. stătŭĕrit: a third foot tribrach is nearly always 'broken' between
more than one word; unbroken elsewhere only at 450 below, *Phoe*
105 (Strzelecki, 61).

201. Pelia: 133 n. Creon counters shrewdly, referring to M.'s treat-
ment of Pelias: also 258 ff. The Latin form Pelia corrects the metre
(Pelias *codd*. would give a fourth-foot spondee): see 35 n. and cf. 276,
Oed 289 'Tiresia'.

203-6: 'I learnt in my royal house how hard it is to turn from wrath
a mind once roused, and how kingly anyone who has proudly
grasped the sceptre thinks it is to persist in his course.' M. generalizes
about the *mores* of kings from the example of her father (209 'quondam nobili fulsi patre'). *hoc* looks forward to *ire*.

207. miseranda: probably abl. with *clade*.

> **obruta . . . :** another characteristic string of epithets: cf. 20-1, 45.

209. fulsi: *fulgere* abstract 'be glorious, illustrious': below, 218, *Oct* 936
(*nomen*), Hor. *C*. iii. 2. 18 (*virtus*).

210. avo . . . Sole: cf. 28-9.

211-16. The geographical limits of Aeetes' kingdom are described by
reference to notable natural features (Phasis, Pontus) and inhabitants
(Amazons).

211 ff. quodcumque . . . Phasis . . . Pontus: similar phraseology
to 44.

> **quodcumque . . . quidquid . . . quidquid:** 'all the country which
> . . .' or similar English phrase, picked up by *hoc omne* 216.

> **placidis:** the same river is called *violenta* at 762. Here a tranquil river
> is recollected in nostalgia, in 762 the river's power yields to her own.

212. a tergo: to a speaker or writer orientated in the Graeco-Roman world the east coast of the Pontus is 'behind' it.

213. The coast is made marshy, and the sea-water diluted, by the outflowing rivers. The sweetness of the Pontic water was widely remarked, e.g. Pliny, *HN* iv. 79 (the Danube freshens the Pontus for forty miles from its mouth), Strabo i. 50, Arrian, *Peripl. M. Eux.* 8, Ammianus, xxii. 8. 46.

214. peltis: the crescent shields traditionally carried by the Amazons (*cohors vidua*): *Phae* 402–3, 'lunata latus / protecta pelta', *Ag* 218 'peltata Amazon', Sil. It. ii. 80 'Thermodontiaca munita in proelia pelta'.

215. Cf. *HF* 246 'regina gentis vidua Thermodontiae'.   **vidua:** 'unmarried'. The Thermodon flowed into the Pontus on the north coast of Asia Minor near Themiscyra. This area was a traditional home of the Amazons (e.g. Aesch. *P.V.* 723–5)—rather far from Colchis, but we must not press Seneca's geography, and the description is conventional.

218 ff. petebant, petuntur: a stylistic feature of the exercises in the rhetorical schools, which is reflected in Seneca's tragedies, is the repetition of the same verb in a different form, especially a change of voice: cf. above, 28–9 'spectat spectatur', *HF* 726–7 'timet timetur', *Tro* 1099–1100 'flet fletur', and see Bonner, *Roman Declamation* 70, 167.

    proci: plural for singular (though M. doubtless had many suitors), as Jason only can be referred to in *qui . . . petuntur*. The anguished Dido similarly reflects: 'rursusne procos inrisa priores / experiar', *Aen.* iv. 534–5. M. cannot bring herself to mention Jason's name to Creon: *ducem* 233, *gener* 240, *comitem* 273, *illi* 276, *maritus* 279. So in Eur. they avoid each other's names when speaking together: see also 441 n.

220. praeceps: 'swift, violent' or perhaps 'rushing down' like a bird, Fortune often being represented as winged: Hor. *C.* i. 34. 14 ff. 'hinc apicem rapax / Fortuna cum stridore acuto / sustulit, hic posuisse gaudet', iii. 29. 53–4 'si celeres quatit / pennas (Fortuna)'.

    eripuit, dedit: sc. *me*.

221 ff. levis . . . casus: the phrase jars somewhat so soon after *fortuna levis*.

    After recalling her own dramatic change of fortune M. speaks ironically of reliance on the material advantages of royal power, which cannot be depended on to last, and then contrasts them with the one great and enduring quality of kings—help and protection for the wretched. She herself illustrates this, for having lost her former royal position at Colchis the only thing she has brought away with her is the realization that she has saved the Argonauts from doom: 'solum hoc . . . extuli, decus illud . . . servasse memet.'

    confide regnis: 'put your trust in royal power': the following words make it clear that she means the wealth and material trappings of kingship. Creon thinks only of these, and by forcing her into exile forgets the real glory of kings, 'prodesse miseris, supplices . . . protegere'. For the thought see Ovid, *Pont*. ii. 9. 11 'regia, crede mihi, res est succurrere lapsis'.

225. Colchico: a less common adjectival form (Hor. *Epode* v. 24, xvii. 35, Pliny, *HN* vi. 29).

   hoc anticipates *servasse memet*, like *hoc . . . prodesse, protegere* 222 ff.

226. florem: a very common metaphor, like ἄνθος in Greek and 'flower' in English. (*et* is the correction of Studemund, generally accepted and probably right.)

227. Achivae: Ovid's Medea calls the Argonauts *pubis Achivae* (*M*. vii. 56).

   deum: the archaic gen. pl., as often at a line-ending in the tragedies.

228. memet: *-met* intensifies: 'I and no other saved them'; cf. 546, 899, 1018. Pronominal forms in *-met* occur several times in the tragedies, but are on the whole avoided by the post-Augustan poets.

   munus: Ovid, *Her*. xii. 203 'dos mea tu sospes, dos est mea Graia iuventus'. M. now names some of the more distinguished Argonauts.

228-9. Orpheus . . . trahit: as a symbol of the power of music over all creation Orpheus has been continually popular with poets: Simonides fr. 27 Diehl, Aesch. *Ag*. 1630, Eur. *Bacchae* 561 ff., Virg. *G*. iv. 510, Hor. *C*. i. 12. 7 ff., Shakespeare, *Henry VIII*, III. i. 3 ff. See also 625 n., and for other references in the tragedies *HF* 569 ff., *HO* 1036 ff.

230. geminum: if this reading of all manuscripts is right it is a sort of hypallage, 'C. and P. are a twin gift', but perhaps *gemini* (Nicolas Heinsius) should be read. On Castor and Pollux see 88-9 n.

231. satique Borea: Calais and Zetes ('Aquilone natos' 634), best known for rescuing Phineus from the Harpies (Ap. Rhod. ii. 240 ff).

231-3. satique . . . Lynceus . . . Minyae: understand *munus meum est/sunt.*

   quique . . . videt: 'and Lynceus who with darting glance sees things remote even beyond the Pontus'. He had the keenest sight of all men (Pindar, *N*. x. 62-3 and many other writers). For *lumine immisso* cf. the description of Lynceus in Val. Fl. i. 463-4 'possit qui rumpere terras / et Styga transmisso tacitam deprendere visu'.

233. Minyae: a legendary and prehistoric tribe associated with Thessaly, whose name was given to the Argonauts from the time of Pindar (*P*. iv. 69, cf. Ovid, *M*. vii. 1, Strabo, ix. 2. 40, Ap. Rhod. iii. 1091 ff.). Apollonius (i. 229 ff.) says the Argonauts were so called because most of them claimed descent from the daughters of Minyas. Apart from these associations tradition mainly connected Minyas and the Minyans with Orchomenus in Boeotia (Hom. *Il*. ii. 511, Pindar, *O*. xiv. 4, Thuc. iv. 76).

nam explains why M. abruptly breaks off her list of individuals with *omnesque Minyae*, for the list is not to include Jason, who was her gift to nobody but herself.

ducum . . . ducem: Sen. is fond of the rhetorical figure in which the same noun is repeated in a different case (polyptoton; cf. note on 218 ff.): 511 'prole prolem', 563–4 'scelerum scelus'. A long list of examples, and of other types of paronomasia, in the tragedies is in Canter, *Rhetorical Elements in the Tragedies of Seneca* 161 ff.

234. hunc . . . imputo: 'I hold no one in my debt for him'.

235. vobis: i.e. 'for you Greeks'.

236 ff. A further rhetorical flavour is now given to the speech as M. puts the charge against herself, and answers it by dramatically recalling the moral dilemma she had found herself in at Colchis, and pointing out the fate of the Argonauts if she had followed the call of *pudor* and her father. Similarly Lycus in *HF* 401 ff. defends his usurpation of the throne of Thebes by posing accusations against himself which he then refutes. Raising objections in order to show how easily they can be demolished has always been a favourite technique of orators.

236–8. incesse: the word is used here only in the tragedies, but is found frequently in Silver writers of attacking with words (see L–S): 'accuse me now and pile on all my misdeeds: I shall confess them; (but) this crime alone can be held against me—the return of the Argo.' Presumably *fatebor* governs *flagitia* understood, but the distinction between the (lesser) *flagitia* and *crimen* is not very clear, e.g. was the murder of Absyrtus one of the *flagitia*? M. certainly regarded this in retrospect as a terrible deed. In view of the following words M. must be suggesting that the Argo was enabled to return because of her most damning fault—disobedience to her *pudor* and her father. This was her real *crimen*, to which her other misdeeds were secondary.

238 ff. Argo: one traditional derivation from ἀργός 'swift' is accepted by L–S–J and Frisk, *Griech. etym. Wört.*; for other views see Roscher, i. 503. s.v.

placeat: conditional subj. (= *si placeat*) followed by fut. indic. of firm prophecy (*ruet, occidet*): 'should the maiden heed modesty and her father, all Greece will perish . . .'. The tenses of *placeat . . . occidet* show that M. is mentally reliving the time in Colchis when she had to make her decision whether to obey her father or her love for Jason, and repeating the words she might have used to herself. Thus the words *hic tuus gener* fit awkwardly into her recollected thoughts, as though in the midst of her mental flash-back she suddenly remembers Creon's presence and Jason's new relationship with him. This fusion of past and present in her words well reflects her mental state.

ducibus: with the loss of her greatest champions Greece will fall.

241. tauri: here and 466, 829 one bull is referred to, though there are two in Apollonius' account (iii. 409 ff.; cf. Pindar, *P*. iv. 225, Eur. *M*. 478, Ovid, *M*. vii. 104 ff.).

242. i.e. whatever doom awaits me: **causam nostram** virtually means *me*. (Avantius' *qua* for *quae* is attractive and simplifies the line.)

243. servasse . . . decus: emphatic repetition of 226-8: if they were a glorious troop, hers was a glorious deed in rescuing them.

244 ff. quodcumque praemium . . . penes te: i.e. Jason was all I gained from my wicked actions and you can decide whether I am to keep him.

246. crimen: '(the cause of) my crime', Jason. M.'s plea to be given her due grows into a refrain: 'redde fugienti ratem / et redde comitem' 272-3, 'redde supplici felix vicem' 482, 'redde fugienti sua' 489.

247. genua attigi: the knees were touched or invoked by suppliants; cf. *Tro* 691 ff. 'ad genua accido / supplex . . . dextram pedibus admoveo tuis', Eur. *M*. 709-10 ἄντομαί σε τῆσδε πρὸς γενειάδος / γονάτων τε τῶν σῶν ἱκεσία τε γίγνομαι, Virg. *Aen*. iii. 607. The Elder Pliny comments on the practice: 'hominis genibus quaedam et religio inest observatione gentium. haec supplices attingunt, ad haec manus tendunt, haec ut aras adorant, fortassis quia inest iis vitalitas' (*HN* xi. 250).

248. fidem praesidis dextrae: 'the security of your protecting hand'. All these words are charged with meanings calculated to sharpen the sting of reproach for Creon: *fides* was commonly the protection one craved of the gods; *praeses* is several times applied to divinities (as in all other passages where it is used in the tragedies); and *dextra* has often the meaning of a pledge of friendship.

peti: for similar contracted perfects at a line-ending see 984 *redit*, 994 *perit*.

249. The text is uncertain but *terra hac* (local abl.) or Gronovius' *terrae* seems likeliest for the first foot, and *miseriis* is guaranteed by *miserias* 253.

angulum: *Ag* 998 'ultimo in regni angulo' (of Electra's imprisonment). *angulus* is used in senses both complimentary (Hor. *C*. ii. 6. 13-14 'ille terrarum . . . angulus', of Tarentum) and insulting (Hor. *Ep*. i. 14. 23, of a wretched plot of land): see *OLD*, s.v. 5 and 6. Seneca's M. is more eloquent here than Euripides', who asks simply τήνδε δὲ χθόνα / ἐᾶτέ μ' οἰκεῖν (313-14).

252-71. In his reply Creon rebuts the suggestion that he is behaving arrogantly—after all, he has accepted an exiled and terror-stricken man as his son-in-law; he reminds M. again of the shameful murder of the aged Pelias, in which Jason had no part; and once more orders her to leave his kingdom.

252 ff. 'By choosing as my son-in-law a distressed and terror-stricken outcast . . . I think I have shown clearly enough that I am not one to rule harshly or trample arrogantly upon misery'. Creon's first words hark back to M.'s opening (203 ff.), with verbal echoes in *sceptra*, *superbo*. As in Eur. (ἥκιστα τοὐμὸν λῆμ' ἔφυ τυραννικόν, / αἰδούμενος δὲ πολλὰ δὴ διέφθορα 348–9) he is concerned to show himself a reasonable and sympathetic man.

254. haud clare parum: *haud* with *parum*: a pompous phrase.

256 ff. quippe: causal ('seeing that A. demands him'), here with indic. of fact, in 438 with subj. of a hypothetical case. (These are the only occurrences of *quippe* in the plays, and it is used rather erratically in poetry generally: see Axelson, *Unpoetische Wörter* 48.)

    poenae . . . leto: datives, forming a hendiadys: 'for punishment by death'.

257. Acastus: 133 n. (According to Ap. Rhod. i. 224 ff. and Hyg. *fab.* 24 Acastus was one of the Argonauts.) This element of fear in Jason's motivation for deserting M., which is strongly stressed in Sen. (see also 415, 521, 526), is not found in Eur., who does not mention Acastus at all and does not refer to Pelias in his corresponding scene. Seneca's Creon twice effectively throws Pelias' murder in M.'s face, here and 201.

258–9. senio . . . senis: the cognates in emphatic positions at beginning and end of successive lines stress the horror of murdering the helpless old man.

261. piae, impium: this type of word-play (here a sort of oxymoron) is exceedingly common in the tragedies: other random examples from this play are 163 'sperare desperet', 472–3 'somno insomne', 503 'innocens nocens'. Here Sen. may be following Ovid, *M.* vii. 339 'his ut quaeque pia est hortatibus impia prima'.

    sorores: i.e. of Acastus. The best known was Alcestis, wife of Admetus.

262–3: 'Jason can defend his cause if you dissociate yours from it': for this use of *tueri* see *Tro* 905–6 'causam tamen / possum tueri iudice infesto meam', Cic. *de Or.* i. 169, Ovid, *Pont.* ii. 2. 56.

265. vestro: the plural suggests 'you and the evil spirits you consort with'.

266. machinatrix: this feminine form occurs here only, but *machinator* is used at *Tro* 750 'o machinator fraudis et scelerum artifex': in both passages Sen. may have had in mind Cic. *Cat.* iii. 6 'horum omnium scelerum improbissimum machinatorem' (see 269 n.). (Did Sen. like coining these forms? There is a similar ἅπ. λεγ. *exprobratrix* at *de ben.* vii. 22, and see also *Tro* 819 *domitrix*, *Phae* 85 *dominatrix*.)

    facinorum: apart from here and 268 *memoria* Sen. only twice elsewhere has a dactyl in the fifth foot: *HF* 408, *Oed* 847. These four lines are also the only ones to end with a proceleusmatic word (‿‿‿‿) —in *HF* and *Oed* also *memoria*. (In 471 below *arietis* the *-i-* is probably consonantal: Strzelecki, 27, 52–3.)

267. cui feminae: there is a clear case for adopting the reading of the Ambrosian palimpsest. *cui feminea ECPSr* gives a clash of ictus and accent in a resolved second foot not found elsewhere in Sen. (see e.g. *HF* 675, *Oed* 18, 394, *Ag* 145): Strzelecki, 48. Note the *variatio* of genitive/adjective *feminae/virile* and cf. *Ag* 958-9 'animos viriles corde tumefacto geris, / sed agere domita feminam disces malo'.

268. nulla . . . memoria: 'no thought of, consideration for your good name'. *memoria* sometimes has this sense of *cura*: Cic. *Cael.* 59 'extremum sensum ad memoriam rei p. reservabat', *fin.* ii. 99.

269 ff. egredere, purga . . . : a clear echo of Cic. *Cat.* i. 10 'egredere . . . liberabis'. Sen. is not limited to fashionable rhetorical techniques, but has studied Rome's greatest orator.

270. herbas: the nurse gives a catalogue of them in 705 ff.

271. sollicita: 'vex, harass' the gods by your unholy acts. M. threatens to do this at 424 'invadam deos.'

272-80. M. bitterly retorts that her guilt is no greater than Jason's.

272 ff. redde . . . redde: 246 n. **vel** has the corrective sense of *vel potius* 'or rather': see L-S, s.v. I. A. 2b.

    comitem: Jason: 218 n.

274. bella: with Acastus if M. remained in Corinth.

275-6. cur . . . distinguis?: as he did 262 ff. 'potest Iason . . . tueri'.

    illi, nobis: dat. of interest or advantage: cf. 507 'placare natis'. This argument that the beneficiary of a crime shares the guilt is used by M. to Jason himself 496 ff.

    Pelia: 201 n.

277. fugam, rapinas: 'my flight from home and theft (of the Fleece)'.

278-9. quidquid . . . : 'whatever (crime) the bridegroom is even now teaching his new wife'. In the rising passion of her defence M. becomes a little hard to follow. She seems to imply with a sneer (note the sardonic plural *coniuges*) that, as she was forced to commit crimes for Jason, so if he chooses another wife this new wife will find herself in the same position. There is thus a slight zeugma in *non est meum*, which goes with *fugam . . . fratrem* as well as with *quidquid*: referring to her own sins the words mean 'not for my sake'; with *quidquid*, something like 'no concern of mine, not prompted by me'. (Herrmann's Budé translation runs 'bref tous les crimes que mon mari enseigne toujours à ses nouvelles épouses' (similarly Thomann), but *etiam nunc* points to the present occasion.)

    coniuges: the plural is intensely bitter, as at 1007-8 'i nunc, superbe, virginum thalamos pete, / relinque matres'.

280. Cf. 503 'tibi innocens sit quisquis est pro te nocens', Ovid, *Her.* xii. 131-2 'ut culpent alii, tibi me laudare necesse est, / pro quo sum toties esse coacta nocens'.

281. seris: 26 n.: here 'contrive' to delay your exile by talking.

282 ff. M. ostensibly accepts the fact that she must go, but asks that her children may not suffer because of her guilt (see introd. note to 179); Creon grants this, and also reluctantly allows her a day's grace to say farewell to them.

283. Later, however, in her interview with Jason M. begs that the children may accompany her into exile (541–3)—perhaps to test Jason's reactions.

285 ff. per ego . . .: the normal word-order in prayers, whereby *ego* is thrown emphatically forward, sometimes, as here, quite widely separated from its verb (*precor*).

  auspicatos: properly 'consecrated by augury', 'begun under a good omen', and hence 'blessed, fortunate, happy': 'by the blessed union of the royal marriage', i.e. of Jason and Creusa. M.'s invocations here form a logical sequence: the marriage should lead to children (*spes futuras*) who, continuing the royal line, will strengthen the kingdom against the shocks of Fortune (*regnorum status . . . vice*).

286. spes: sc. *tuas*, or with *thalami*.

  regnorum: probably no specific reference, though including Corinth, as 287 seems to be a generalization.

287. dubiă: with *Fortuna*; *varia* probably abl. with *vice*.

288. largire: 'generously bestow', 'give as an "extra"', in contrast with *reddere*, 'give what is due', 246 n.

289. natis oscula: Sil. It. xii. 738 'natis infigunt oscula matres'.

290 ff. The throwing back and forth several times of the key word *tempus* is typical of stichomythia.

291. tempore exiguo: for extent of time the abl. is regular in Silver Latin.

292. malis: generalizing masc. dat. 'for the wicked'. There are oddly similar sentences in *NQ* iii. praef. 3 'nullum enim non tam magnis rebus tempus angustum est', and Sen. Elder *Contr.* ii. 3. 7. 'nullum tempus uni verbo angustum est'—perhaps all are echoes of a popular 'tag'.

293. Strictly **negas** goes with **miserae** and **parum** with **lacrimis** ('do you refuse an unfortunate woman even a respite which is too short for her sorrow?'), but the word order evokes other sense patterns: 'too little for a pitiable woman', 'denies her tears'. Translation scarcely captures the taut ambiguity of the Latin.

296. recidas . . . licet: 'even if you shorten that day'.

297–8. et ipsa propero: there may be a veiled reference to her revenge: see notes on 24 ff. and 37–40.

  capite . . .: Eur. *M.* 352 ff. εἴ σ' ἡ 'πιοῦσα λαμπὰς ὄψεται θεοῦ . . . θανῇ; Ennius, *Medea* fr. 274–5 V 'si te secundo lumine hic offendero / moriere'.

  attollat: *Phae* 571 'Hesperia Tethys lucidum attollet diem'.

299. sacra thalami: what these are is not certain, as the main *sacra* should now be over (see note on 59 ff.), but Creon may refer to certain symbolic acts which took place in both Greek and Roman weddings on the arrival of the bride at the bridegroom's house. Or he may refer to a personal sacrifice and prayer.

300. Hymenaeo: 67-70 n.: constructed with *festus*, in the sense of *sacer*, 'Hymen's holy day' (not with *precari*, which seems never to take the dat. of the divinity addressed). Cf. Ovid, *F.* v. 670 'ex illo est haec tibi (sc. Mercurio) festa dies', Tac. *A.* xiii. 15 'festis Saturno diebus'.

301-79. Creon retires with his retainers, M. apparently (see 380 *tectis*) enters her house, and the Chorus sings a lyric on the boldness of the first navigator. It recalls the simpler life of men before the seas were conquered, relates the perils undergone by the Argo, and finally (364 ff.) shows that navigation has led to intercommunication among peoples, and predicts a complete exploration of the world.

The invention of navigation was traditionally one sign of the end of the Golden Age: Aratus, *Phaen.* 110-11 (and cf. Hesiod, *Op.* 236-7), Virg. *G.* i. 136 ff., Tib. 1. 3. 37 ff. (K. F. Smith's note gives extensive references), Ovid, *M.* i. 94 ff.; and the theme of the hazards of sea-faring was a stock one in the schools, e.g. Sen. Elder, *Suas.* i 'deliberat Alexander an Oceanum naviget'. In particular this lyric has strong echoes of Horace, *C.* i. 3 'sic te diva potens Cypri', which treats the same topic (see Nisbet-Hubbard, 43-4). The first word *audax* recalls the repeated *audax* in Horace's poem: 'audax omnia perpeti / gens humana ruit per vetitum nefas. / audax Iapeti genus / ignem fraude mala gentibus intulit' (25-8): for other resemblances see notes below. (See also A. O. Lovejoy and G. Boas, *Primitivism and Related Ideas in Antiquity* (Baltimore, 1935) 263 ff., for a discussion of this chorus and several other passages in Seneca as documents of Stoic primitivism.) Thus the Chorus continues in its second song (as in the first) to treat a theme relevant to the play, though in traditional style moving on to more general reflections, and it continues to express violent hostility to M. ('maiusque mari Medea malum' 362). Dramatically the song gives us an emotional rest between the vigorous exchanges of M. and Creon and the Nurse's description of M.'s passionate, unhinged behaviour 380 ff.

The metre is anapaestic dimeters (lines of four anapaests or equivalent spondees or dactyls), with monometers (two feet) at 317, 328, 379. Often Seneca's anapaestic systems consist of dimeters thus irregularly interspersed with monometers: below 787 ff., *Phae* 1 ff., *Ag* 57 ff. It should be noted that though the dactyl regularly replaces the anapaest Seneca, following the practice of other Silver Latin poets, does not admit four consecutive short syllables (i.e. dactyl followed by anapaest), such as we find frequently in Roman comedy: see D. S. Raven, *Latin Metre* 115-17. Synaphea or strict metrical continuity between lines is observed throughout. Line 301 is quoted by the fourth-century grammarian Diomedes as an example of an anapaestic lyric: 'anapaesticum choricum habemus in Seneca: audax . . . primus' (511.23K).

301 ff. The implied reference may be to Tiphys (see 3 n. and refs.), but *primus* is probably the first unknown who put out to sea in a small skiff, the Argonauts being the first to make an extensive voyage ('vasto ponto' 318–19). At 596 'mare qui subegit' is Jason. Horace's similar passage is unspecific: 'ille . . . qui fragilem truci / commisit pelago ratem / primus' (*C.* i. 3. 9 ff.). For the first navigator see too Prop. i. 17. 13 ff., Ovid, *Am.* ii. 11. 1 ff., Val. Fl. i. 648 ff., Claudian, *Rapt. Pros.* i. praef. (other references in Nisbet–Hubbard on Hor. *C.* i. 3. 12).

    rate . . . fragili: from Horace.   **rupit:** 'cleft.'

303: 'seeing his native shore slip away behind him'.

304. credidit: *Phae* 530 'nondum secabant credulae pontum rates' (in the Golden Age).

306 ff.: 'could trust to a narrow board, drawing a too slender division between the paths of life and death': i.e. only the thickness of the wooden boat kept him from death by drowning. For the same idea see Juv. xii. 57 ff. 'i nunc et ventis animam committe, dolato / confisus ligno, digitis a morte remotus / quattuor aut septem, si sit latissima taeda' with Mayor's note, Sen. Elder, *Contr.* vii. 1. 10, 'scitis nihil esse periculosius quam etiam instructa navigia: parva materia seiungit fata', Aratus, *Phaen.* 299 ὀλίγον δὲ διὰ ξύλον Ἄιδ' ἐρύκει, Diog. Laert. i. 103 (the sage Anacharsis on learning that a boat was four fingers' breadth thick) τοσοῦτον ἔφη τοῦ θανάτου τοὺς πλέοντας ἀπέχειν, Sen. *Ep.* 49. 11.

    Leo deleted 305–6 as a dittography with 301–2, but the repetition is not remarkable, and **ligno** clarifies the meaning of **limite**. After 308 Richter (followed by Leo) against all manuscripts inserted 329–34, making ignorance of the stars (309 ff.) part of the simple honest life of earlier times. But this ignorance has more point following on 308: the first sailor's temerity was the greater because he lacked the navigational aid of the stars. The traditional order is defended by M. Müller, *In Senecae tragoedias quaestiones criticae*, Berlin, 1898, 22 ff., C. Knapp, *CR* xvii (1903), 44–7.

309 ff. sidera . . . stellis: 'constellations', '(individual) stars'.

312. Hyadas: Ὑάδες ('rainers' ὔειν), a group of stars in Taurus. The name was due to their rising and setting occurring at rainy seasons—times to avoid sailing—and is emphasized by *pluvias*, as at Virg. *Aen.* i. 744: cf. Tennyson, *Ulysses* 10–11 'Thro' scudding drifts the rainy Hyades / Vext the dim sea'.

313. Oleniae caprae: Amalthea transformed into a star (note on 63 ff.) which also rose in the rainy season: she was sometimes thought to be the daughter of Olenus, hence the recurring epithet (Ovid, *F.* v. 113, Manilius, v. 130).

    The run of the sentence suggests that *vitare* governs *plaustra* as well as *Hyadas* and *lumina*, and while there seems to be no reason for navigators to avoid the Wain, the constellation Boötes, closely associated with it, rose and set in stormy weather (Plautus, *Rud.* 70-1). Boötes (Arcturus) and the Kids are similarly linked as weather signals by Hor. *C.* iii. 1. 27-8 'nec saevus Arcturi cadentis / impetus aut orientis Haedi', Virg. *G.* i. 204 ff.

314 ff.: 'the northern Wain which sluggish old Boötes follows and controls'. The Wain or Great Bear was imagined to be attended by the near-by constellation Boötes ('ox-driver'), who is often called *tardus* or *piger* because of the time he takes to set in a roughly perpendicular position (G. R. Mair on Aratus, *Phaen.* 583 (Loeb edn.), and see Hipparchus ii. 2. 29); cf. Hom. *Od.* v. 272 ὀψὲ δύοντα Βοώτην, Cat. 66. 67-8 'vertor in Occasum, tardum dux ante Boöten / qui vix sero alto mergitur Oceano', Ovid *M.* ii. 176-7. Seneca's lines recall Ovid, *M.* x. 447 'flexerat obliquo plaustrum temone Boötes'.

Arctica: *P* is probably right (ἀρκτικός 'of the Bear, northern'), though it is a rare technical word which occurs e.g. in Hyginus' work on astronomy; also Mart. Cap. viii. 823: see *TLL*, s.v. The rarity of the word explains the many corruptions in the manuscripts. *Attica E* is adopted by some editors, who explain it as an epithet transferred from Boötes who was sometimes identified with the Athenian Icarius: cf. Val. Fl. ii. 68 'Actaeus . . . Boötes'.

318 ff. Tiphys: 3 n. By learning to make use of the winds Tiphys in a sense controlled them, and so is said to have prescribed 'new laws' for them: similarly at 364-5 the sea 'submits to laws' when navigation is widespread.

ausus: (sc. *est*) is followed by **pandere** and **scribere:** the other four infinitives down to 325 are attached rather loosely to explain **leges . . . ventis**, 'made laws for the winds (so that men were able) now to strain the ropes . . . now . . .'.

320 ff. The first pair **nunc . . . nunc** describe two angles at which the sail is set by adjusting the sheets (*pedes*), or ropes which fasten the sail to the sides of the boat: either the sail is set square so as to be stretched out taut with a breeze from astern, or one sheet is carried forward (*prolato pede*) so that the sail is set obliquely to catch the cross-winds. The second pair **nunc . . . nunc** describe two positions of the yards (*antemnas*), at half-mast or at top-mast, whereby the sail is partially or completely unfurled. For this whole passage cf. the operation in Lucan, v. 426 ff. 'totosque rudentes / laxavere sinus, et flexo navita cornu / obliquat laevo pede carbasa summaque pandens / sipara velorum perituras colligit auras'.

320. lina: 'ropes, cordage' of a ship (Ovid, *M.* xiv. 554, *F.* iii. 587): not 'sails' as many translators take it. The ropes become taut when the sail fills with the wind (*sinu toto*).

322. notos: winds in general, not specifically south winds.

323. tutas: translate adverbially 'prudently', not running headlong with full sail before the wind, in contrast with the 'avidus nimium navita' below.

325. loco: i.e. *malo*, but the repetition is avoided.

326. navita: this form is much commoner in the tragedies than **nauta**.

327–8. alto ... velo: 'the lofty canvas of the scarlet topsails flutters': *alto velo* is a rather otiose descriptive phrase. For scarlet topsails see Lucian, *Nav.* 5 τοῦ ἱστίου τὸ παράσειον πυραυγές, Athen. v. 206c, C. Torr, *Ancient Ships* 90 and 98.

328. sipara: 'topsails'. *siparum* (σίφαρος) seems first to appear in the first cent. A.D. and is used elsewhere by Sen. at *HO* 699, *Ep.* 77. 1 and 2 (a distinctive feature of Alexandrian mail-boats). It is often confused with an earlier word *supparus*, a linen garment. (The many confusions of spelling of the two words are discussed with characteristic vigour by Housman, *CQ.* xiii (1919), 149 ff., who firmly distinguishes and limits the forms to *sip(h)arum* 'topsail', and *supparus* 'garment'.)

329 ff. Although not explicitly a description of the Golden Age (like *Phae* 525 ff.) this passage clearly belongs in the category of the many accounts of that ideal early existence which we find in Greek and Latin literature: see, for example, Hesiod, *Op.* 109 ff., Aratus, *Phaen.* 100 ff., Plato, *Politicus* 271 d ff., Virg. *E.* iv, *G.* i. 125 ff. and ii. 532 ff., Ovid, *M.* i. 89 ff. (and cf. Cat. 64. 385 ff.), Sen. *Ep.* 90. 36 ff. The Golden Age was associated with the reign of Saturn, and two of its notable characteristics were the production of food-crops for mankind by the earth of its own accord, and the absence of seafaring.

329. candida: perhaps combines the ideas 'pure, honest' and 'happy, fortunate'.

331. sua litora tangens: might mean 'keeping close to his own shores' (like Horace's 'premendo litus', *C.* ii. 10. 3–4), i.e. not venturing far out to sea (which could also be the meaning of *Phae* 530–1 'nondum secabant credulae pontum rates: / sua quisque norat maria'), but the tradition of the land-bound men of the Golden Age suggests 'staying *on* his own shores'. Ovid has a similar line: 'nullaque mortales praeter sua litora norant' (*M.* i. 96).

333. parvo dives: an oxymoron of a familiar type, like Horace's 'simplex munditiis' (but see Nisbet-Hubbard on *C.* i. 5. 5). Juvenal moralizes in a similar vein: 'saturabat glaebula talis / patrem ipsum turbamque casae ... nunc modus hic agri nostro non sufficit horto' (xiv. 166–72). We find the happiness of the stay-at-home extolled from Theognis onward (ὄλβιος ὅστις παιδὸς ἐρῶν οὐκ οἶδε θάλασσαν / οὐδὲ οἱ ἐν πόντῳ νὺξ ἐπιοῦσα μέλει 1375–6: cf. Eur. fr. 793N μακάριος ὅστις εὐτυχῶν οἴκοι μένει), and the picture of contentment and self-sufficiency derived from one's ancestral land has had a long currency, at least from Horace (*Epode* ii. 1 ff. 'beatus ille qui procul negotiis, / ut

prisca gens mortalium, / paterna rura bubus exercet suis') to Pope
(*Ode on Solitude* 'Happy the man whose wish and care / A few
paternal acres bound'). For the later development of this theme see
M.-S. Røstvig, *The Happy Man: Studies in the Metamorphoses of a
Classical Ideal*, Vol. I (2nd edn., Norwegian Universities Press, 1962).

335 ff.: 'the covenants of the well-separated world': a condensed
expression meaning the lands and seas well separated before by the
laws of nature (*mare sepositum* 339), which the Argo 'drew together'
by enabling men to travel on the sea. So Hor. *C*. i. 3. 21 ff. 'nequi-
quam deus abscidit / prudens Oceano dissociabili / terras, si tamen
impiae / non tangenda rates transiliunt vada', Lucan iii. 193 ff. 'cum
rudis Argo / miscuit ignotas temerato litore gentes . . . fatisque per
illam / accessit mors una ratem' (cf. 'partemque metus nostri' below), Columella i. praef. 8. *foedera mundi* recurs below, 606, and
Claudian has a similar phrase: 'nam cum dispositi quaesissem foedera
mundi' (*in Rufinum* 4). According to early Greek cosmologists
original chaos was succeeded by an orderly separation of the natural
elements: the chorus means that the Argo violated this natural
division.

   Thessala pinus: the Argo was built of timber from the slopes of
Mt. Pelion in Thessaly: *Ag* 120 'Thessalica trabe', Cat. 64. 1 'Peliaco
quondam prognatae vertice pinus', 609 n.

337. verbera: of the oars.

338–9. partemque . . . sepositum: 'the sea which had been inviolate
became part of our fear' (*sepositum* suggesting a thing apart, unsullied
by human contact): navigation was a new hazard to be added to
mankind's stock of terrors. The thought is something of a commonplace from Augustan times onwards: Prop. iii. 7. 31–2 'terra parum
fuerat, fatis adiecimus undas: / fortunae miseras auximus arte vias',
Lucan l.c. above, Sen. *NQ* v. 18. 8 'quid maria inquietamus? parum
videlicet ad mortes nostras terra late patet . . . itaque eamus in pelagus
et vocemus in nos fata cessantia'. See too *Ep*. 90. 43 (in contrast with
the Golden Age) 'nunc magna pars nostri metus tecta sunt'.

339–40. illa . . . improba: the Argo.

341 ff. duo montes: the Symplegades, rocks situated at the Bosporus
which were thought to clash together. The Argo managed to pass
between them with the loss of only part of her stern, and the rocks
thereafter remained fixed. Some accounts put the incident during the
voyage out (Pindar, *P*. iv. 208 ff., Ap. Rhod. ii. 549 ff., Theocr. xxii.
27–8, Val. Fl. iv. 561 ff.), others on the way home (Hom. *Od*. xii.
69–70, Eur. *Med*. 432 ff., 1263 ff., Ovid, *Am*. ii. 11. 3: cf. below, 456).
These rocks are probably to be distinguished from the Wandering
Rocks (610 n.), though the confusion between them in the poets
goes back to Homer: see Page on Eur. *Med*. 2, Stanford on *Od*. xii.
59 ff.

claustra profundi: 'barriers, gates of the deep', being situated at the entrance to the Euxine: *HF* 1210–11 'illa quae pontum Scythen / Symplegas artat'.

The following lines describe the booming crash, as of thunder, caused by the impact of the rocks coming together, and the column of sea water which is thus shot up to the sky. There is a similar description of this phenomenon at *HF* 1212 ff.: it should be borne in mind that descriptions of storms and shipwreck were stock subjects in the schools, and Sen. is also remembering Apollonius: ταὶ δ' ἄμυδις πάλιν ἀντίαι ἀλλήλῃσιν / ἄμφω ὁμοῦ ξυνιοῦσαι ἐπέκτυπον. ὦρτο δὲ πολλὴ / ἅλμη ἀναβρασθεῖσα, νέφος ὥς· αὖε δὲ πόντος / σμερδαλέον· πάντῃ δὲ περὶ μέγας ἔβρεμεν αἰθήρ (ii. 564–7).

344. astra *CPS* (*astris Ee*) has troubled editors (*arces* Leo, following Madvig, *austris* Peiper), but the hyperbole is in the Senecan manner and quite consonant with *nubes ipsas*: cf. *Phae* 1007–8 'vastum tonuit ex alto mare / crevitque in astra', *Ag* 471 'in astra pontus tollitur', Virg. *Aen.* iii. 423 'sidera verberat unda' (Charybdis), Lucan x. 320 'spuma tunc astra lacessis' (the Nile). Possibly Silius imitated our passage with 'sparsuras astra procellas / parturit unda freti' ix. 283–4.

346. palluit audax: the striking juxtaposition recalls the same words in Hor. *C.* iii. 27. 28 (Europa, also fearful of the sea): Sen. has Horace in mind throughout this lyric—and Statius may be recalling Sen. at *Th.* v. 412–13 'clavumque audire negantem / lassat agens Tiphys palletque'.

346–7. omnes . . . misit habenas: 'relinquished all control', i.e. dropped the tiller: 3 n. Or *habenae* may be literally 'ropes', as at Ovid, *F.* iii. 593, Val. Fl. iv. 679.

348. Orpheus and his lyre (357 n.) are pictured on the Argo on a metope of the Treasure House of the Sicyonians at Delphi: Homolle, *Fouilles de Delphes* IV. fasc. i. 2 (art archaïque), planche IV (top).

torpente: 'lying idle': the word suggests that the lyre shared the general stupefaction.

349. vocem: the Argo could speak with a human voice as a beam from one of the talking oaks of Dodona had been incorporated into her stem by Athena: Ap. Rhod. i. 524 ff., iv. 580 ff.

350, 355. quid cum . . . : used in rhetorical enumeration, 'and what about . . . ?'

350 ff. virgo: Scylla, the maiden-monster who dwelt off Pelorus, the north-east promontory of Sicily. The description of the fiendish dogs around her womb follows the same tradition as the accounts in Virgil (*E.* vi. 74 ff., *Aen.* iii. 424 ff.) and Ovid (*M.* xiv. 59 ff.): they do not appear in Homer's description (*Od.* xii. 85 ff.). (The Virgil and Ovid passages should be compared with Seneca's lines for possible verbal suggestions.) These descriptions are the direct ancestors of Milton's account of Sin, *P.L.* ii. 650 ff.: 'The one seem'd Woman to the waste, and fair, / But ended foul in many a scaly fould / Voluminous and vast, a serpent arm'd / With mortal sting: about her middle round / A cry of Hell Hounds never ceasing bark'd / With wide Cerberean mouths full loud, and rung / A hideous Peal: yet, when they list, would creep, / If aught disturb'd thir noyse, into her woomb'; and Spenser's similar picture of Errour, *Faerie Queene* i. 1. 14-15.

   virgŏ: notice the scansion, as in 49. The shortening of a final -ō, especially in an iambic dissyllable, originally reflected the pronunciation of spoken Latin, and was used increasingly widely from the Augustan poets onwards for metrical convenience. At first we find iambic dissyllables affected, like *modŏ*, then cretics, e.g. *nesciŏ*, and spondees as here. (The first spondaic example is Prop. iii. 9. 35 *findŏ*: see Housman, *J. Ph.* xxi (1893) 160.) Sen. extended still further the range of words with shortened -ō, e.g. *imagŏ* (*Ag* 874), *ratiŏ* (*Oed* 696), *retineŏ* (*Phoe* 105), *vincendŏ* (*Tro* 264), and was followed by later dactylic writers. For more details and references see Austin on *Aen.* ii. 735.

351. rabidos succincta canes: *succincta* is a 'middle' participle governing a direct object *canes*. This use of a passive verb like the Greek middle with a direct object in the accusative is probably native to Latin, and is to be distinguished from the use of the accusative of 'respect', esp. with adjectives and passive participles, which derives from Greek usage. The latter type is particularly common with parts of the body (cf. *totos horruit artus* below), and seems to have been first used extensively by Virgil: he has many examples of both kinds of accusative with a passive verb, e.g. 'exuvias indutus' (object) *Aen.* ii. 275; 'mentem formidine pressus' ('respect' with a pure passive) *Aen.* iii. 47; and many others where the two constructions are blended. See K-S i. 285 ff., R. D. Williams on *Aen.* v. 135.

   utero: local abl., 'at, around her womb'.

352. hiatus: often used of the wide open mouth of animals, and of Tantalus at *Thy* 157.

354: '(who did not shudder) at the multiple howling of that single monster?'

355 ff. pestes: the Sirens, half women, half birds, who lived on an island near Scylla and Charybdis (hence *Ausonium mare*), and by their enchanting singing enticed sailors to their death. Orpheus, who had been mute with fear at the Symplegades, now rose to the challenge of rival musicians and out-charmed the Sirens, so that the Argonauts escaped their clutches: Ap. Rhod. iv. 902 ff., Apollod. i. 9. 25. (Odysseus by a different ruse had also saved his men from them.) William Morris imagined a long amoebean singing-contest between Orpheus and the Sirens: *The Life and Death of Jason*, Book XIV.

356. mulcerent: the subj. is probably potential, the sense being: 'and what about the time when the Sirens would be calming the sea (and thus retarding the ship), when O. nearly compelled them to follow the Argo?' The imperfect *mulcerent* is thus vivid for the pluperfect, and we have an 'inverse *cum*' construction which is virtually equivalent to a *nisi*-clause: 'they would have . . . if he had not . . .'.

357. resonans: 'echoing, sounding back' with his own music to the Sirens: Apollod. i. 9. 25 Ὀρφεὺς τὴν ἐναντίαν μοῦσαν μελῳδῶν τοὺς Ἀργοναύτας κατέσχε.

Pieria (adj.): Orpheus was associated with this area of north Greece, near Mt. Olympus: Ap. Rhod. i. 32 ff. Ὀρφέα . . . Πιερίῃ Βιστωνίδι κοιρανέοντα.

cithara is here clearly synonymous with *lyra* in 348, though strictly the cithara was a slightly different and more elaborate form of the lyre: see D–S iii. 2, s.v. *lyra* p. 1438, *OCD*, s.v. 'Music' pp. 709–10.

358 ff. solitam . . . : 'nearly forced the Sirens to follow, though they were used to holding ships fast by their song'.

360. Sirena: Σειρῆνα, Greek acc. sing. (like *Titana* 410) used collectively.

362: 'and M., a greater evil than the sea, a reward worthy of the first ship', an ironical way of saying that the Argo's temerity was suitably punished by bringing back M. The alliteration in 362 is notable: it may be a contemptuous jingle, but readers' reactions will vary. Alliteration is not a feature of Seneca's style, but cf. 190, 933–4.

364 ff.: today sailing is commonplace and there is intermingling among once scattered peoples.

nunc iam: a strong transition to the chorus's own time; but not many years have elapsed since the Argo's voyage for this dramatic expansion in seafaring, and the impression we have is of the poet speaking *in propria persona* in this concluding passage (e.g. in the reference to *ultima Thule*).

365. leges: cf. 319. **Palladia manu:** 2 n.

non: strictly with *quaeritur*, but virtually equals *nulla* (*Argo*): 915 n. The description of the Argo is balanced and asyndetic, the words *compacta* and *referens inclita* being centrally placed in their phrase units.

366–7. regum referens remos: 'rowed home by princes', i.e. completing its mission. Madvig's *regumque ferens*, adopted by some editors, is quite unnecessary and against the united manuscript tradition (see Damsté, *Mnem.* 46 (1918), 407–8).

quaeritur: 'is needed'.

368: 'any little skiff roams freely on the high seas'.

369. motus: sc. *est*.

urbes: Greek colonization started during the eighth cent. B.C. Elsewhere Sen., using colonization as an example of voluntary exile, remarks 'illud utique manifestum est, nihil eodem loco mansisse quo genitum est. adsiduus generis humani discursus est; cotidie aliquid in tam magno orbe mutatur: nova urbium fundamenta iaciuntur . . .' (*Cons. Helv.* 7. 5).

371 ff.: 'the world now a thoroughfare has left nothing in its former place'.

372-4: the geographical identification of a people by naming a local river whose waters they drink (cf. 80 ff.) is widespread in Greek and Latin poetry and goes back to Homer, *Il.* ii. 825-6 πίνοντες ὕδωρ μέλαν Αἰσήποιο / Τρῶες: cf. Pindar, *O.* vi. 85 Θήβαν . . . . τᾶς ἐρατεινὸν ὕδωρ πίομαι, Hor. *C.* iv. 15. 21 'qui profundum Danubium bibunt', ii. 20. 20 'Rhodanique potor', Sen. *Oed* 427-8 'qui bibit Gangen niveumque quisquis / frangit Araxen'. See Fraenkel on *Agam.* 1157, who refers to Norden, *Berl. Sitzgsb.* 1917, 673 n. 2. (The phrase *gelidum potat Araxen* is repeated at *Phae* 57-8, though exact repetitions are not notably frequent in the tragedies: see Summers in *CR* xix (1905), 42 ff.) There is a further rhetorical point here: the chorus states as coming true an occurrence which was one of the stock ἀδύνατα, natural impossibilities, exemplified in Virg. *E.* i. 60 ff. 'ante leves ergo pascentur in aethere cervi, / et freta destituent nudos in litore pisces; / ante pererratis amborum finibus exsul / aut Ararim Parthus bibet aut Germania Tigrim, / quam nostro illius labatur pectore vultus'. The chorus is in effect saying that the miracle is now realized—and further miracles will follow. The Araxes, now the Aras, was a river of Armenia; Albis, the Elbe. Seneca's Corinthian chorus talks like a Roman surveying the ends of his empire.

374 ff. annis . . . seris: 'in distant years to come': the whole phrase resembles 'veniet lustris labentibus aetas' in the prophecy of Jupiter, Virg. *Aen.* i. 283. Navigation will reveal that the earth is much larger than hitherto suspected, and this is expressed by saying that the Ocean 'will loosen the fetters, or barriers, of the world': the rest of the sentence elaborates the thought. Cf. Sen. Elder, *Suas.* i. 4 'de Oceano tamen dubitant utrumne terras velut vinculum circumfluat'. The diction has a Lucretian flavour: e.g. 'effringere ut arta / naturae primus portarum claustra cupiret' (i. 70-1), and Tennyson has a similar image in *Columbus* 210-11 'the Atlantic sea, / Which he unchain'd for all the world to come'.

376. laxet . . . : the subjunctives are consecutive.

377. Tethys: sister and wife of Oceanus, often personifying the sea.

379. Thule: a land in the far north, representing the limits of geographical knowledge (cf. Virg. *G.* i. 30 'tibi [Caesar] serviat ultima Thule'). Strabo (i. 63) quotes the Greek traveller Pytheas as saying that Thule was six days' sail north of Britain, and modern guesses favour Iceland or Norway as its identity.

Farnaby reports that Abraham Oertel (the sixteenth-century Flemish geographer) regarded this passage as a prophecy by a

Spaniard of the discovery of America by his fellow countrymen. Thinking on the same lines Ferdinand Columbus wrote in the margin of his copy of Seneca's tragedies 'haec prophetia expleta est per patrem meum Christoforum Colon almirantem anno 1492' (Damsté, *Mnem.* 46 (1918), 134).

380–430. M. emerges with passionate haste from her house, accompanied by the Nurse, who describes and tries to allay her mistress's frenzy. M. pays no attention, and in a brooding self-apostrophe strengthens her own resolution for revenge.

382 ff. M. ignores her appeals, and the Nurse proceeds to describe the frenzy she cannot calm: cf. the later chorus 849 ff., and for a similar picture of a woman's jealous passion see the description of Deianira, *HO* 233 ff. It is good declamatory stuff, but Sen. was interested too in the pathology of extreme anger, as the treatise *de ira* shows: the outward signs are described as follows to show that those possessed by anger are really insane: 'flagrant ac micant oculi, multus ore toto rubor exaestuante ab imis praecordiis sanguine. labra quatiuntur, dentes conprimuntur, horrent ac subriguntur capilli, spiritus coactus ac stridens, articulorum se ipsos torquentium sonus, gemitus mugitusque et parum explanatis vocibus sermo praeruptus et conplosae saepius manus et pulsata humus pedibus et totum concitum corpus' (i. 1. 4). See also *Ep.* 18. 14–15. In our passage the stock metaphors are used of a raving maenad, breaking wave, and overflowing water, and the speech with its vivid account of M.'s physical movements (which would have been visible to an audience at a stage production) is one of those which point firmly to recitation of the tragedies.

incerta qualis . . . : 'as a distracted maenad roams frenziedly, now maddened by the onset of the god . . . so M. rushes . . .'.

entheos: *entheus* (ἔνθεος) is exactly 'recepto deo' 383 and Horace's 'tui [Bacchi] plenum' (*C.* iii. 25. 1–2), 'filled with a god, divinely inspired'. A similar passage is *Tro* 673 ff. 'qualis deo / percussa Maenas entheo silvas gradu / armata thyrso terret' (Andromache), and further examples of the Bacchante as an image of a frenzied woman are Deianira (*HO* 244, 701), Dido (*Aen.* iv. 301 ff.). *maenas* is used of M. again at 806, 849: for this element in her character see 123 n.

384: favourite haunts of Dionysus and his acolytes. Pindus was a major mountain range in Thessaly, Nysa a mountain, located in various lands from Thessaly to India, where Dionysus was nursed by the nymphs (cf. *Oed* 404, 435: a dithyramb).

385. recursat: the verb is rather rare, esp. in the literal sense, and occurs only here in the tragedies.

386. lymphati: 'frenzied, demented'. For the old association of *lympha*, *lymphatus* with νύμφη, νυμφόληπτος 'crazed by the nymphs', see E–M, s.v. *lympha*.

387. flammata facies: sc. *est* (rather than take *facies* as subject of *citat*, or as acc. of reference).

  spiritum . . . : 'she breathes with deep pants'.

389. omnis . . . capit: 'she contains proof of every passion, is clearly subject to every emotion'. The words probably look forward to the next line, rather than summarize the previous clauses. On the punctuation and other problems of these lines see Carlsson, *Class. et Med.* x (1948), 47–8, and Zwierlein, *Rezitationsdramen* 209–10.

391. quo . . . verget? : 'whither shall the weight of her wrath incline?' The metaphor is of an evenly poised balance, and there is a possible imitation of this passage in Lucan, viii. 280 'expromam mentisque meae quo pondera vergant'.

393 ff.: 'it is no simple or moderate crime which she plots: she will outdo herself': cf. 49–50, 904 ff.

396. Furoris: virtually = *Furiae* (cf. 386, 392).

397–8. M. reflects that her hatred must now be as boundless as once her love for Jason was. As the Chorus later puts it, 'frenare nescit iras / Medea, non amores' 866–7.

398–9. egone ut . . . patiar?: a 'repudiating' subjunctive question, often as here and 893, 929, introduced by *-ne ut*, and suggesting an idea which is strongly rejected by the speaker: 'am I really to . . .?' (Handford, *The Latin Subjunctive* 70 ff.).

  faces: 67 n.

399. segnis . . . : 'shall this day pass in idleness which was sought and granted by such insistence?' (285 ff.).

401 ff. So long as the natural order of the universe persists my passion for revenge shall never cease. Passages like this which express fixity of duration by reference to the immutable laws of nature are extremely common (cf. at random Virg. *Aen.* i. 607 ff., *Oed* 503 ff.): lists of ἀδύνατα ('sooner shall rivers run backwards, lions mate with ewes etc. . . .') are a variant on this idea and serve the same purpose: notes on 372–4, 762.

401. terra media: the geocentric view of the universe was of course widely held, though Aristarchus of Samos had first proposed a heliocentric system in the third cent. B.C.

402. nitidus: the word suggests that the movements of the stars are meant.

404. sequentur: *sequi* in the sense 'attend, be inseparable from', rather than 'follow after': see Duff on *Cons. Helv.* 6. 1.

  siccas: a stock description of the Bears which did not set, and so remained 'dry' above the ocean: such descriptions go back to the Homeric (Ἄρκτος) ἄμμορός ἐστι λοετρῶν Ὠκεανοῖο *Il.* xviii. 489, *Od.* v. 275. In spite of the precession of the equinoxes the Bears still do not set in Aegean latitudes.

406. cessabit in poenas: 'will cease to exact vengeance'; a rare construction with *cessare*: *Oct* 247 'in tam nocentem dextra cur cessat tua?', Virg. *Aen.* vi. 51 'cessas in vota precesque'.

407. immanitas: a very rare word in poetry: see Quicherat, s.v.

408. Charybdis: a fearsome whirlpool near to Scylla, described by Circe to Odysseus *Od.* xii. 101 ff.

    Ausonium mare: 355–6.

410. Titana: Enceladus, who however was a Giant, but the Titans and Giants were often confused. After the Giants were defeated in battle by the Gods he was pinned under Etna, and his writhings were imagined to cause the volcanic eruptions: see Virg. *Aen.* iii. 578 ff. The more usual version of the legend has Typhoeus buried under Etna and Enceladus under Inarime, but *HO* 1157 ff. 'feret Aetnaeos inde caminos . . . Enceladus' suggests that Sen. here too follows Virgil.

    tantis: 'so great as mine'.

411. non . . . non: 365 n.

415. timuit: sc. Jason. As when talking to Creon, she does not name the man who fills her thoughts and whose memory is hourly becoming more bitter to her. This soliloquizing debate on Jason's conduct recalls 137 ff., but her resentment has now hardened.

    Thessalici ducis: Acastus: see notes on 133, 257.

417: 'but grant that he was forced to give way and surrender', i.e. to accept Creusa as the condition of safety: the subjunctives are concessive. In Eur. M. says to Jason himself χρῆν σ᾽, εἴπερ ἦσθα μὴ κακός, πείσαντά με / γαμεῖν γάμον τόνδ᾽, ἀλλὰ μὴ σιγῇ φίλων (586–7).

418. certe: 'at least'; in 420 'surely'.

419: 'this too the hero was afraid to do': *ferox* is tartly ironic and pointedly juxtaposed to *extimuit*.

420: 'to relax, i.e. delay, the time of my cruel exile': an unusual use of *laxare*, but cf. Quint. x. 5. 22 'longiore potius dierum spatio laxabit ('extend') dicendi necessitatem'.

421. genero: after Creon's casual reference to Jason as his *gener* 184 M. picks up the word with increasing scorn at 240, here, and—very bitterly—at 460 'regius iussit gener'; but she has not relinquished her status as his wife, *coniugem* 418.

421–2. liberis . . . duobus: ostensibly to say good-bye to them, but the context of a similar phrase in *Cons. Marc.* 14. 2 'quid minus potest quam unum diem duobus filiis dare'—a single day's grief observed by L. Bibulus for the death of his two sons—suggested to Anliker (*Prologe* n. 101) the possibility of a sinister interpretation of M.'s words here. Her following words might support this view, or they may express only vague plans for vengeance: it is hard to say when the idea first dawns which is crystallized at 549–50 (see also notes on 23 ff., 37–40). In any case resolution returns to her with *non queror*.

423. multum patebit: 'it will stretch far': cf. *brev. vit.* 1. 4 'aetas nostra bene disponenti multum patet', 15. 5 'sapientis ergo multum patet vita'.

424. nullus: sc. *dies.*

invadam deos: by deeds of witchcraft abhorrent to them: 271 n., 673.

425–6: 'you must control your feelings, shattered though they are by your woes'. Cf. Phaedra's nurse: 'recipe iam sensus, era' *Phae* 733.

426–8. sola . . . obruta / trahere . . . libet: this *sententia* appears in many different forms in Sen. and elsewhere, and must have been popular in the schools (cf. Sen. Elder, *Contr.* ix. 6. 2 'morientibus gratissimum est commori'): *Ag* 202 'mors misera non est commori cum quo velis', *HO* 350 'felix iacet quicumque quos odit premit', *NQ* vi. 2. 9 'si cadendum est cadam orbe concusso . . . quia ingens mortis solatium est terram quoque videre mortalem', *de clem.* ii. 2. 2 (referring to the Greek verse ἐμοῦ θανόντος γαῖα μιχθήτω πυρί, trag. adesp. 513N), *de ira* i. 1. 1; cf. too fr. inc. 159R 'pereant amici dum inimici una intercidant', Lucan, vii. 654–5, trag. adesp. 362N.

trahere: sc. *omnia, ceteros,* or the like.

429–30: the Nurse in despair is driven back to her earlier warnings of the odds against her mistress, 164 ff.

431–559. Jason enters and there follows the major central scene of the play, as he and Medea confront each other, he attempting to defend his treatment of her and she throwing at him every argument she can think of to induce him to flee with her from Corinth. His rejection of this plan, based ostensibly on his fear of Creon and Acastus, and more particularly his refusal to part from his children, harden M.'s resolution for vengeance and suggest the means to achieve it.

At first Jason does not notice her presence, and he begins with a monologue on the harshness of fate and his own difficult position. At sight of him M. seems for the time being to forget thoughts of vengeance, and she launches into a long appeal based on the cruelty of her own predicament and her past services to him. For the rest of the scene their shorter exchanges embody a fast-moving and bitter dispute in which Jason is finally driven merely to reiterating his fears. M., having failed to move him, offers a pretended reconciliation: Jason gladly accepts it and departs. They do not meet again until the climax of the play, and thus Sen. has greatly reduced their confrontation compared with Euripides' play, where they meet twice (446–626, 866–975) before the end. There are many reminiscences of Eur. in this scene, the more important of which are mentioned in the notes.

432. ex aequo malam: with *sortem,* 'equally evil'.

433–4. remedia . . . peiora: perhaps another *sententia* of the declaimers: Sen. Elder, *Contr.* vi. 7. 2 'quaedam remedia peiora ipsis periculis sunt'; cf. *Oed* 517 'ubi turpis est medicina sanari piget'. But although we know that poets and rhetoricians borrowed from each other, Leo (I. 153) rightly enjoins caution in so explaining similarities in commonplace reflections.

434 ff. vellem . . . nollem: not present 'unreal' but past 'ideal' conditionals: Jason puts the choice he faced when he made his decision. Cf. *Cons. Marc.* 22. 6 'quid faceret? si vivere vellet, Seianus rogandus erat'. The triple repetition of *fides* is significant.

437. misero: dat. of agent, sc. *mihi*.

438. pietas: 'father-love'. Jason stresses this feeling again at 545, and at 943–4 M.'s *pietas* towards her children fights against her *ira*. For Jason's claim to have his children's interests at heart see Eur. *M.* 559 ff.

    quippe: 256 n.   **necem:** with *parentum*.

440. Iustitia: Astraea, the constellation Virgo.

441. quin: 'why', 'indeed'.

    ipsam: cf. the unspecific *iratam* 444: Jason only once refers to M. by name, 496.

442. ferox: 186 n.

443. consulere . . . thalamis: 'put her children's safety above her marriage rights'.

444. animus: sc. *meus*.

445. Jason and M. appear to catch sight of each other simultaneously.

446. totus . . . dolor: cf. 52 n., *HO* 247–8 'in vultus dolor / processit omnis'.

447. Without greeting or preamble M. bursts upon Jason with the thought now uppermost in her mind—her continued wandering which has not yet brought her lasting happiness.

    fūgimus . . . fŭgimus: 'I have been an exile, Jason: I still am'. The first *fugimus* is perfect, the second is present. *fŭgimus . . . fūgimus* would give a first foot tribrach formed by a tribrachic word, which occurs nowhere else in Sen. (Strzelecki, 68–9, who, however, reads *fūgimus . . . fūgimus*, omitting *hoc*).

449 ff. pro te: in contrast with the next line.

    discedo . . . : the contrast is expressed in abrupt asyndeton: '(but this time) I leave, I go forth, driven by you to fly from your own home (emphatic *tuis*); and to whom do you return me?' (Linking 450 and 451—'to whom do you return the woman whom you are forcing . . . ?'—leaves *discedo*, *exeo* rather awkwardly isolated.)

450. prŏfŭgĕre: for the 'unbroken' third foot tribrach see 200 n.

451 ff. Cf. Eur. *M.* 502 ff. νῦν ποῖ τράπωμαι; πότερα πρὸς πατρὸς δόμους . . . ; Ap. Rhod. iv. 378 πῶς ἵξομαι ὄμματα πατρός; Ennius, *Medea* fr. 276–7 V 'quo nunc me vortam? quod iter incipiam ingredi? / domum paternamne anne ad Peliae filias?'; and for similar female laments Cat. 64. 177 ff. (Ariadne), Virg. *Aen.* iv. 534 ff. (Dido), Ovid, *M.* viii. 113 ff. (Scylla).

petam: (and 457) whether deliberative subjunctive or future indicative of factual question (like *remittis, iubes, monstras*) hardly matters.

452–3. quaeque . . . arva: the context suggests that Sen. refers to the variant of the legend in which Absyrtus was killed in Colchis, though this version put the murder in the *palace*: see n. on 131 ff.

quas . . . iubes?: quoted by Quintilian to illustrate a rhetorical question which expresses bitter reproach: 'interrogamus etiam . . . invidiae gratia, ut Medea apud Senecam: quas peti terras iubes?' (ix. 2. 8–9).

454. fauces: sc. *monstras*, sardonically suggesting an answer to the last question.

455. revexi: again the proud note of her achievement: see 235, 243, and introd. note on 179–300.

456. adulterum secuta: with taut and bitter brevity the two words point up their joint moral responsibility: he seduced her and she was willing.

Symplegadas: the 'Clashing Rocks': 341 n.

457. parvam: the point of the epithet is not clear, and it contradicts the Homeric description of Iolcos as ἐϋκτιμένη and εὐρύχορος. Perhaps it merely contrasts the town with the wider extent of Aeetes' kingdom (451 ff.), now closed to M. (Mr. D. A. Russell suggests to me *pergamne*.)

Tempe (Τέμπη: Gk. neut. pl.) seems to have no particular connection with the Medea legend, but is named as a notable feature of Thessaly which M. can never revisit. (Iolcos and Tempe appear together also in the song of the captive Trojan women, speculating on where their future homes will be, *Tro* 814 ff.)

458. Scylla similarly rages in Ovid, *M.* viii. 113 ff., especially 117–18: 'obstruximus orbem / terrarum, nobis ut Crete sola pateret'.

459–60. exuli . . . das: 'you impose exile on one already exiled, but give no place to go'. These words are quoted by Ennodius, bishop of Pavia in the early sixth century: 'adulescentiae meae memini me legisse temporibus de quodam dictum: exuli exilium imperas nec das' (*pro synodo* 38 in Vogel, *Mon. Germ. Hist.* vii. p. 54)—whose quotation supports the reading *exuli*.

460 ff.: from *eatur* to *patiar* 465 M. is passionately ironical about her own deserts—'Well, I have my orders, I must go. I have more than deserved the worst punishments that can be devised for me'—before her real feelings burst out again with *ingratum caput*.

eatur: the Latin impersonal is used both in elevated poetry (like *itur* at Virg. *Aen.* vi. 179, ix. 641) and in everyday speech (*passim* in the comedians): here it suitably expresses M.'s tragic pose, 'Let me then make my way'.

gener: 421 n.

462. paelicem: a married man's mistress, so the word is applied to herself with peculiar bitterness here and at 495: it is used of Creusa at 920 (as by Hor. *Epode* v. 63).

464: 'immured for ever in a dark cavern'—the fate with which another Creon threatened Antigone: Soph. *Ant.* 773 ff.

465. caput: a common form of address at most literary levels. The same rebuke is in her last words to him, 'ingrate Iason' 1021. Studley's version here illustrates the lush diffuseness of the Tudor translators:

'O thou uncurteous Gentleman, consider in thy mynde
The flamy puffes, and firy gaspes of gastly gaping bull,
And Aetas catell rych with Fleece of gorgeous golden wooll,
That went to graze amid so great and mighty feares in fielde,
Of uncontrouled Nation, whose soyle doth armies yeelde. . . .'

466 ff. M. similarly lists her services to Jason in Eur. *M.* 476 ff., Ovid, *Her.* xii. 107 ff.: cf. the lines, probably from Ennius' *Medea*, 'non commemoro quod draconis saevi sopivi impetum, / non quod domui vim taurorum et segetis armatae manus' (274–5V).

467–8. The lines are a little awkward (Leo had some excuse for deleting them): 'amid the fearsome terrors of the unconquered race Aeetes' fiery beast in the field teeming with arms': *-que* in *interque* must introduce an explanatory expansion of '*igneos tauri halitus*'; *gentis* must refer to the Colchians (not to the armed warriors, as Leo seems to have taken it, I. 211); and *pecus* is a loose repetition of *tauri* (though *pecus* can mean one beast, and elsewhere too in the play only one bull is mentioned, 241 n.). Three terrifying elements in Jason's ordeal are recalled in this densely written couplet: the hostile crowd of assembled Colchians, the fire-breathing bull, and the field teeming with armed men.

metus: here the cause of fear, 'terrors', as at 516 and *Phae* 29 'metus agricolis . . . aper'.

469. subiti: 'suddenly springing up'.

470. Cf. Ovid *M.* vii. 141 'terrigenae pereunt per mutua vulnera fratres'.

471. Phrixei: the ram with the golden fleece had brought Phrixus to Colchis.

arietis is probably trisyllabic, 'Phrixĕ(i) āriĕtĭs': see 266 n.

472–3. somnoque . . . insomne: for the word-play see 261 n.

473: 'and in that one crime a crime not only once performed': Absyrtus was not simply killed but cut to pieces and strewn on the sea.

475–6. Cf. 259–61.

477. Leo perhaps rightly transposed this line to follow 482. Here it is a natural and effective climax to M.'s list of her services to Jason, 'seeking a kingdom for another I abandoned my own', but after 482 it would certainly smooth the transition in 483.

478. liberum: probably defining genitive, 'hopes consisting in your children', rather than subjective or objective ('your children's hopes', 'your hopes of (future) children'). The idea of hope continues in **certum larem:** 'by the settled home (you seek)'. In her earlier curse on Jason she wished him to be 'incerti laris' 21.

479. manus: sc. *meas.*

481. caelum, undas: there were various accounts of the location of M.'s and Jason's union: according to Apollonius (iv. 1128 ff.) it took place in a cave on the island of the Phaeacians.

  coniugi: for the contraction (to avoid a fourth-foot anapaest) cf. *supplicis* 743, 1015, and 248 n.

482. vicem: goes closely with *felix*: 'you are happy, give me my turn now (to be happy)'. (Cf. *HF* 1337–8 'gratiam meritis refer / vicemque nostris', Ovid, *Am.* i. 6. 23 'redde vicem meritis'.) She probably means 'come away from Corinth with me': see 273–5, 524 'innocens mecum fuge'.

483. Scythae: M. regards her people as belonging to the far-ranging Scythian tribes. (There was another ancient theory that the Colchians were related to the Egyptians: see How and Wells on Hdt. ii. 104–5, and cf. Diod. Sic. i. 28.) *raptas* suggests plunder, but in historical times Phasis was the terminus of an established trade route from India: Pliny *HN* vi. 52. Pliny also reports a later phase of the Colchian love of loot: 'iam regnaverat in Colchis Saulaces Aeetae suboles, qui terram virginem nactus plurimum auri argentique eruisse dicitur in Suanorum gente, et alioqui velleribus aureis incluto regno. et illius aureae camarae, argenteae trabes et columnae atque parastaticae narrantur victo Sesostri Aegypti rege . . .' (*HN* xxxiii. 52).

484. perustis: from being supposedly nearer to the sun: *Oed* 122–3 'Phoebus et flamma propiore nudos / inficit Indos', *Thy* 602 'Phoebi propioris Indus'. (There is a similar remark about the Ethiopians at *NQ* iv. 2. 18.) Sen. was himself interested in India: Pliny the Elder tells us (*HN* vi. 60) that he wrote a treatise on the country—and repeats the same theory about sun-scorched Indians (vi. 70).

485: an awkward line: lit. 'which treasures since the crammed palace scarcely holds (we deck the trees with gold)'. The wealth from the east, overflowing Aeetes' palace, was hung on trees—as was the Golden Fleece. (*auro* seems to have a wider reference than just to the fleece.) A memorable passage in Apollonius describes the fleece shining like the sun as it hangs on an oak tree: τὼ δὲ δι' ἀτραπιτοῖο μεθ' ἱερὸν ἄλσος ἵκοντο, / φηγὸν ἀπειρεσίην διζημένω ᾗ ἔπι κῶας / βέβλητο, νεφέλῃ ἐναλίγκιον ᾗ τ' ἀνιόντος / ἠελίου φλογερῇσιν ἐρεύθεται ἀκτίνεσσιν (iv. 123–6).

  gaza abl. (Bentley, Wilamowitz) gives a smoother construction but is not essential.

487. impendi tibi: for the construction see *Cons. Helv.* 18. 9 'quanto iustius sit te illi servari quam mihi impendi'.

488. tĭbĭ pătrĭa: the first foot is a proceleusmatic, which is very rare in Senecan iambics and occurs only in this foot: cf. 670 'păvĕt ănĭmus'.

   pater, pudor: cf. 238–9.

489. hac dote: cf. Ovid, *Her.* xii. 199 ff. 'dos ubi sit quaeris? . . . aureus ille aries, villo spectabilis aureo, / dos mea: quam dicam si tibi redde, neges; / dos mea, tu sospes; dos est mea Graia iuventus', and M.'s similar argument to Creon 225 ff. Tarpeia and Scylla also refer to the homelands they are betraying as a dowry: Prop. iv. 4. 56, Ovid, *M.* viii. 67–8.

   sua: 'her due': 482 n. (Farnaby suggested an anachronistic reference to the Roman law of divorce.) M.'s speech is framed by emphatic appeals to her plight as a refugee: *fugimus* 447, *fugienti* here.

490. With no defence for his general conduct Jason clutches at the one action for which he claims credit, but M. has already heard of it from Creon, 183–4. Similarly Jason in Eur.: κἀγὼ μὲν αἰεὶ βασιλέων θυμουμένων / ὀργὰς ἀφῄρουν καί σ' ἐβουλόμην μένειν . . . τοιγὰρ ἐκπεσῇ χθονός (455–8).

492. Sen. may be recalling Ovid, *M.* ii. 99 (Phoebus to his son) 'poenam, Phaethon, pro munere poscis', where, however, the words have not M.'s heavy irony.

494–5. hoc . . . Creusae: 'this exile you urge on me is a gift to Creusa': the following words explain her meaning.

   paelicem: 462 n.

496. Medea: 441 n.: even when he utters her name Jason puts the question in the third person.

   amores: sc. *Creusae.* Jason picks up the hint in *paelicem*, but the fatuity of his question reveals his indefensible position.

497. tandem: often adds a note of impatience to a question.

498 ff. M. repeats her argument to Creon (275 ff.) that Jason must share the blame for her crimes.

500–1. cui . . . fecit: cf. *Tro* 870–1 'ad auctorem redit / sceleris coacti culpa'.

501 ff. M. abandons dialectics and suddenly becomes a wife pleading pitifully with her husband for support against an accusing world. The lines contrast strongly with her prevailing *furor* throughout the play.

503. Cf. 280 n. Note the balanced symmetry of this very Senecan line: *quisquis* in the centre, flanked by *sit/est, innocens/nocens, tibi/pro te.*

504 ff. To M.'s reminder of the crimes she committed on his behalf Jason retorts that life won in this shameful way is unwelcome. M.'s rejoinder is swift and unanswerable: 'why then cling to it?' and Jason then shifts his ground to their children.

506. quin only here in the tragedies emphasizes an imperative, adding a note of impatience. The idiom seems to derive from colloquial language and was introduced by Virgil into high poetry: see Austin on *Aen.* iv. 99, and an interesting discussion by Sonnenschein in *CR* xvi (1902), 165 ff.

507. placare: 'middle' imperative, 'calm, reconcile yourself', like *accingere* 51.

  natis: dat. of interest, 'for the children's sake'. Jason believes them to be his best weapon: see 443.

  abdico . . . : sc. *natos.* A purely emotional reaction: contrast 541 ff.; but these words *abdico . . . dabit* are the first hint of a feeling which takes possession of her shortly before she murders her first son, when she speaks of her children as now belonging to Creusa, 921 ff. 'quidquid ex illo tuum est, / Creusa peperit . . . liberi quondam mei . . .'.

509. regina, potens: with both understand *fratres dabit.*

510. miseris: sc. *natis.*

512. Phoebus was M.'s grandfather, Sisyphus the founder of Corinth.

  nĕpōtĭbŭs: Sen. shared the general dislike of iambic writers for an iambic fifth foot in trimeters, and there are only about half a dozen examples in his plays. With one doubtful exception (*HF* 20) these lines all end with a quadrisyllable. Richter may have been right to delete 512 as an interpolation: the only other example in the *Medea* is 709 *Promethei.* (See Hardie, *Res Metrica* 83, Strzelecki, 27.)

513. exilium: this is the reading of all manuscripts: editors usually accept Avantius' conjecture *exitium,* but M. is trying to induce Jason to leave Corinth with her (482 n., 524), and he rejects the thought of further wandering. *meque teque* is emphatic: 'don't involve both of us in your banishment: off with you.'

515. vel scelus: the understood thought is 'as I did for you'. He should be prepared to commit even a crime for her, though all she asks him is to have the courage to break away from Creon's protection.

516. rex: 'on either side a king', Creon and Acastus (521): sc. *est* or *instat.*

  his: if the right reading, *his* is probably abl.: M. says she is a more formidable adversary than the kings. (It might be dat.: 'M. is more to be feared by them (than they are by you)', but this seems a less natural interpretation.)

  metus: 467 n.

517. †confligere: a thorny problem: *confligere* has no construction and the metre is faulty (a fourth foot anapaest). There have been many suggestions but no clear solution. The general sense is clear: M. suggests pitting herself in contest against the kings, with Jason as prize for the victor. Gronovius' *conferre certamen sine* is probably on the right lines. For a discussion of the passage see W.-H. Friedrich, *Untersuchungen* 141 ff.

518. cedŏ: the *-o* must be short (350 n.) to avoid a fourth-foot spondee.

519. expertos: sc. *tibi.*

520. So the true Stoic *rex* 'tuto positus loco / infra se videt omnia' *Thy* 365–6.

521. Creon is of course *hostis* only to M., but her state of mind does not maintain a logical argument.

523. caede cognata: by killing his cousin Acastus.

524. fuge: 482 n., 513 n.

525. et introducing a surprised or indignant question is quite common in the tragedies, e.g. *Tro* 429, 598, *Phae* 673.

528. Scythas: 483 n.   **Pelasgis:** 127 n.

   dabo: causative with perf. part. like *reddo*: 'I shall overwhelm'; cf. Virg. *Aen.* xii. 436–7 'te mea dextera bello / defensum dabit', Livy, viii. 6. 6 'stratas legiones Latinorum dabo'.

529. ne . . . : i.e. do not make the plea of fear of royal power a cloak for ambition to acquire it: a shrewd thrust, for Jason is an exiled prince.

530. amputa: 'cut short'. *amputare* is often used in phrases indicating conciseness of language or style: Sen. *Ep.* 114. 17, Tac. *Dial.* 32, Pliny, *Ep.* i. 20. 19.

   Their argument has reached deadlock and Jason lamely tries to end it. M., desperate at the failure of her appeals and stung by the realization that Jason does not even want to be seen talking to her, launches into a wild prayer to Jupiter to destroy one or other of them.

531 ff. For the prayer cf. those of Hercules, 'nunc parte ab omni, genitor, iratus tona . . .' *HF* 1202 ff., and Hippolytus, 'cur dextra, divum rector atque hominum, vacat . . . in me tona' *Phae* 680 ff.; the phrase *vindice flamma* is used by Jupiter at Ovid, *M.* i. 230.

534–5: 'and let not your weapons be poised in a hand that chooses me or him', i.e. distinguishes between us. She goes on to stress their joint guilt: see her words to Creon 'cur sontes duos / distinguis?' 275–6 and 456 n.

538–9. Jason makes a similar offer in Euripides (459 ff., 610 ff.) which is similarly rejected, though in Eur. he offers to give her something χρημάτων ἐμῶν, while in Sen. his complete dependence on Creon is stressed by *ex soceri domo*. M.'s *unicum solamen* is her children (945–6).

540. animus: sc. *meus.*

541 ff. liberos . . . : either M. has changed her mind about her children since talking to Creon (282–3) or she makes this request to observe its effect on Jason. In Eur. she asks that her children may stay in Corinth (780 ff., 939–40)—for her own sinister purpose. See introd. note to 179–300.

543. profundam: final subj.

545 ff. Jason again stresses the claim of his *pietas* towards his children (438 n.). It can be assumed to be genuine: he was speaking to himself in the earlier passage, and to let M. have the children would have been the easier course and one less fraught with tension for his future ménage with Creusa.

546. rex et socer: Creon's two claims to Jason's obedience.

547. haec, hoc: not simply his children, but having them with him. Jason thus reveals his basic self-centredness, for having offered M. a *solamen* for her exile he claims as his own *levamen* the one thing she asks for.

    perusti: with *curis*: 'consumed, seared with trouble'. Sen. is fond of this verb in the *Medea*, though elsewhere (484, 966, 997) it is used literally.

549 ff. A powerfully dramatic moment in which we have the first clear indication of M.'s vengeance: Jason's expression of love for his children reveals the way to make him suffer (see notes on 23 ff., 37–40, 421). So in Eur., in answer to an aghast question of the chorus about killing her own children M. says οὕτω γὰρ ἂν μάλιστα δηχθείη πόσις (817). However, the idea lies dormant in her mind until much later (921 ff.—though there are passing hints at 808 ff. and 848), when it recurs to her at the thought that her children are passing under Creusa's control. It seems a weakness in M.'s characterization, even allowing for her over-wrought condition, that she appears to forget for so long such a striking and gruesome idea. On the other hand, perhaps, as yet, she thinks only of smuggling them away with her and so causing him grief.

550. bene est, tenetur: 'good: I have him!' The same words are used by Ulysses of the pretended capture of Astyanax, *Tro* 630, and the whole line smacks of hunting or gladiatorial language. The words *sic . . . locus* are of course an aside.

551. certe: 'at least'.   **abeuntem:** sc. *me.*

553. et illud: 'even that', with *gratum est*. Or possibly take *et illud . . . peto* together.

554 ff. Eur. *M.* 869 ff. Ἰᾶσον, αἰτοῦμαί σε τῶν εἰρημένων / συγγνώμον' εἶναι.

    dubius: 'unstable, distracted': so in 942 'dubiumque fervet pelagus' describes the blind raging of a stormy sea.

555–6. melioris . . . nostri: for adjectival agreement with objective gen. of a personal pronoun see Ovid, *Her.* xi. 106 'amissae [*al.* admissi] memores sed tamen este mei'.

    haec: sc. *verba.*

557. oblitterentur: a mainly prose word, but it occurs in Cat. 64. 232, and two surviving fragments of Accius: fr. 42–4R 'inimicitias Pelopidum / extinctas iam atque oblitteratas memoria / renovare', fr. 162–3R.

557 ff. Jason eagerly clutches at the offered reconciliation and loses no time in bringing the conversation to an end. His embarrassment and consciousness that he has not justified his shabby behaviour are shown in the banal admonishment to M. and his hasty departure.

560 ff. oblitus . . . : cf. 122 'adeone credit omne consumptum nefas?' and note.

561. excidimus tibi?: 'have you forgotten me?': a common meaning of *excidere*, and elsewhere in the tragedies at *Tro* 204, 714, *HO* 1332 (the same phrase).

562. hoc age: a call to action or attention (cf. 905, 976), but with sinister undertones of the original ritual meaning. *hoc age* was the formula spoken at Roman sacrifices at the moment of killing the victim: Plutarch (*Coriol.* 25. 2) explains this ritual meaning (see also Ovid, *F.* i. 321–2), and Suetonius (*Calig.* 58, *Galba* 20) records that these or similar words were uttered on two occasions when an emperor was struck down. Sen. quotes a gruesome pun on the phrase by Sulla in the senate, while a mass butchery of his enemies was taking place near by: 'hoc agamus, patres conscripti, seditiosi pauculi meo iussu occiduntur' (*Clem.* i. 12. 2). The phrase became general, but coming from M. at this moment it must, despite the anachronism, retain its sacrificial flavour.

563–4. fructus . . . putare: 'the fruit of your crimes is to consider nothing a crime'. Somewhat similar is *Tro* 422–3 'hic mihi malorum maximum fructum abstulit, / nihil timere'.

565–6. hac . . . timere: i.e. do something too unimaginably terrible to be guarded against.

567. Cf. Cat. 76. 16 'hoc facias, sive id non pote sive pote' (with Fordyce's note): no doubt different forms of a popular asseveration.

568. The Nurse has been a silent witness of the confrontation between M. and Jason since 430.

570. palla: a robe features in most accounts of M.'s gifts to Creusa (Hyg. *fab.* 25 and Ovid, *Ibis* 605 mention a *corona* only).

Reading **aetherium** (explained by *datum a Sole* below) we have *-que* in *decusque* linking *domus* and *regni* (cf. Hor. *C.* ii. 19. 28 'pacis eras mediusque belli, iii. 4. 11 'ludo fatigatumque somno', *CS* 22): this position of *-que* is unparalleled in Sen. (Axelson, *Korruptelenkult* 14 n. 8), and if this is felt as a difficulty *aetheriae* (*domus*) is quite acceptable.

pignus . . . generis: 'a pledge of his birth': Eur. *M.* 954–5 κόσμον ὅν ποθ' Ἥλιος / πατρὸς πατὴρ δίδωσιν ἐκγόνοισιν οἷς.

572–4. auro . . . comae: 'a gleaming necklace of twisted gold (a kind of torque), and a golden hair-band set with sparkling jewels'. The words *quodque . . . comae* probably describe a different object, though some critics (Gronovius, Bentley, Herrmann in his Budé translation) have taken the words *auro . . . comae* together as describing one article. In Eur. there are two gifts only (λεπτόν τε πέπλον καὶ πλόκον χρυσήλατον 786), but *monile* is strictly a neck ornament, and the repetition of *aurum . . . auro* referring to the same object is awkward and flat. Sen. may have had in mind the list of gifts in Virg. *Aen.* i.

648 ff., which includes 'pallam signis auroque rigentem . . . colloque monile / baccatum et duplicem gemmis auroque coronam'.

576. diris artibus: virtually concrete, 'poisons': at *Tro* 582–3 *diras artes* are tortures.

577–8. Hecate: see notes on 6–7, 750. The Nurse is now forgotten and M. is entering her own world of witchcraft: these lines foreshadow the mood of her next appearance in the incantation scene, 740 ff.

letifica: the reading of *E* is followed instead of the more familiar variants: the word is very rare (not recorded in L–S), occurring also at Lucan ix. 901—perhaps a first-century coinage.

flamma: from the *arae*.

tectis: presumably M.'s house, though *evasit* 676 might suggest that her rites took place somewhere outside. At any rate M. and the Nurse apparently now retire into her house, making way for the third song of the chorus.

579–669. The chorus, stirred by M.'s increasing fury and the possibility that Jason will suffer in her plan of vengeance, sings a lyric that falls into two parts: (*a*) 579–606: there is no violence in nature equal to that of a wronged wife; may the gods spare Jason, who having conquered the sea is in danger of paying for his temerity as Phaethon did; (*b*) 607–69: the other Argonauts have suffered terrible fates for breaking the laws of the sea ('exigit poenas mare provocatum' 616), but their punishment is enough: let Jason be spared as he was under orders to go. This lyric thus contains in part the theme of the second chorus 301 ff., on the beginnings of navigation, though here the emphasis is not so much on sailing as over-bold adventuring but as a crime against cosmic laws for which the gods exact retribution. By setting Jason's danger against the background of the fate of the other Argonauts the chorus creates an atmosphere of doom, and starts a crescendo movement (punctuated by only one more short lyric)—M.'s incantation, the report of Creusa's death, and the murder of the children. The list of the Argonauts and their fates also illustrates the sort of learned catalogue and mythological detail which is common in Seneca's choruses.

Metrically this chorus is interesting: each of the two main themes has a separate metrical form. 579–606 consist of seven sapphic stanzas of the usual type (three hendecasyllables and an adonius). This is the only place in the tragedies where Sen. uses the standard form of sapphic, and it is his only 'strophic' chorus, though of course without any responsion (see n. on 75 ff.). 607–69 apparently consist of seven stanzas, each of eight hendecasyllables and an adonius, but certainty about this is difficult because of the textual trouble at 660 (see notes). In using sapphics elsewhere Sen. wrote either a continuous stretch of hendecasyllables only (e.g. *Phae* 274–324), or hendecasyllables interspersed irregularly with an adonius (e.g. *Oed* 110–53).

579 ff. For the fury of the wronged wife cf. Eur. *M.* 265–6 ὅταν δ' ἐς
εὐνὴν ἠδικημένη κυρῇ, / οὐκ ἔστιν ἄλλη φρὴν μιαιφονωτέρα, Ovid, *A.A.*
ii. 373 ff.

580. metuenda: attributive, sc. *vis est tanta.*

581. viduata taedis: 'bereft of her marriage, divorced': for *taedae*
'marriage' cf. *Ag* 259 'nec regna socium ferre nec taedae sciunt', and
67 n. The word survived in English as *tead(e)* or *tede* until the seventeenth century, e.g. Spenser, *Epithalamium* 25–7 'Hymen is awake . . .
With his bright Tead that flames with many a flake'.

583. nebulosus: a characteristic epithet of this wind which is *nubilus*
in Prop. ii. 16. 56, Ovid, *P.* ii. 1. 26.

585. Hister: the lower Danube: 724 n.

586. i.e. floods its banks.

587. Silius It. describes the Rhône: 'ingentemque extrahit amnem /
spumanti Rhodanus proscindens gurgite campos, / ac propere in
pontum lato ruit incitus alveo' (iii. 448–50).

590. Haemus: a high mountain range in Thrace which appears itself
to be dissolving as the melting snow runs down it: the point here is the
force of the down-rushing mountain torrents so caused.

591: 'blind is the fire of love when spurred on by wrath'. *ignis* is jealous
love (so *ardet* 582): in a similar vein the chorus later reflects on love
and rage combined: 'frenare nescit iras / Medea, non amores; / nunc
ira amorque causam / iunxere: quid sequetur?' 866–9.

592 ff.: for *nec* . . . *-ve* . . . *aut* cf. Prop. iv. 1. 103–6 'neque . . . aut . . .
aut . . . -ve' where *neque* similarly governs the following connectives.

595. parcite: *parcere* more often has an expressed object; here it is a
general appeal which becomes more explicit in the following prayer.

596. qui: Jason: n. on 301 ff.

597–8: the chorus shows that the wrath of Neptune lay behind the
disasters to the Argonauts described in 607 ff., even where nothing
in the traditional stories suggests this.

    regna secunda: after the defeat of Kronos the universe was
divided by lot between his sons Zeus, Poseidon (Neptune), and
Hades, who received respectively the sovereignty of the sky, the
sea, and the underworld: Hom. *Il.* xv. 187 ff. Similar references to
Neptune's 'second kingdom' occur at *HF* 599, *Phae* 904.

599–602: 'the youth who dared to drive the everlasting chariot forgot
the limits of his father's course, and himself received the fire which
he wildly scattered over the heavens'. The fate of Phaethon, the type
of reckless presumption (n. on 32 ff.), forms an analogy to the punishment of the Argonauts.

    currus: prob. 'horses' here and 787, as elsewhere (e.g. Virg. *Aen.*
xii. 287, Lucan, vii. 570).

    metae: virtually means 'course', as at Stat. *Ach.* i. 456, Manil. i.
199.

ignes ipse recepit: cf. Ovid, *M.* ii. 311–13 '[Jupiter] dextra libratum fulmen ab aure / misit in aurigam: pariterque animaque rotisque / expulit, et saevis compescuit ignibus ignes'.

603: 'the beaten track has cost no one dear'. With the next line Bothe compares Lucian, *Dem. Enc.* 22 χρὴ μέντοι καθάπερ ὁδὸν θαρραλεωτάτην εἶναι τὴν συνηθεστάτην.

605. violente: 'impetuous as you are': the generic singular for mankind, not an appeal to Jason. The predicate is 'attracted' to the vocative by a common idiom (cf. 106, 704), e.g. Theocr. xvii. 66 ὄλβιε κοῦρε γένοιο, Tib. i. 7. 53 'sic venias hodierne', Virg. *Aen.* ii. 283, Hor. *C.* i. 2. 37: see K–H i. 255–6.

sacro . . . sancta: the reading of *E* is usually accepted instead of *sancti . . . mundi CPS*, in spite of the tmesis *sacro-sancta*. Such word-division is fairly rare and generally occurs with *quocunque* (Virg. *Aen.* ii. 709, Hor. *C.* i. 7. 25) or words compounded with a preposition ('inque ligatus', *Aen.* x. 794), but we also find 'septem subiecta trioni' at Virg. *G.* iii. 381 (also Ovid, *M.* i. 64) and *sacroque sanctum* at Pliny, *HN* vii. 143. (The fact that L–S and Quicherat quote no examples of the compound *sacrosanctus* in poetry suggests that it should be treated as two words here, and O–P–C list the elements separately.)

606. foedera mundi: 335 n. The next section of the chorus exemplifies the precept by telling of the doom of those who broke these laws. Hyginus, *fab.* 14. 25–9, also gives an account of the fate of some of the Argonauts.

607. nobiles: a sort of hypallage, the epithet referring to the oarsmen: cf. 366–7 'regum remos', 455 'nobilem regum manum'.

608 ff. nemorisque . . .: Ennius, *Medea*, fr. 246 ff.V, 'utinam ne in nemore Pelio securibus / caesae accidissent abiegnae ad terram trabes . . .', translating Eur. *M.* 3 ff.; also 336 n.

Pelion: 'still thickly tree-clad', Page on Eur. *M.* 3.

610. scopulos vagantes: the Wandering Rocks (Planctae), frequently confused with the Symplegades (341 n.). They were sometimes thought to lie at the Straits of Messina near Scylla and Charybdis (Hom. *Od.* xii. 59 ff., Ap. Rhod. iv. 924, Apollod. i. 9. 25); other writers explicitly identified them with the Cyanean Rocks (and thus with the Symplegades) at the Bosporus (Hdt. iv. 85, Arrian, *Peripl. M. Eux.* 25). This uncertainty is summed up by Pliny, *HN* vi. 13 'insulae in Ponto Planctae sive Cyaneae sive Symplegades'.

611: cf. Sil. It. iv. 53–4 'pelagi terraeque laborem / diversum emensos'.

612. barbara: see on *barbarae* 127, though from the unsympathetic chorus the word may include the meaning 'savage'.

religare is the technical word for tying a ship's cable to the shore.

613. rediturus ironically expresses their hopes, for some did not return.

617 ff. Tiphys died of a sickness while the Argonauts were among the Mariandyni in Bithynia (Ap. Rhod. ii. 854 ff.). **domitor profundi**

perhaps suggests that he died for presuming to set himself up to equal
the true *dominus profundi* 597.

618. indocto magistro: In Apollonius (ii. 894 ff.) and Hyginus the
place of Tiphys at the helm is taken by Ancaeus, son of Neptune;
in Val. Fl. (v. 65) by Erginus. But far from being *indoctus* Ancaeus
is said by Apollonius to be an outstanding steersman: the chorus
may here contrast him with Tiphys who had been taught by Pallas
herself, 2–3 above.

    regimen: 'rudder'.

619–20. paternis regnis: Tiphys came from Siphae in Boeotia.

622. The Boeotian port Aulis, at which the assembled Greek fleet was
delayed before setting out for Troy, is said to have caused this delay
in revenge for the loss of Tiphys. This connection between the two
expeditions (and making Tiphys king of Aulis) seems to be Seneca's
invention, and if the present *retinet* is taken strictly and the Greek
fleet supposed to be already assembled at Aulis, he has imagined the
Trojan expedition as taking place very soon after the voyage of the
Argo. Alternatively one can treat *retinet* as a 'prophetic' present (cf.
mactas 645). See further Leo I. 135, who compares *Thy* 586–7 'et
putat mergi sua posse pauper / regna Laertes Ithaca tremente';
W. R. Hardie, *J. Ph.* xxxiii (1914), 95 ff.

623. lentis: 'tenacious, delaying', as though the harbour were literally
gripping the ships: Hor. *Epode* xv. 6 'lentis adhaerens bracchiis'.

624: 'chafing at their idleness'.

625. ille: Orpheus: for his power over nature see 228 n. He was said
to be the son of the Muse Calliope. The chorus here refers to the
well-known legend that he was torn apart by maddened Thracian
women and his head floated away still singing on the river Hebrus:
Virg. *G.* iv. 520 ff., Ovid, *M.* xi. 1 ff. The story of Orpheus features
at length in two other Senecan choruses: *HF* 569 ff., *HO* 1031 ff.

    Camena: for Calliope: the Camenae were apparently old Roman
water-goddesses who were identified with the Muses since the time
of Livius Andronicus.

    vocali: 'tuneful', applied to Orpheus himself by Hor. *C.* i. 12. 7;
cf. Milton, *Lycidas* 86 'vocall reeds'.

626: 'at the sound of his lyre, touched by the plectrum': *Tro* 833
'tinnulas plectro feriente chordas'.

632. notam: because of his previous visit to Hades to rescue Eurydice
(Virg. *G.* iv. 464 ff., Ovid, *M.* x. 11 ff.)—but this time there is no return.

634 ff. Seneca's preoccupation with the many-sided legend of Hercules,
the great champion of mankind, establisher of peace by crushing
monsters and tyranny (637), and Stoic hero, can be seen in the two
plays *Hercules Furens* and *Hercules Oetaeus*. Here Hercules illustrates
the chorus's theme in his role of an Argonaut who killed three of his
fellow sailors and himself met a horrible end.

634. Alcides: the name is explained as either an ordinary patronymic, H.'s grandfather being Alcaeus, or a variant of the name Alcaeus ('Valiant'), a lesser hero with whom H. was identified (see *OCD*, s.v. 'Heracles').

Aquilone natos: 231 n. They were slain by H. in revenge because they persuaded the other Argonauts to abandon him in Cios, where he was looking for Hylas: Ap. Rhod. i. 1298 ff. Studley translated the line with gusto: 'Alcydes banging bat did bringe the Northern laddes to grounde'.

635: the reference is to Periclymenus, who was killed when H. ravaged Pylos (Ovid, *M.* xii. 556 ff., Apollod. i. 9. 9, with Frazer's note in the Loeb edn.); but this Periclymenus was a son of Neleus and grandson of Neptune. Sen. may be confusing him with another P., son of Neptune and defender of Thebes (Eur. *Phoe.* 1156–7), or he may be misled by the legend that Neptune gave the Argonaut P. the power to change his shape at will.

636. innŭmĕras: a resolved long syllable here in a sapphic is most unusual, but may also explain *Ag* 817 'tardius celeres agitare currus' (in a polymetric lyric). Sen. allowed himself a fairly free hand in writing aeolic metres, e.g. in *Oed* 882 ff. the central double short of the glyconics is sometimes contracted to a long. In any case the Latin sapphic since Horace regularly had a long fourth syllable, so that its equivalent could be regarded as two shorts, rather than one short as in the Greek and Catullan sapphic. See further Raven, *Latin Metre* 148–50.

637: for Hercules as the bringer of peace to the world see *HF* 250, 882 ff.

638: i.e. after the capture of Cerberus: this labour is singled out to illustrate H.'s power over even the underworld.

Ditis: the Romans adopted the Greek underworld god, either using the same name Pluton (Πλούτων) or translating it as Dis (contracted from *dives* 'the Rich One').

639 ff. Hercules had given his wife Deianira to the centaur Nessus to carry across a river, and when Nessus tried to assault her H. shot him with an arrow poisoned with the blood of the Lernaean hydra. As he died Nessus gave Deianira a garment dipped in his blood to use as a love charm on her husband. Later, when jealous of Iole, she sent H. the garment, but the poison on it caused him such agony that he cremated himself on a funeral pyre which he built on Mt. Oeta. There are many literary treatments of the legend, e.g. Soph. *Trachiniae*, Ovid, *M.* ix. 103 ff., and the *HO*.

639. ardenti: because of the burning pyre. Oeta was a range in central Greece, between Thessaly and Aetolia.

641. gemini: alluding to the hybrid form of the centaur, not (the usual view) to the mingled blood of Nessus and the hydra.

642. munere: in ironic apposition to *tabe*: this was her real gift to him.

643–4. Ancaeus was an Arcadian, son of Lycurgus, who was killed in the Calydonian boar-hunt: Ovid, *M.* viii. 391 ff.

644–6. Meleager, son of Oeneus and Althaea, was the leader of the boar-hunt just alluded to. One version of his death was that after he had dispatched the boar he quarrelled with and killed his mother's brothers, and she accordingly threw on the fire a brand on which his life depended. The whole story of the hunt and Meleager's end is told by Ovid, *M.* viii. 270–525; see also Apollod. i. 8. 2 ff., below, 779–80.

   matris . . . matris: the repetition stresses the unnaturalness of his deed and its punishment alike.

   mactas morerisque: 'prophetic' presents, suggesting that the hand of doom is already upon him: see n. on *retinet* 623.

646 ff.: 'they all deserved the charge for which the tender boy . . . atoned by his death'. When the Argonauts on their outward journey arrived at Cios in Mysia, Hercules' page Hylas went to fetch water from a spring, and was drawn under by a water-nymph who fell in love with his beauty. While Hercules was vainly searching for him his companions pursued their journey: 634 n., Ap. Rhod. i. 1207 ff., Theocr. xiii. Delrius noted that out of this catalogue of casualties Hylas alone died solely because he had shared in defying the seas. Note the pathos of the repeated *puer*. There is a verbal similarity to Ovid, *A.A.* ii. 110 'Naiadumque tener crimine raptus Hylas'. (Some editors punctuate with a stop after *cuncti* and a query after *undas*: this is possible but seems weaker.)

649. tutas: supposedly so, in contrast with the expected dangers of the sea.

650–1: as frequently *i(te) nunc* is ironic (cf. 1007): 'go now, heroes, plough the waters of the deep, though even a spring is dangerous.'

652 ff.: a confusion: the seer Idmon was killed by a boar while the Argonauts were among the Mariandyni in Bithynia (Ap. Rhod. ii. 815 ff. and other writers); he had joined the Argonauts although he foresaw his fate. It was Mopsus who was killed by a snake in Libya (Ap. Rhod. iv. 1502 ff.). Accordingly there have been various attempts to emend the text (see Leo's amusing and sensible remarks, I. 24–5), but it is simpler to suppose that here as elsewhere (635 n.) Sen. is careless about mythological details. Likewise the Argonaut Mopsus, another seer from Thessaly, seems to be confused with the Theban Mopsus, grandson of Tiresias; but it is not clear that the two were distinct.

653. condidit: 'brought to his grave'.

654: he could foresee the fate of all but himself: cf. Ap. Rhod. iv. 1503–4 ἀδευκέα δ' οὐ φύγεν αἶσαν | μαντοσύναις· οὐ γάρ τις ἀποτροπίη θανάτοιο.

656–63: the chorus use alleged prophecies of Mopsus (*ille*) to foretell disasters yet to befall Peleus, Nauplius, Oileus, and Admetus. On this assumption the following verbs are all printed as futures, though emendation is necessary for *errabit, cadet* (Gruter), and *impendes* (Gronovius). The whole passage bristles with difficulties:

(1) There must be a strong presumption that Sen. followed the seven regular sapphics (579–606) with seven stanzas consisting each of eight hendecasyllables and an adonius. Working backwards from 669 we arrive at *crimine poenas* as the probable adonius for the sixth long stanza, which leaves a half-line lost before . . . *patrioque pendet* and one line too many in this stanza. W. R. Hardie (*J. Ph.* xxxiii (1914), 99–100) suggested deleting 656, and Housman (*CQ* xvii (1923), 167) supported Leo's deletion of 657, partly on the grounds that *erravit* is absurd in the context of prophecy and *errabit* is absurd as Peleus had already suffered his exiles. (But see next note.) Certainty is impossible but 657 seems the likeliest candidate for expulsion.

(2) The missing half-line must have contained a reference to Ajax, as it is clearly his death which is here described as a cause of grief to his father Oileus, not Oileus' own death. (That *Oileus* could here stand for Ajax is adequately refuted by Hardie and Housman in the articles just cited.) Again we cannot solve the problem, but Housman's suggestion is worth considering: 'patrio ⟨gnatus proprio⟩que pendet / crimine poenas / fulmine et ponto moriens Oilei'. For a recent discussion see E. Courtney in *CR* xx (1970), 200.

657. Peleus' earlier exiles were for the murder of his half-brother Phocus and subsequently for killing his father-in-law Eurytion. But there was a further tradition that later in life he was banished by Acastus or his sons: Eur. *Tro.* 1126 ff., Apollod. *Epit.* vi. 13, Dictys Cret. vi. 7–9, and this story may have been the subject of Sophocles' lost *Peleus*. For P. as a well-known figure of tragic exile see Hor. *A.P.* 96 'Telephus et Peleus, cum pauper et exsul uterque . . .'.

658–9. Nauplius was the father of Palamedes, and to avenge his son's fate at Troy he lured the returning Greek fleet by false beacons to destruction on the rocks off Euboea: Hyg. *fab.* 116, Apollod. *Epit.* vi. 7–11, Sen. *Ag* 557 ff. Of his own death Apollodorus says (though he seems to conflate this and an earlier N.) συνέβη οὖν καὶ αὐτὸν τελευτῆσαι ἐκείνῳ τῷ θανάτῳ (ii. 1. 5).

Argis: 'Greece' generally, just as *Argivus* and *Argolicus* frequently mean 'Greek'.

660–1: if, as seems certain, Ajax lurks behind the corrupted text, the chorus suggests that his death was a punishment to his father. The usual story was that this Ajax ('the Lesser', to distinguish him from the son of Telamon) was killed by Pallas or Poseidon during a ship-wreck because of his violation of Cassandra or his boastfulness against the gods: *Od.* iv. 499 ff., Virg. *Aen.* i. 39 ff., Sen. *Ag* 528 ff. (cf. esp.

'fulmine et ponto' with *Ag* 556 'igne victus et pelago iacet'—a firm pointer to Ajax in our passage too).

662–3: a legend of wifely devotion, Alcestis gave her life to save from death her husband Admetus, king of Pherae in Thessaly. So Ovid, *A.A.* iii. 19–20 'fata Pheretiadae coniunx Pagasaea redemit / proque viro est uxor funere lata viri'. That she was a daughter of Pelias is coincidental here: the point is that her death will be a punishment to the Argonaut Admetus.

664 ff.: the chorus ends with the fate of Pelias (133 n.), who set the whole expedition going.

ustus accenso . . . arsit: there is a certain relish in the grim repetition.

angustas vagus: a rather strained 'point'.

668–9: a final prayer for Jason ends the lyric and links the two parts of it (see 595 ff. 'parcite, o divi . . . vivat'): here the chorus pleads that he was only obeying orders. Jason similarly pleads compulsion when confronting Aeetes in Ap. Rhod. iii. 388 ff. and Val. Fl. v. 481 ff.; and for the thought cf. *Tro* 870–1 'ad auctorem redit / sceleris coacti culpa'.

670–739. The Nurse returns full of excitement and horror and gives a vivid description of M.'s preparations of a poison to beat all poisons. Her speech is largely a catalogue of deadly snakes (684–704) and evil herbs (705–30), which M. has mixed all together into a ghastly concoction, accompanying her actions by magic formulas 731–8. At 738 the Nurse hears the sounds of M.'s approach.

Witches and witchcraft had a firm place in Greek and Latin literature and go back to Circe in Homer. Theocritus (*Id.* ii) and Virgil (*Ecl.* viii) have left extended treatments of practical magic, Horace knew some notable witches (the sinister preparations in his fifth Epode may be compared with the Nurse's speech), and Apuleius' *Metamorphoses* is a world of magic. The most famous practitioners, at least in literature, were the Thessalian witches (Thessaly was a centre of the cult of Hecate: see Farnell, *Cults*, ii. 505, and Pliny's interesting discussion, *HN* xxx. 6–7), and the most extensive extant reference to these formidable ladies occurs in Seneca's own day at Lucan, vi. 436 ff. Clearly the subject lent itself to rhetorical treatment, and Sen. gave his fancy full rein in the Nurse's description and M.'s incantation which follows. The incantation scene seems to be unique in extant classical tragedy, and the same is true of the divination scene in *Oed* 303 ff.—the same play has also a long description of necromancy 530 ff. (see Mary V. Bragington, *The Supernatural in Seneca's Tragedies* 83 ff.). Earlier treatments of the Medea story varied in the stress laid on this side of her character: e.g. it is on the whole played down in Eur. compared with Sen., but strongly emphasized in Ovid, particularly in the incident of the rejuvenation of Aeson, *M.*

vii. 179 ff. It suited Seneca's interests and purpose to enlarge on her supernatural powers: see further Leo I. 169–70. The late Virgilian cento of the Medea story has a messenger describe Medea the witch preparing her magic (321 ff. in Baehrens, *PLM* iv. 232). Lucan too enjoyed describing a witch's brew (vi. 670 ff.—the whole passage should be compared), and the most famous witches in English drama must have had everything desirable in their cauldron (*Macbeth* iv. i. 5 ff.).

Literature reflects life, and the place of magic and divination in the everyday life of the ancient world is clearly shown in the numerous magical papyri which have been found in Egypt. These contain recipes for magic, and though dating from the second century A.D. onwards they embody much older material: see Gow on Theocr. ii (preface), and in general *OCD*, s.v. 'Magic' and references given there.

670. păvĕt ănĭmus: for the scansion see 488 n.

671. immane quantum: like *mirum quantum*, θαυμαστὸν ὅσον: '(it is) frightful how much . . .': Hor. *C.* i. 27. 6, Tac. *H.* iv. 34.

dolor: sc. *Medeae*.

673. aggressam deos: 424 n.

674. caelum: i.e. the heavenly bodies: it was part of the standard repertoire of the Thessalian and other witches to draw them down from the sky (Aristoph. *Nubes*, 749–50, Plato, *Gorgias* 513 a (see Dodds's note), Hor. *Epode* v. 45–6, Virg. *E.* viii. 69, Lucan, vi. 499 ff., Apul. *Met.* i. 8). M. herself says 'te quoque, Luna, traho' at Ovid, *M.* vii. 207.

675. evasit: the Nurse apparently saw M. leave her house and perform her rites at her private 'deadly shrine'—the *arae* of 578. But the location of this shrine is not clear. *evasit* might refer to her leaving the stage at 578, and the shrine might be indoors: see note on *tectis* 578.

677. opes: 'resources of magic'.

678 promit: the present tenses show the Nurse's increasing absorption in the horrible scene she has just witnessed, which remains vividly before her eyes as she recounts it.

explicat suggests the deployment of troops for an offensive.

679. arcana . . . : in strict apposition with *turbam*, and loosely with *malorum*.

680. The line makes doubtful sense because of the uncertainty in the reading *comprecans* and in the meaning of *sacrum*.

sacrum may be M.'s altar (578, 785), or possibly the assembled ingredients of her witches' brew, the central feature of her rites, but it is less natural to say that she 'supplicates' these.

laeva manu must be 'touching, or gesturing, with her left hand'— *laeva* because M.'s purpose is evil and the powers she appeals to are chthonic: see 740 ff. (So in the necromancy scene of the *Oedipus* Tiresias 'fundit et Bacchum manu / laeva' 566-7.)

complicans *CPSQ²e* is intelligible ('stirring' the brew?), but seems to jar with *explicat* 678 and to anticipate a later stage in the ritual which comes at 731 ff. There are many unconvincing conjectures.

681. pestes: 'deadly, destructive things' in general, like *monstrum* 684: they are elaborated as snakes 684 ff. and herbs 705 ff.

682 ff. Libyae . . . Taurus: all regions of the earth, from hottest to coldest, yield offerings to M.'s poisonous brew. For the snakes of Libya see the long and fearful description of Lucan, ix. 619 ff.: both he and Ovid (*M.* iv. 617 ff.) derive the large number of snakes in Libya from the drops of blood which fell into the ground from the head of Medusa when Perseus flew with it over that country. Taurus is an extensive mountain range in Asia Minor.

683. frigore Arctoo rigens: the phrase is imitated at *Oct* 234. Sen. is quite fond of *arctous*, which is not found before his tragedies and is almost exclusively poetical: cf. *Arctica* 315.

685. squamifera: Sen. is extremely fond of compounds in -*fer* and -*ger* and uses about thirty of the former: cf. *mortifer* three times below in less than forty lines, 688, 717, 731.

687. trifidam: the conventional description of a serpent's tongue: Ovid, *M.* iii. 34, Sil. It. vi. 222–3.

ex(s)ertare is the rare frequentative of *exserere*, 'keep thrusting out'.

689. tumidumque . . . plicat: these words describe the bunching up of the snake's body as it stops in its tracks at the sound of M.'s chant, and 'cogitque in orbes' shows the snake settling at rest on its coils, the second action following immediately on the first. Sen. may be recalling the writhing snake in Virg. *Aen.* v. 278–9 'pars vulnere clauda retentat / nexantem nodis seque in sua membra plicantem'; and Lucan describes a snake uncoiling: 'squamiferos ingens haemorrhois explicat orbes', ix. 709.

690. inquit: *inquit* is used very unevenly in the tragedies. Of the fifteen occurrences all except here and *Tro* 452 are in the *HO*, which has been suspected on many grounds not to be by Sen. (See, for example, the discussion by Summers in *CR* xix (1905), 40 ff., and Axelson, *Korruptelenkult.*)

691. vile: 'common, ordinary', much like *vulgari* 693.

693: 'to stir up something that passes the limits of ordinary crime': **altius** also suggests M.'s new sphere of activity in the heavens. She now summons serpents from the constellations, and three others famous in legend, Python, Hydra, and the guardian of the Golden Fleece with which she had already dealt.

694 ff. Draco appears to coil sinuously between the Bears, *duae ferae*: the comparison with a river is made by Aratus, *Phaen.* 45–6 τὰς δὲ δι' ἀμφοτέρας οἵη ποταμοῖο ἀπορρὼξ / εἰλεῖται μέγα θαῦμα, Δράκων . . .

(translated by Cicero, *ND* ii. 106). Cf. *Thy* 869-70 'et qui medias dividit Ursas, / fluminis instar lubricus Anguis'.

697. The Greeks used the Great Bear to find the north, the Phoenicians (more reliably) the Little Bear. Aratus, discussing the Bears, says (*Phaen.* 36-9) καὶ τὴν μὲν Κυνόσουραν ἐπίκλησιν καλέουσιν, / τὴν δ' ἑτέρην Ἑλίκην. Ἑλίκῃ γε μὲν ἄνδρες Ἀχαιοὶ / εἰν ἁλὶ τεκμαίρονται ἵνα χρὴ νῆας ἀγινεῖν, / τῇ δ' ἄρα Φοίνικες πίσυνοι περόωσι θάλασσαν (so too Ovid, *Tr.* iv. 3. 1-2). We are told that it was Thales who first found out for the Greeks the navigating importance of the Little Bear: Diog. Laert. i. 23.

698-9. Ophiuchus: 'Snake-holder', a constellation sometimes identified with Asclepius and imagined to be gripping a serpent in both hands. M. urges him to release it and let its poison flow. The close linking of **pressasque . . .** with the preceding lines suggests that Sen. is conflating Draco and this serpent, though they are of course distinct.

700. When Leto was pregnant with Apollo and Diana she was pursued by Python, the dragon of Delphi, and finally gave birth safely on Delos. Apollo subsequently killed Python. **gemina numina** therefore seems to refer to the unborn Apollo and Diana. The legend is widely cited, e.g. Apollod. i. 4. 1, Eur. *IT* 1245 ff., Hyg. *fab.* 53, 140.

701-2. Hercules disposed of several serpents in his career, but the words **caede . . . sua** should apply only to the Hydra of Lerna which he killed as his second labour: **omnis succisa serpens** might therefore be the many heads of the Hydra which grew again as soon as cut off, rather than different snakes ('let the Hydra return with all its serpent-heads'), but the meaning is a little uncertain.

703-4. The Colchian dragon is the climax of a formidable list, and M.'s proved power over him suggests her power over anything like him.

    pervigil: *insomne* 473; Ovid, *M.* vii. 149 'pervigilem superest herbis sopire draconem'. **sopite:** for the voc. see 605 n.

705 ff. After the snakes come M.'s poisonous herbs, **frugis infaustae mala:** here *mala* is clearly more restricted in meaning than at 679, where it covers all the elements of the brew.

707. Eryx: a mountain in the west of Sicily, the highest in the island next to Etna. It seems to have no special association with witchcraft or its tools, but rather with a celebrated temple of Venus.

    saxis: probably with *generat* rather than with *invius*: Gronovius suggested *inviis saxis*.

708-9. In Apollonius M. gives Jason a strength-inducing drug, taken from a plant which grew on Caucasus from the dripping blood of Prometheus (Ap. Rhod. iii. 844 ff.): this time the drug must be as different as M.'s purpose.

    Prŏmēthĕï: for the scansion see 512 n.

710–11. Gronovius' transposition of these lines, adopted by many editors, is certainly an improvement, taking *Medus* and *Parthi* with *linunt* rather than *fert*.

　　leves: 'fleet, nimble' (rather than 'light-armed'), with reference to their well-known tactics of fighting in retreat, as at Virg. G. iv. 314 'prima leves ineunt si quando proelia Parthi'.

　　quis: *ea* (*mala*) *quibus*.

　　divites: the Arabians were proverbially rich (see Otto, *Sprichwörter*, s.v. 'Arabs') because the southern part of the country, Arabia Felix, exported its own famous precious stones and spices and re-exported others from India.

712. sucos: used of poisonous juices, as by Lucan, vi. 581 'pollutos cantu dirisque venefica sucis'; of restorative juices by Ovid, *M.* vii. 215.

713. Suebae: notice the fem. Suebi was an inclusive name used, e.g. by Tacitus, for a number of tribes inhabiting northern and eastern Germany: the most important groups were the Semnones, Hermunduri, Marcomani, and Quadi (see Tac. *Germ.* 38 ff. and Anderson's note on 38. 1). But if *Hyrcaniis* is right Sen. has muddled his geography (as often: see Leo I. 202–3). The Hyrcani lived on the south-east coast of the Caspian Sea, so Sen. probably confused the name with the *Hercynia silva*, the extensive mountain range running across Germany from the Rhine to the Carpathians. But we may vindicate him by supposing with Avantius that he wrote *Hercyniis*: manuscripts are notoriously unreliable with proper names.

714. nidifico: 'nest-building', a charming epithet of springtime which occurs nowhere else, but for this evidence of spring's arrival cf. Virg. G. iv. 307, Hor. *C.* iv. 12. 5–6.

715. discussit: cf. *HO* 383 'et saeva totas bruma discussit [*al.* decussit] comas'. The compound *decutio* is common in this sense, e.g. Virg. G. ii. 404 'frigidus et silvis Aquilo decussit honorem', but there is no need to adopt Gronovius' *decussit* (countenanced by *TLL*).

718. dirusve or *dirusque* seems the likeliest reading, though it may represent a corrupted relative (*cuiusve* Vahlen, *cuiusque* Müller). In any case a relative must be understood from the previous clauses in the catalogue: 'whatever ghastly juice . . .'.

　　tortis: either pictorial, 'twisted', or more probably 'squeezed, pressed', i.e. the poisonous sap is wrung out of the roots.

719. attrectat has for objects all the relatives from *quaecumque* 707. *attrectare* often contains the idea of pollution or violation, as at *Phoe* 224, the only other occurrence in the tragedies. It is almost absent from high poetry: the only epic instance is Virg. *Aen.* ii. 719.

720 ff. As usual Sen. enjoys a geographical catalogue, and, as often, he is not strictly accurate—Mt. Athos is not in Thessaly but in the eastern promontory of Chalcidice. (By a similar blunder Pindus is called

Thracian at *HF* 1285 and *Oed* 434-5.) The evocative and wide-
ranging names of mountains and rivers stress the extent of M.'s
repertoire of drugs (n. on 682 ff.). Ovid similarly gives a list of
mountains and rivers from which M. culled herbs for the rejuvenation of Aeson (M. vii. 224 ff.), but only Pindus is common to the
two lists.

Haemonius: Haemonia was strictly only a part of Thessaly but
was commonly used in poetry for the whole country. So in Lucan
(also of Medea) 'terris hospita Colchis / legit in Haemoniis quas non
advexerat herbas' (vi. 441-2). In our context the (inaccurate) epithet
is more significant than the name Athos, as Thessaly was a notorious
land of witches (introd. note on 670-739): hence too the mention of
Pindus (384 n.).

pestes: 681 n.

721. illa: sc. *pestis*. The change of construction is a conscious attempt
at rhetorical *variatio*. Mt. Pangaeus was on the southern coast of
Thrace, near the mouth of the Strymon.

722. teneram: the epithet does not suit the baneful nature of the plant,
and is due to Sen.'s wish for a shock-contrast with *cruenta*: notice too
the chiastic arrangement of the two nouns and their adjectives.

cruenta: prob. 'savage' or 'polluted' (by association with M.), as
there is no reason why the sickle should be literally bloody: cf.
Prop. iv. 1. 112 'Atrides vela cruenta dedit'. For the *falx* (usually of
bronze, 728 n.) used in gathering magic herbs see Virg. *Aen.* iv.
513-14 'falcibus et messae ad lunam quaeruntur aenis / pubentes
herbae', and in connection with M. herself Ovid, *M.* vii. 227 'partim
succidit curvamine falcis aenae', and Soph. 'Ριζοτόμοι fr. 491N αἱ δὲ
καλυπταὶ / κίσται ῥιζῶν κρύπτουσι τομάς, / ἃς ἥδε βοῶσ᾽ ἀλαλαζομένη /
γυμνὴ χαλκέοις ἦμα δρεπάνοις.

723 ff. The four rivers go some way towards symbolizing the bounds
of the known or civilized world.

723. gurgitem ... premens: 'checking its waters', so as not to flood
or sweep away the plants on its banks. Similarly in obedience to M.'s
power the Hister 'compressit undas' 764.

aluit is understood also with *Danuvius, Hydaspes, Baetis*.

724. Danuvius: strictly the upper Danube, above the Iron Gates
(Djerdap in Yugoslavia), the lower Danube being known as Hister
(585).

plagas: *plăga* is used, mainly in poetry, of a tract or region on the
earth or in the skies. Referring to the earth it means either one of the
five 'zones' (Virg. *Aen.* vii. 226, Ovid, *M.* i. 48), or more generally
'district, region', as here, Lucr. v. 31 'Bistoniasque plagas', Virg. *Aen.*
xi. 320, 'celsi plaga pinea montis'. The connection with *plăga* 'snare'
is debatable: see Nettleship, *Contributions to Latin Lexicography*, 551-2,
E–M, s.v.

725. Hydaspes: now the Jhelum, a tributary of the Indus. To the poets the name conjured up the wealth and romance of the East: *gemmifer* here, *dives H. HO* 628, *fabulosus H.* Hor. *C.* i. 22. 7–8, 'dives Hydaspeis augescat purpura gemmis' Claudian, *III Cons. Hon.* 4.

726. Sen. might be retailing tradition and travellers' tales about the Hydaspes, but he was on home ground with the Baetis, now the Guadalquivir, as his birthplace Corduba lay on that river in the province of Baetica in southern Spain. So for once a geographical detail (727) in Sen. may be an eyewitness report: at any rate his fellow Spaniard Martial agrees with *languenti* in calling the Baetis *placidus* (ix. 61. 2).

727. Hesperia: 'western' in this case means 'Spanish', as in Hor. *C.* i. 36. 4. Strictly speaking, to the Nurse in Corinth the 'western land' would be Italy, as it usually was from a Greek point of view, but the meaning here is relative to Sen. writing in Italy.

728 ff.: 'this one suffered the blade while Phoebus was bringing the day; the stalk of that one was cut in the depths of night; whereas this other one was slit and cropped by her enchanted fingernail'. These lines are not merely a rhetorical elaboration of M.'s routine, but reflect traditional ideas of witchcraft. (i) The time of gathering magic herbs is important: in particular, some were most potent if gathered by moonlight: Virg. *Aen.* iv. 513–14 'messae ad lunam . . . herbae', Hor. *S.* i. 8. 20–2 'has nullo perdere possum / nec prohibere modo, simul ac vaga luna decorum / protulit os, quin ossa legant herbasque nocentes', Pliny, *HN* xxiv. 12 'quidam id religione efficacius fieri putant prima luna collectum e robore sine ferro' (here the plant—the mistletoe—is benign), Val. Fl. vii. 364 ff., Achilles Tatius, v. 26 διανυκτερεύσειν γὰρ ἔλεγεν εἰς τὸν ἀγρὸν βοτανῶν ἕνεκεν χάριν, ὡς ἐν ὄψει τῆς σελήνης αὐτὰς ἀναλάβοι; cf. Lucian, *Philops.* 14. This must be the point of *alta nocte* here. The reason for collecting the plants by moonlight was presumably to secure the influence of Hecate, but there was also a curious belief that when the moon was drawn closer to the earth by witchcraft it emitted a venomous slime upon herbs which thus increased their potency: Lucan, vi. 505–6, Val. Fl. vi. 447. (ii) Apparently it was important not to use an implement in gathering certain plants, which must be pulled up by hand: see the passage from Pliny quoted above, and his remarks about a plant called *selago*: 'legitur sine ferro dextra manu' (*HN* xxiv. 103: see W. H. S. Jones' Loeb note ad loc.). So too M. in Ovid, 'partim radice revellit, / partim succidit', (*M.* vii. 226–7).

728. ferrum: should mean loosely 'blade, knife', not 'iron', as implements of magic were of bronze not iron: see Macrobius, v. 19. 11 'omnino autem ad rem divinam pleraque aenea adhiberi solita, multa indicio sunt et in his maxime sacris quibus delinire aliquos aut devovere aut denique exigere morbos volebant'; Virg. *Aen.* iv. 513

(with Austin's note), Ovid, *M.* vii. 227, Soph. fr. 491N (all quoted in n. on *cruenta* 722).

730. at marks the contrasted method of culling this plant.

cantato: 'enchanted', applied literally to something which has had a magic spell sung over it: cf. Ovid, *Her.* vi. 84 (Medea) 'diraque cantata pabula falce metit'. Here used rather oddly of part of the enchantress's own body.

732. saniem: used elsewhere of the blood of serpents or the corrupt matter resulting from their venom: Virg. *Aen.* ii. 221, Ovid, *M.* iv. 494, Lucan, ix. 770.

miscetque: *-que* probably links *miscet* with *aves* only, with *et* = 'also'. Otherwise *miscet* governs *saniem* as well: 'she squeezes out the serpents' gore and mingles it and ill-omened birds'.

obscenas: 'ill-omened', probably the original meaning of the word, though the derived sense of 'filthy, disgusting' is often present as well: Virg. *Aen.* iii. 241 (the Harpies), iv. 455 (sacrificial wine turning to blood), *G.* i. 470 (dogs portending Caesar's death), Ovid, *Her.* v. 119 (the ship which took Helen to Troy). It seems better to punctuate after *aves* and understand *sunt* with *exsecta* 734.

733. bubonis, strigis: the owl was widely regarded as a sinister harbinger of doom: *HF* 687-8 'luctifer bubo gemit / omenque triste resonat infaustae strigis', Virg. *Aen.* iv. 462 'ferali carmine bubo' (see Pease's exhaustive list of references). Throughout English literature the bird is sinister: Chaucer, *Parlement of Foules* 343 'The oule eek, that of dethe the bode bringeth', Spenser, *Faerie Queene* ii. 12. 36 'The ill-faste Owle, deaths dreadfull messengere'; and Shakespeare is full of boding owls, e.g. Lady Macbeth's 'It was the owl that shriek'd, the fatal bell-man, / Which gives the stern'st good-night' (*Macbeth* II. ii. 3-4). Moreover, witches turned into owls: Ovid, *F.* vi. 139 f. 'est illis strigibus nomen . . . seu carmine fiunt / neniaque in volucres Marsa figurat anus', Apul. *Met.* iii. 21 'fit bubo Pamphile'. The owl has therefore a natural and traditional place in M.'s brew here and in Ovid, *M.* vii. 269 (see too Hor. *Epode* v. 20, Prop. iii. 6. 29), just as a 'howlet's wing' is among the ingredients in the witches' cauldron in *Macbeth* (IV. i. 17).

The *bubo* was the eagle-owl: Pliny discusses its funereal associations and its eerie cry (*HN* x. 34). The *strix*, conventionally and imprecisely translated 'screech-owl', is hard to identify, and here Pliny shows an honest doubt: 'esse in maledictis iam antiquis strigem convenit, sed quae sit avium constare non arbitror' (*HN* xi. 232). See S. G. Oliphant in *TAPA* xliv (1913), 133 ff. for an interesting discussion of the mythical nature of the *strix* in Augustan and later poets, and the suggestion that it may have been the bat.

734. scelerum: M.'s own repeated description of her acts: see n. on *quae scelere* 55.

haec seems to refer generally to the articles mentioned in 731-4, which are then further characterized in *his . . . his.* The use of these pronouns is a little imprecise, but *illis* 737 refers clearly to *venenis.*

735. discreta ponit: emphatic periphrasis for *discernit:* 'separates into different heaps'.

736. pigri: *piger* is often used of water, standing or flowing; here of the inertness or numbing effect of icy frost: cf. Lucr. v. 746, Tib. i. 2. 29.

737-8. Cf. Lucan vi. 685-6 (of the witch Erictho) 'tum vox Lethaeos cunctis pollentior herbis / excantare deos confundit murmura'.

738-9. sonuit . . . : 'hark, I heard her maddened steps: she is chanting her spells': cf. Virg. G. iii. 191 'gradibusque sonare' (of a colt)— M.'s frenzied pacing adds a down-beat to her incantation.
    vesano: 123 n.

740-842. M.'s incantation, embodying appeals to infernal powers, in particular Hecate, and a description of the consuming fire she has prepared for Creusa, falls into four sections which are distinguished formally by changes of metre.

740-51 (trochaic tetrameters): address to Hell and its dismal inmates; let the famous criminals of legend be freed from their torments to attend Jason's nuptials; invocation to Hecate.

752-70 (iambic trimeters): M.'s power to reverse the laws of nature under Hecate's inspiration.

771-86 (iambic trimeter and dimeter couplets): M.'s offerings to Hecate, mainly relics of sinister creatures of legend; the altars respond favourably.

787-842 (anapaests): Hecate appears to the summons as a lurid moon; M. describes the ritual at the altar of Hecate, including shedding her own blood; she names Jason as the sole cause of the summons (812-16); the fiery poison prepared for Creusa is described (817 ff.); Hecate gives signs that M.'s prayer will be granted and Creusa destroyed.

With this promise of success M. then briefly sends for her children and despatches them to Creusa with the gifts (843-8).

This long and powerful monody has no parallel in classical drama, though other passages suggest themselves for comparison apart from the treatments of magic mentioned in the introd. note to 670-739: the preparations of Dido's priestess, *Aen.* iv. 509 ff.; M.'s invocation before rejuvenating Aeson in Ovid, *M.* vii. 192 ff.; Erictho's chant before revitalizing a corpse in Lucan, vi. 695 ff. The passage shows Senecan versatility at its best. Frequently his longer monodies and choruses are turgid in content and metrically boring. Here theme and pace are varied within the incantation, while the grim figure of Hecate dominates and links the strands of thought: she is addressed throughout, she makes her grisly appearance at 787 ff., and she barks three times and shoots up the sacrificial flames at the climax 840-2. Noteworthy is the variety of names by which she is addressed: Phoebe 770, Trivia 787, Dictynna 795, Perseis 814, Hecate 833, 841.

740 ff. Sen. only twice elsewhere uses trochaic tetrameters and in both passages there is a somewhat similar tone of frenzied or sinister excitement: at *Phae* 1201-12 the half-crazed Theseus invokes destruction upon himself, 'pallidi fauces Averni vosque Taenarei specus . . .'; at *Oed* 223-32 Creon describes the chill terror he experienced when consulting the oracle of Phoebus, 'sit, precor, dixisse tutum visu et auditu horrida . . .'. The metre has a steady rhythmic pound which gives an impressive opening to M.'s chant. (On Sen.'s trochaics see further Hardie, *Res Metrica* 108-10, Raven, *Latin Metre* 76.)

Studley let himself go in this passage, and the English 'fourteener' comes into its own in reproducing the weight and drive of the Latin trochaic:

'O flittring Flockes of grisly ghostes that sit in silent seat
O ougsome Bugges, O Gobblins grym of Hell I you intreat:
O lowrying Chaos dungeon blynde, and dreadfull darkned pit,
Where Ditis muffled up in Clowdes of blackest shades doth sit,
O wretched wofull wawling soules your ayde I doe implore,
That linked lye with gingling Chaynes on wayling Limbo shore,
O mossy Den where death doth couche his gastly carrayne Face . . .'

740. silentum: *silentes* are 'the dead', as frequently. The shades of the dead were (poetically at least) held to be dumb or possessed of only a vestigial voice, e.g. Virg. *Aen.* vi. 264-5 'di, quibus imperium est animarum, umbraeque silentes / et Chaos et Phlegethon, loca nocte tacentia late . . .', 492-3 'pars tollere vocem / exiguam: inceptus clamor frustratur hiantes', Val. Fl. vii. 402 'per chaos occurrunt caecae sine vocibus umbrae'. Homer's shades can only squeak like a bat until they have drunk blood, when they become articulate: *Il.* xxiii. 101, *Od.* xi. 36 ff., xxiv. 5 ff.

741. Chaos caecum: the same phrase at *Oed* 572, *HO* 1134, *Oct* 391: *caecum* is 'dark, dim'—a picture of murky confusion.

Ditis: 638 n. This line somewhat recalls the possibly contemporary little poem *Precatio Terrae* 7 'tu Ditis umbras tegis et immensum chaos'.

742. A difficult line: if right, the words must mean something like 'the caverns of mournful Death bounded by (possibly 'adjoining') the shores (i.e. limits) of Tartarus', i.e. the realm of death which extends over the whole abode of the damned. Thomann translates 'die an die Ufer des Tartarus geketteten Höhlen des grausigen Todes', and explains *ligatos* as an epithet transferred from *Mortis* to *specus*. But *Tartari ripis* is an odd phrase: can Tartarus here stand for the river Phlegethon which flowed round Tartarus (*Phae* 1227, Virg. *Aen.* vi.

550-1), to give the normal meaning to *ripis*? Many editors accept modifications by Haase and Peiper to read '. . . domum. / Tartari ripis ligatae squalido [or -dae] Mortis specu / supplicis, animae, remissis . . .'. H. W. Garrod (*CQ* v. (1911), 216-17) suggested 'Taenari rupi ligatos squalidae mortis specus', comparing *HF* 664 ff.; but the reference to Tartarus is natural as the special abode of sinners. On the whole the paradosis should be respected here, though the Haase–Peiper changes are tempting.

743. supplicis: the contracted form of *suppliciis* (to avoid a dactyl in the first foot): 481 n., 1015. It forms an abl. abs. with **remissis**: 'released from your punishments'.

   novos: 'strange', a sinister new kind of marriage when the bride meets a horrible death: for this undertone in *novus*, cf. 894 'nuptias specto novas', *Tro* 900 'thalamis Troia praelucet novis' (of Polyxena's supposed marriage with Pyrrhus).

744 ff. Similar lists of the famous sinners and their tortures recur in the tragedies—they are almost formulaic in their use for rhetorical amplification: *HF* 750 ff., *Phae* 1229 ff., *Ag* 15 ff., *Thy* 4 ff., *HO* 942 ff., 1068 ff., *Oct* 621 ff. For the cessation of their punishments see *HO* 1068 ff., Ovid, *M.* x. 41 ff. (both recounting Orpheus' visit to Hades). Ixion tried to rape Hera; Tantalus killed his son Pelops and served him as food to the gods. There are various stories of Sisyphus' wickedness: one version accounts for his punishment by his revealing to Asopus Zeus' abduction of his daughter Aegina (Apollod. i. 9. 3). The daughters of Danaus were punished for killing their husbands on their wedding-night: their appearance in this invocation is thus particularly apt for M.'s purpose.

745. i.e. let Tantalus enjoy his former life in Corinth, drinking waters that do not elude him. Tantalus is usually said to have been a king of Lydia, but **Pirenidas** shows that Sen. is following a version of his story which made him king of Corinth (Servius ad *Aen.* vi. 603)—an account of more local interest to a play which is set there, and linking him with Sisyphus who founded Corinth (512). Pirene was the famous and beautiful spring at Corinth, so well known that the name is used periphrastically for 'Corinth', as here, Pindar, *O.* xiii. 61, Ovid, *Pont.* i. 3. 75. For its site see How and Wells on Hdt. v. 92.

746-7. There is some awkwardness in interrupting the list of those whose punishments are to be relaxed in order to ask that Sisyphus' be intensified. Accordingly Bothe put these lines after 749, and Gronovius suggested *solvat* for *volvat* (with *Tityi* for *uni* in 746, thus breaking the link between the two lines). Bothe might be right, but tidiness is not always characteristic of Senecan choruses, and the Danaids make a good climax in the context of M.'s design.

   Sisyphus is excepted from the remission of penalties because he, the legendary founder of Corinth, seems to be regarded here as also an ancestor of Creon. **socero** must refer loosely to him, not to Creon: if the latter, he would be supposed to suffer vicariously for Sisyphus, which is flat. (The statement by some scholars that S. was the father or ancestor of Creon seems unsupported in any other sources, and may go back to an unconfirmed consultation of Lemprière.)

sedeat: 'be fixed, settled firmly'.

volvat: the stone is not merely to roll backwards but to carry S. with it.

748-9. The Danaids' task was to fill a jar endlessly with water, and the cause of their eternal frustration according to most authorities was that the jar was leaky and emptied as fast as they tried to fill it (e.g. Lucr. iii. 1008-10, Hor. C. iii. 11. 26-7, Tib. i. 3. 79-80, Lucian, *DMort.* 11. 4, *Tim.* 18). This passage seems to be the earliest reference to another version in which the Danaids had to use holed or broken pitchers in which to carry the water, and other accounts which mention this detail are rare and late: Zenobius, ii. 6 (s.v. ἄπληστος πίθος) καὶ κόραι δέ, ἃς Δαναΐδας λέγουσιν, πληροῦσαι ἐν κατεαγόσιν ἀγγείοις ὕδωρ πρὸς αὐτὸν φέρουσι τετρημένον; Porphyrius, *Abst.* 3. 27 ὡς εἰ αἱ Δαναΐδες ἠπόρουν τίνα βίον βιώσονται ἀπαλλαγεῖσαι τῆς περὶ τὸν τετρημένον πίθον διὰ τοῦ κοσκίνου λατρείας. The disputed lines in Juv. vi. 614A-614B Clausen 'semper aquam portes rimosa ad dolia, semper / istud onus subeas ipsis manantibus urnis' seem to follow this version; the other reference in Sen. at *HF* 757 'urnasque frustra Danaides plenas gerunt' is ambiguous. This account no doubt links the Danaids in some way with the uninitiated and other classes of sufferers in the underworld, who are condemned to endless water-carrying with sieves or broken pitchers (Plato, *Gorgias* 493 b, *Rep.* 363 d, Paus. x. 31. 9): see further Dodds on *Gorgias* 492 d 1-493 d 4 *ad fin.*, Campbell Bonner in *HSCP* 13 (1902), 129 ff.

At *HF* 498 ff. Megara, threatened with marriage to Lycus, similarly calls upon the Danaids: 'nunc, nunc, cruentae regis Aegypti nurus, / adeste multo sanguine infectae manus. / dest una numero Danais: explebo nefas.'

750-1. Hecate is summoned to ensure the efficacy of the poisons—a regular petition in magic (see Gow on Theocr. ii. 15 f.). M. claims Hecate as a close associate in Eur.: τὴν δέσποιναν ἣν ἐγὼ σέβω / μάλιστα πάντων καὶ ξυνεργὸν εἱλόμην, / Ἑκάτην, μυχοῖς ναίουσαν ἑστίας ἐμῆς (395-7), and calls upon her in Ovid: 'tuque triceps Hecate, quae coeptis conscia nostri / adiutrixque venis' (*M.* vii. 194-5). Similar too are Simaetha's invocation χαῖρ', Ἑκάτα δασπλῆτι, καὶ ἐς τέλος ἄμμιν ὀπάδει / φάρμακα ταῦτ' ἔρδοισα χερείονα μήτε τι Κίρκας / μήτε τι Μηδείας μήτε ξανθᾶς Περιμήδας (Theocr. ii. 14-16), and Canidia's 'o rebus meis / non infideles arbitrae, / Nox et Diana, quae silentium regis / arcana cum fiunt sacra, / nunc, nunc adeste' (Hor. *Epode* v. 49-53).

vocata, induta: fem. agreeing with *Hecate* or an equivalent name understood, with *sidus* in apposition. (So Phaedra's nurse addresses Hecate as 'clarumque caeli sidus et noctis decus' *Phae* 410.) *induta* is a 'middle' partic. governing object *vultus*: 351 n.

non una = *triformis* 7.

752 ff. M. justifies her appeal to Hecate for aid in this her crowning performance by recounting her powers over nature in the past, which she has owed to the goddess. The topic is natural for M. here— the plea for further help supported, as it were, by a list of her own testimonials—and Sen. would have known in Ovid two descriptions of M.'s powers, her own words at *M.* vii. 199 ff. and Hypsipyle's bitter account of her at *Her.* vi. 83 ff., as well as a detailed description of a witch in *Amores* i. 8. Note that one conventional achievement is missing from our list, the charming down of the moon from the sky—a tactful omission, as M. is appealing to Hecate/Luna herself.

This section of the honorific address to Hecate is formally framed by the words *tibi/tuis*, just as the next section 771–86 is framed by *tibi/dea*.

752. vinculo . . . comam: 'letting my hair flow freely'.

gentis is usually taken to mean 'my race' (Farnaby thought it meant the race of witches), though Herodotus tells us (ii. 104) that the Colchians were οὐλότριχες, 'curly- or woolly-haired'. But we need not see a difficulty here, as M. is simply painting the conventional picture of a witch in action, with loose hair and bare feet: so too Virg. *Aen.* iv. 509 'crinis effusa sacerdos', Hor. *S.* i. 8. 24 'Canidiam pedibus nudis passoque capillo', Ovid, *M.* vii. 183 (Medea) 'nuda pedem, nudos umeris infusa capillos'. The reason for the unconfined feet and hair seems to be that ancient magical (and many religious) rites had to be free from all constrictions and knots: Servius ad *Aen.* iv. 518 remarks 'in sacris nihil solet esse religatum, praecipue eius quae amore vult solvi'. For a variation on the idea see Callim. *H.* vi. 124–5 ὡς δ' ἀπεδίλωτοι καὶ ἀνάμπυκες ἄστυ πατεῦμες, / ὡς πόδας, ὡς κεφαλὰς παναπηρέας ἔξομες αἰεί. Pease on *Aen.* iv. 509 and 518 has a full discussion of the matter with extensive references.

753. lustravi: 'paced'. On this interesting word see Warde Fowler, *The Death of Turnus* 96 ff. Originally applied to ritual processions, and often retaining the sense of slow and dignified movement, the word is also used of quick, wild activity, as probably here, below, 864 'cursu furente lustrat', Virg. *Aen.* ii. 528 'fugit et vacua atria lustrat' (Polites desperately fleeing from Pyrrhus).

755–6. egique . . . : a variation of Ovid's 'concussaque sisto, / stantia concutio cantu freta' (*M.* vii. 200–1). The words **Oceanus . . . dedit** amplify the preceding clause and mean 'the Ocean has withdrawn his mighty waves, his tides overcome (by me)', not 'the Ocean, outdoing his (former) tides, has driven his mighty waves further inland' (Kingery, Miller).

757. pariter: either 'likewise' or 'at the same time', strengthening *et . . . et.*

758-9. vetitum . . . ursae: 404 n.: as a symbol of cosmic perturbation also in *Thy* 476-7 'aetherias prius / perfundet Arctos pontus', 867-8, Ovid, *M.* ii. 171-2, Claudian, *Rapt. Pros.* ii. 189-90.

temporum: 'seasons'.

760. floruit: i.e. spring flowers appeared in summer.

761. 'Ceres (goddess of grain and fruits) was forced to see her harvest in winter.'

762. M. particularizes Ovid's 'amnes / in fontes rediere suos' (*M.* vii. 199-200), and Ap. Rhod. iii. 532 καὶ ποταμοὺς ἵστησιν ἄφαρ κελαδεινὰ ῥέοντας. Power over rivers was standard in the repertoire of witches, and rivers flowing backwards was a common ἀδύνατον, the most famous example being Eur. *Med.* 410 ἄνω ποταμῶν ἱερῶν χωροῦσι παγαί, which was much imitated and adapted (see Otto, *Sprichwörter* 139, Pease on Cic. *Div.* i. 78 and on Virg. *Aen.* iv. 489).

763. Hister: 724 n. The outflow of the Danube impressed the ancients, who variously estimated the number of its mouths (five, Hdt. iv. 47, six, Pliny, *HN* iv. 79, seven, Strabo vii. 3. 15). There are now three principal mouths, but they may well have varied in the past.

truces: applied to the sea by Hor. *C.* i. 3. 10, Cat. 4. 9.

765 ff. Some editors assume that these lines refer to the present mood of the elements in response to M.'s chant. This would give a smooth link to the climax of this section, *adesse . . . tuis* 770, but there is no clear indication that the lines are not a continuation of M.'s description of her powers over nature, and the presence now of Phoebus in the sky (768) would add some pictorial confusion to her address to the Moon.

766. tacente vento: 'though the wind is silent'.

domus: this passage shares with *HF* 239 and *Oed* 228 a separate section in the *TLL* entry, V. i. 1972, 12 ff., 'poetica translatione de silva'. It is an odd use of *domus*, but not unnatural in view of the sheltering nature of woods and the belief in spirits dwelling there. In our passage at least **nemoris antiqui** is a defining genitive, and the phrase means something like 'the ancient sheltering wood'. Such a place is naturally dark, but M.'s magic banishes its shade. (The reading of *E* 'decus domus' shows in *decus* an intrusive marginal gloss, perhaps recalling 715-16—or it may go back to Seneca's own second thoughts on the line.) Taking *tacente vento* also with this clause *umbras* could be 'leafage, foliage' here (cf. *Phae* 967-8 'arbustis / redeant umbrae', *HO* 1619, 'fagus umbras perdit').

768: 'abandoning day-time (i.e. normal daylight hours) the sun has stood still in mid heaven': cf. *Phoe* 86-7 'noctem afferet / Phoebea lampas, Hesperus faciet diem', *HO* 462 'nox media solem vidit et noctem dies' (a passage also listing magic achievements). **die relicto**

is a slightly odd phrase (*die reducto* Leo, linking it with the preceding lines), but perhaps undeserving of the attention it has received (see M. Müller, *In Sen. trag. quaest. crit.*, Berlin, 1898, 24 ff., F. Levy in *Berl. Phil. Woch.* 39 (1919), 911). M. simply means that she caused the sun to shine at night and the constellations to be shaken from their positions.

769. There seems to be no special significance in naming the Hyades (312 n.): they typify the effect on the constellations of M.'s chant, and perhaps the effect of the sun's unnatural presence in the night sky.
   labant: 'tremble, totter', rather than 'set'.

770. Phoebe: *Phoebē* of course, the Moon.

771–86. Sen. does not elsewhere use the iambic trimeter/dimeter combination, though he has a run of iambic dimeters at *Ag* 759–74. It is rare in Greek but Horace used it for his first ten Epodes—another link between Horace and Seneca's lyrics (see Hardie, *Res Metrica* 85).

771–2. The list of grisly offerings begins with garlands entwined with nine serpents (or nine each if the distributive is literal): the unspecified nature of the *serta* is probably less important than the details given in *cruenta manu* and *novena serpens*.

   novena: three—and therefore multiples of three—is the ritual number *par excellence* (e.g. for invocations, libations, magic chants), and especially appropriate to Hecate (see Rose in *OCD*, s.v. 'Numbers, Sacred', Gow on Theocr. ii. 43 and xxx. 27). In Ap. Rhod. Hecate answers a sacrificial summons by Jason, and as she appears πέριξ δέ μιν ἐστεφάνωντο / σμερδαλέοι δρυΐνοισι μετὰ πτόρθοισι δράκοντες (iii. 1214–15).

773–4. Typhoeus or Typhon was a hundred-headed monster, born of Earth and Tartarus, who terrorized the gods until Zeus blasted him with a thunderbolt: Hes. *Theog.* 820 ff., Apollod. i. 6. 3 ff. For his terrifying *membra* and snake-heads see Hesiod's description: οὗ χεῖρες μὲν †ἔασιν ἐπ' ἰσχύι ἔργματ' ἔχουσαι, / καὶ πόδες ἀκάματοι κρατεροῦ θεοῦ· ἐκ δέ οἱ ὤμων / ἦν ἑκατὸν κεφαλαὶ ὄφιος, δεινοῖο δράκοντος, / γλώσσῃσι δνοφερῇσι λελιχμότες· ἐκ δέ οἱ ὄσσων / θεσπεσίης κεφαλῆσιν ὑπ' ὀφρύσι πῦρ ἀμάρυσσεν (823–7), and Apollodorus' (l.c.): χεῖρας δὲ εἶχε τὴν μὲν ἐπὶ τὴν ἑσπέραν ἐκτεινομένην τὴν δὲ ἐπὶ τὰς ἀνατολάς· ἐκ τούτων δὲ ἐξεῖχον ἑκατὸν κεφαλαὶ δρακόντων. τὰ δὲ ἀπὸ μηρῶν σπείρας εἶχεν ὑπερμεγέθεις ἐχιδνῶν, ὧν ὁλκοὶ πρὸς αὐτὴν ἐκτεινόμενοι κορυφὴν συριγμὸν πολὺν ἐξίεσαν. See also 410 n.

   tibi: sc. *sunt, dicantur*, or the like.

   discors: 'rebellious'.

775–8. For the story of Nessus and Hercules' death see on 639 ff.
   istic: adv. 'therein', indicating another offering.

   vectoris . . . perfidi / Nessus: at *HO* 514 he is called 'infide vector'.

   sanguīs: the older long final syllable (= *sanguins*), as always in Lucretius, and sporadically in later writers, e.g. Virg. *Aen.* x. 487,

Lucan, ii. 338, vii. 635, ix. 702, x. 128, Val. Fl. iii. 234, Sil. It. ix. 555, x. 23. It is *sanguis* at 808 below.

777: 'to (lit. with) these ashes collapsed the pyre on Oeta'.

779-80. Cf. 644-6 and n. This *fax* is a little out of place among the monstrous relics which M. is offering, but soon M., like Althaea, will slay her offspring.

    piae . . . impiae: the epigram recalls Ovid's Althaea: 'incipit esse tamen melior germana parente, / et, consanguineas ut sanguine leniat umbras, / impietate pia est' (*M.* viii. 475-7).

781-2. The Harpies (*Ἅρπυιαι*, 'snatchers'), storm-winds in Homer, are portrayed as monstrous birds with women's faces. They had tormented the Thracian king Phineus by devouring or defiling his food until they were driven away by the Argonauts Calais and Zetes: see 231 n., Williams on Virg. *Aen.* iii. 211-12. For the detail **invio specu** Sen. may be thinking of Ap. Rhod. ii. 298-9 αἱ μὲν ἔδυσαν / κευθμῶνα Κρήτης Μινωίδος (though their flight was then over). **Hārpȳiă** is trisyllabic.

783-4. Stymphalidos: sc. *avis*. One of Hercules' labours was to dispose of the birds which infested Stymphalus in Arcadia: most accounts say he shot them with his arrows, which had been dipped in the blood of the Lernaean hydra killed in another of his labours. This venom is therefore the same as that which killed Nessus and infected his blood, 775-6: see on 639 ff. This is clearly the point of **Lernaea passae spicula,** but even in life the birds had frightful feathers which they discharged like arrows at their enemies (Ap. Rhod. ii. 1088, Hyg. *fab.* 30.6), which may give added significance to **pinnas.**

785-6. The altars sound in response and the tripods tremble, which M. recognizes as a sign of Hecate's favour.

    sonuistis may refer to the noise of sacrificial fires whose behaviour was important in judging the efficacy of ritual: so Manto reports to Tiresias 'immugit aris ignis et trepidant foci', *Oed* 383, and the altar flame responds in Virg. *E.* viii. 105-6 'aspice: corripuit tremulis altaria flammis / sponte sua, dum ferre moror, cinis ipse. bonum sit!' At 841-2 M. is sure of success when Hecate makes the sacrificial flames blaze up brightly.

    tripodas: cf. 86 (Apollo) 'tripodas movet', and n. M., who wants a kind of oracular response from Hecate, uses equipment which recalls the great oracle of Delphi.

787 ff. The anapaests (see on 301-79) accelerate the pace for this last climactic section of M.'s chant, where Hecate's favouring presence is felt, and details of the grim ritual and the poison for Creusa are described.

787. Triviae: Trivia, *Τριοδῖτις*, was a very common name for Hecate, who was worshipped at the meeting of three ways—a notoriously haunted place (Rose, *Handb. Gk. Myth.* 121–2). Here she appears as a ghastly moon, reflecting in her aspect the rites she comes to witness. In contrast, the moon should shine brightly upon lovers or those weaving love-spells: Theocr. ii. 10–11, *A.P.* v. 191 (Meleager). **currus:** 599 n.

788 ff. Cf. the description of the moon at *Phae* 744 ff. (quoted in n. on 96–8). The contrast is between the clear bright full moon and the lurid mournful look (*facie / luridǎ maestā*) of the moon in semi-eclipse, when 'harassed by the threats of the Thessalian witches she sweeps through the sky on a tighter rein' (to keep firmer control of her chariot) or 'with reins nearer to us' (being pulled towards the earth): 674 n., *Phae* 420–1 'sic te regentem frena nocturni aetheris / detrahere numquam Thessali cantus queant'.

792 ff. M. encourages the moon in her present state (*sic*) to witness the horrible rites she is performing, and she then invokes aid to release the moon from her eclipse (795–6). The true explanation of eclipses was known as early as Anaxagoras (42.9D–K: see Bailey on Lucr. v. 751 ff.), but there was a widespread belief that the moon's eclipse was due to witches' incantations, which could be counteracted by the loud clattering of metal, especially bronze, or blaring of trumpets, presumably to make the spells inaudible: *Phae* 790–2, Livy, xxvi. 5, Tib. i. 8. 21–2, Mart. xii. 57. 16–17, Pliny, *HN* ii. 54, Stat. *Theb.* vi. 685 ff., Juv. vi. 442–3, Plu. *Mor.* 944B, *Aem.* 264B, Tac. *A.* i. 28 (an interesting case of this superstition among the mutinous Pannonian legions in A.D. 14). This is only a special case of the general apotropaic force against evil which the clash of metal had in ancient magic (see Gow on Theocr. ii. 36).

795. Dictynna: a cult name of Artemis (Diana), which she shared with the Cretan goddess Britomartis with whom she was associated or identified: Aristoph. *Ranae* 1359, Eur. *IT* 126–7, *Hipp.* 146 (see Barrett's note), Callim. *H.* iii. 189 ff., *Ciris* 286 ff.

796. Corinthi: this is natural in view of the setting of the play, but **pretiosa** refers to the high esteem in which Corinthian bronze was held, as an alloy of gold, silver, and copper. It is discussed by Pliny (*HN* xxxiv. 6–8), who says that this alloy was accidentally produced by a fusion of the metals when Corinth was burnt by Mummius in 146 B.C.—of course centuries after the Medea legend, and the epithet is pointless here anyway.

797 ff. For the hymnic anaphora of *tibi* see note on 71 ff.

797. caespite: an altar of turf, especially an improvised as opposed to a permanent one: Hor. *C.* i. 19. 13–14 'hic vivum mihi caespitem . . . ponite', iii. 8. 3–4; at Ovid, *M.* vii. 240–1 Medea 'statuitque aras de caespite binas, / dexteriore Hecates, ast laeva parte Iuventae'.

798. sollemne: 112 n.

799. sepulcro: 'pyre': *Oed* 550–1 (preparations for necromancy) 'tum

effossa tellus, et super rapti rogis / iaciuntur ignes', *HF* 102-3 'Megaera
. . . vastam rogo flagrante corripiat trabem', Ovid, *M.* vi. 430 (at the
ill-omened wedding of Tereus and Procne) 'Eumenides tenuere faces
de funere raptas'.

800-1. mota caput flexā . . . cervice: ritual movements attending
the magic words. In Ovid she turns round three times and kneels down
before her invocation to Hecate and other powers (*M.* vii. 189 ff.).

802-3. M. as priestess of Hecate wears the sacerdotal **vitta**, woollen
band, on her head. Here the words **funereo de more** suggest that it
is entwined with cypress-leaves, associated always with death and
burial. (In Hor. *Epode* v. 18 Canidia calls for 'cupressos funebres'.)
Very different is this *vitta* from those she said good-bye to before she
fled from Colchis with Jason: 'ultima virgineis tunc flens dedit oscula
vittis', Val. Fl. viii. 6.

   iacens is difficult: 'lying, placed over' the hair, or perhaps 'with
hanging or dangling ends', adding to her dismal and dishevelled
appearance.

805. ramus: probably the yew, *taxus*, which like the cypress was
associated with the underworld and death (e.g. Ovid, *M.* iv. 432-3,
Lucan, vi. 642-5).

806 ff. maenas: the same description of M. is given by the Nurse at
382 ff. (see note) and by the chorus at 849. At Ovid, *M.* vii. 258 she
'Bacchantum ritu flagrantes circuit aras'. Here her action is like that
of the votaries of the old Roman war-goddess Bellona, who frenziedly
slashed their own arms during their rituals: Tib. i. 6. 45 ff., Lucan,
i. 565-6, Val. Fl. vii. 636. Her own blood is an offering (**sacrum
laticem**), and it is tempting to read into her words **assuesce . . .
cruores** a reference to the killing of her own children: see on 549 ff.

   feriam: probably fut., the completed action being signified by
'percussa dedi' 811.

810. cruores: the plur. only here in the tragedies, but it is fairly
common, especially in the Silver poets, in the senses 'drops of blood'
or 'bloodshed' (see Austin on Virg. *Aen.* iv. 687).

   laticem: a word applied to any liquid, but there seems to be no
other instance of its referring to blood as here.

814. Perseï: voc. of the patronymic *Perseis*. One legend made Hecate
daughter of Perses: Hes. *Theog.* 409 ff. Sen. knew his Apollonius,
and there may be in these lines a consciously ironic recollection of
a very different prayer to Hecate on behalf of Jason, the 'causa una
atque eadem semper': ναὶ δὴ τοῦτό γε πότνα θεὰ Περσηὶ πέλοιτο, /
οἴκαδε νοστήσειε φυγὼν μόρον· εἰ δέ μιν αἶσα / δμηθῆναι ὑπὸ βουσί, τόδε
προπάροιθε δαείη, / οὕνεκεν οὔ οἱ ἔγωγε κακῇ ἐπαγαίομαι ἄτῃ (Ap. Rhod.
iii. 467-70).

815. arcus: a sudden switch from the darker side of the goddess to her
Artemis/Diana aspect: the bow is the huntress's characteristic weapon

and symbol of her power. The plural *arcus*, like τόξα, is common for the singular.

817. tinge: in Eur. M. plans to do this herself: τοιοῖσδε χρίσω φαρμάκοις δωρήματα (789—which creates a staging difficulty in that play: see Page ad loc.).

820 ff. M. has in a golden phial a burning poison compounded of fire she has received from Prometheus; she has also flames from Phaethon, the Chimaera, and the scorching breath of the Colchian bull mixed with venom from Medusa. The whole passage expands the Nurse's words 'rapax vis ignium' 735.

820. auro: probably a phial containing the fiery poison until used, but it may refer to the golden gifts which accompany the robe for Creusa (572 ff.) and are now also impregnated with the venom.

821 ff. caeli . . . furta: the Titan Prometheus stole fire from the gods hidden in a fennel-stalk to give to men (Hes. *Op.* 50 ff., *Theog.* 565 ff.). Zeus punished him by chaining him to a rock, where an eagle fed on his liver which grew again as fast as it was consumed: his punishment is the theme of Aeschylus' *Prometheus Vinctus*.

822. feto: 'reproducing itself, ever-growing', an extension of the usual meaning of *fetus* 'pregnant, productive': the sense is the same as Virgil's 'fecundaque poenis / viscera' and 'fibris renatis' (*Aen.* vi. 598 ff., of Tityus' similar punishment).

824. arte: probably with *condere*, not *docuit*, but it is significantly juxtaposed to the name Prometheus (Προμηθεύς, 'forethinker').

   dedit et: postponement of connective particles (*at, et, nam, sed,* etc.) goes back to Catullus and the *neoterici* (though Catullus does not postpone *et*). It was mainly a metrical device, following the Hellenistic practice of postponing connectives like ἀλλά and καί: see Norden, *Aeneis vi* Anh. III 402 ff. For a repeated *et*-postponement see Virg. *Aen.* iv. 512 ff. 'sparserat et . . . falcibus et . . . quaeritur et . . .'.

824–5. tenui . . . ignes: 'flames reeking of sulphurous fumes'. Flames and sulphur also played a part in the rejuvenation of Aeson: 'terque senem flamma, ter aqua, ter sulphure lustrat' (Ovid, *M.* vii. 261).

   Mulciber was a cult-name for Vulcanus. Festus' derivation is generally accepted: 'Mulciber: Volcanus a molliendo scilicet ferro dictus. mulcere enim mollire sive lenire est' 129.5L.

826–7. For Phaethon's adventure see notes on 32 ff., 599 ff. He was M.'s *cognatus* as the son of Phoebus, who was her grandfather.

   vivacis: 'ever-living, enduring', or merely an intensifying epithet of *flammae* 'brightly burning' (cf. Ovid *M.* iii. 374 'admotas rapiunt vivacia sulphura flammas').

   fulgura flammae is a Lucretian phrase: i. 725, vi. 182.

828. Chimaera (Χίμαιρα 'she-goat') was a fire-breathing, triple-bodied monster, lion in front, goat in the middle, and serpent behind, killed by Bellerophon: Hes. *Theog.* 319 ff., Hom. *Il.* vi. 180 ff. ἡ δ' ἄρ' ἔην θεῖον γένος, οὐδ' ἀνθρώπων, / πρόσθε λέων, ὄπιθεν δὲ δράκων, μέσση δὲ χίμαιρα, / δεινὸν ἀποπνείουσα πυρὸς μένος αἰθομένοιο. This description was apparently taken to mean that the fire emanated from its middle: so too Ovid, *M.* ix. 647–8 'quoque Chimaera iugo mediis in partibus ignem, / pectus et ora leae, caudam serpentis habebat'.

829–30. Cf. 241 and n.

831 ff. Medusa, the fearful monster whose eyes could turn onlookers into stone, was killed by Perseus and her blood was used both as a deadly poison and as a powerful restorative for men: Eur. *Ion* 1001 ff., Apollod. iii. 10. 3.

    tacitum . . . malum: the effect is to be subtle and unperceived: so *condita* 834, *fallant* . . . 835.

834. semina flammae: cf. Hom. *Od.* v. 490 σπέρμα πυρὸς σώζων, Pind. *O.* vii. 48 σπέρμα φλογός, Virg. *Aen.* vi. 6–7 'semina flammae / abstrusa in venis silicis', and the Lucretian technical phrase *semina ignis* (iv. 330, vi. 160, 200–1). Notice the build-up of words meaning fire or heat in this clinching appeal to Hecate (*flammae, calor, fument, flagrante, faces*), as in the messenger's account of Creusa's end in Eur. (1186 ff.).

835. fallant, ferant: sc. *semina.*

837. stillent: 'dissolve': cf. Eur. *M.* 1200–1 σάρκες δ' ἀπ' ὀστέων . . . ἀπέρρεον.

839. faces: her wedding-torches: 67 n.

840. vota tenentur: 'my prayers are being granted' or 'are acceptable': for this use of *tenere* cf. Cic. *Fam.* i. 1. 3 'teneri enim res aliter non potest' 'for we cannot otherwise carry our point'. Rather less likely is the meaning 'my offerings are accepted'.

    latratus: Hecate was regularly associated with hell-hounds, and their or her own barking manifested her presence: *Oed* 569–70 'latravit Hecates turba; ter valles cavae / sonuere maestum', Ap. Rhod. iii. 1216–17 (as Hecate appears to Jason) στράπτε δ' ἀπειρέσιον δαΐδων σέλας· ἀμφὶ δὲ τήνγε / ὀξείῃ ὑλακῇ χθόνιοι κύνες ἐφθέγγοντο, Virg. *Aen.* vi. 257–8. Moreover, dogs were sacrificed to her, and dogs' flesh included in the offerings of food which were put out for her at cross-roads: Plut. *Mor.* 277b, 280c, 290d.

    For **ter** see on 772.

841–2. Hecate makes the altar fires blaze up with her own torch, and this shows that the ritual has been successful: see on 785–6.

    lucifera: 685 n. But this seems a weak epithet and perhaps we should read *luctifera.*

843–8. After the favourable sign from Hecate M. notices the Nurse, to whom presumably the words *huc . . . feras* are addressed. We must then suppose a short pause until the children arrive, and M. then enjoins them to take the fatal gifts to Creusa.

843: 'the whole potency of my drugs has been achieved'. **vis** has here the special meaning of the power or potency of a drug, or the drug itself: *HO* 563 'prolata vis est '(of Nessus' venom), Val. Fl. vii. 450 'Perseasque vires' and 460 'ille manu subit et vim corripit omnem' (of the drugs M. gave to Jason in Colchis).

844. feras: note the second person: with the deadly gifts now fully prepared M. distances herself from their presentation to Creusa.

846–7. placate ...: in Eur. their plea to Creusa is to be more specific as they are included in M.'s banishment: ἀλλ', ὦ τέκν', εἰσελθόντε πλουσίους δόμους / πατρὸς νέαν γυναῖκα, δεσπότιν δ' ἐμήν, / ἱκετεύετ', ἐξαιτεῖσθε μὴ φυγεῖν χθόνα, / κόσμον διδόντες (969–72)—but *novercam* is more ominous than νέαν γυναῖκα.

847–8. We are not told of their return, but they are again present by 945.

ultimo amplexu: cf. 552 'ultimum amplexum dare', but now there must be a sinister ambiguity in *ultimo*.

849–78. In its final lyric the chorus describes the physical symptoms of M.'s manic frenzy, longs for her departure from Greece, and prays for the swift ending of this terrible day.

The metre is an irregular system of catalectic iambic dimeters (⌣⌣ – ⌣ – ⌣ – ✕), with three lines one syllable shorter (857, 865, 878: – – ⌣ – ⌣ –). Sen. is following the normal Greek practice of closing an iambic stanza or period with a line shorter by a syllable (Raven, *Greek Metre* 38, Wilamowitz, *Griech. Versk.* 133). (This is better than regarding the lines as anacreontics or 'anaclastic' ionic dimeters, as Leo did, I. 136.) Thus the chorus is again given a different metre for its last lyric—all four lyrics being metrically different from each other—and the song itself is varied by the irregularly spaced shorter lines. This is another example of Sen.'s greater care in this play to avoid lyric monotony: cf. introd. note to 740–842.

The theme is the recurrent topic of M.'s *furor* and its expression in her outward behaviour, which resembles a Bacchante's (849): see 123, 382 ff., 806, and notes to those lines. Here the concentrated excitement of the short staccato lines, packed with vivid details, and with few wasted words, builds up tension towards the climax of the messenger's arrival. It is a characteristic function of a tragic chorus to span an interval like this, and as we hear it we know that something horrible is happening elsewhere. (See also the discussion by J. D. Bishop in *CJ* 61 (1965), 315–16, who regards this description of M.'s *furor* as a document for Stoic psychology.)

849. cruenta: perhaps literal here, in view of 806 ff.

853–4: 'her features are glazed, set hard, in the turmoil of her anger': **citatus** and **riget** are awkwardly coupled, perhaps in an intentional 'point'.

858–61. Pallor and blushes alternate under the influence of powerful

emotions: Ap. Rhod. iii. 297-8 ἁπαλὰς δὲ μετετρωπᾶτο παρειὰς / ἐς
χλόον, ἄλλοτ' ἔρευθος, ἀκηδείῃσι νόοιο (M. first smitten with love for
Jason), Ovid, M. viii. 465-6 'saepe metu sceleris pallebant ora futuri, /
saepe suum fervens oculis dabat ira ruborem' (Althaea), Hor. C. i. 13.
5-6 'tum nec mens mihi nec color / certa sede manet' (see Nisbet-
Hubbard ad loc.), HO 251-3 'nunc inardescunt genae, / pallor
ruborem pellit et formas dolor / errat per omnes' (perhaps an
imitation of our passage: see Summers in CR xix (1905), 48); cf. also
the symptoms quoted from the de ira in n. on 382 ff.

servat: sc. *illa.*

862. Cf. 'feror huc illuc ut plena deo' from Ovid's *Medea* (123 n.).

863-5. The rage or grief of a bereaved mother animal is a familiar image,
e.g. Ovid, *M.* xiii. 547-8, *F.* iv. 459-60. Here the language recalls
Ovid's Procne (a different simile about another mother about to kill
her child), who 'traxit Ityn, veluti Gangetica cervae / lactentem
fetum per silvas tigris opacas' (*M.* vi. 636-7), and we meet the Ganges
tigress again at *Oed* 458, *Thy* 707-8. In Eur. M. is described as a
lioness (187, 1342).

lustrat: 753 n.

866 ff. The chorus reflects on the two ungovernable passions of M.'s
soul, as she herself did, 397-8.

867. amores: the plur. (also 496) is used in prose as well as poetry,
not always with any special significance: see further K. F. Smith on
Tib. ii. 2. 11. Her feelings of love drive her to action as irresistibly
as her angry thoughts (*iras*), and now they act in concert.

non: sc. *scit (frenare)*, understood loosely from *nescit.*

871. Colchis: fem. sing. nom. So Eur. *M.* 132 τᾶς δυστάνου Κολχίδος,
and in the Latin poets M. was the 'Colchian woman' *par excellence.*

873. reges: 'royal family', or more specifically Creon and Jason.

874-8: let this day—the one day granted to M. to remain in Corinth,
295—quickly come to an end.

874. Phoebe: *Phoebĕ*, the sun: contrast 770.

875. loro: usually plur. in the sense of 'reins', as at 34, though the
sing. is used of a dog-leash, *Thy* 498, Grattius, *Cyn.* 213.

876. alma: 'kindly' night, which brings peace and sleep. This is a
standard adjective with words meaning day and earth, as cherishing
or fostering men and beasts, but Sen. uses it elsewhere of the night,
Tro 438, *Ag* 74.

878. dux noctis: Sen. likes to ring the changes on this idea: 71 'gemini
praevia temporis', *Phae* 750-1 'nuntius noctis . . . Hesperus', *Thy*
794-5 'serae nuntius horae . . . Vesper'.

879-92. A messenger arrives and abruptly announces to the chorus
the deaths of Creon and Creusa, and the total destruction by fire of
the royal palace, as a result of M.'s gifts to Creusa. The Nurse urges
M. to flee at once.

It is characteristic of Greek tragedy that a messenger should arrive at a climactic point and deliver a long and elaborate account of some event vital to the plot which has happened off-stage. Sen. too uses this technique elsewhere, e.g. *Phae* 1000–1114, where a messenger reports at great length the appalling fate of Hippolytus; but in our play he is terse and gives only a bald outline of the disaster. (Contrast Eur., whose messenger speaks, with a few interruptions, for over a hundred lines, 1121–1230.) The reason seems to be that Sen. does not wish to halt the gathering momentum of the play, now moving towards the greater climax of the killing of the children which marks M.'s completed revenge. In a sense the extended report has been replaced by the incantation scene, with its circumstantial predictions of Creusa's sufferings, 817–19 and 836–9; and there is another long and agonized speech of M. to come, 893 ff., before the final scene.

The excitement of this scene is marked by the division of lines between speakers, which emphasizes the speed and abruptness of question and answer (157 n.).

A minor problem is the presence or absence of M. during the announcement. Elsewhere Sen. seems to allow a chorus to speak to a messenger only if no one else is supposed to be present, but the Nurse seems the natural speaker of 891–2 (see note), and M. knows the facts when she speaks at 893 ff. The question is an unreal one in view of the nature of the plays (and scene-headings in the manuscripts are unreliable), but we can suppose that M. and the Nurse are in the background and overhear the conversation between chorus and messenger. For a discussion of this point see Zwierlein, *Rezitationsdramen* 91 n. 11, 102–3.

879. periere: note the impact of the word, emphatically first in the line, like ὄλωλεν in Eur.'s messenger's words ὄλωλεν ἡ τύραννος ἀρτίως κόρη 1125.

status: 'the condition, public order, framework' of the kingdom: *status civitatis* or *reipublicae* frequently has this meaning, esp. in Cicero's letters and speeches.

880. Eur. *M.* 1220 κεῖνται δὲ νεκροὶ παῖς τε καὶ γέρων πατήρ.

882. donis: emphatic—first in the line and before a pause. The gnomic flavour of the reply recalls the proverbial ἐχθρῶν ἄδωρα δῶρα κοὐκ ὀνήσιμα Soph. *Ajax* 665, which M. varies in Eur.: κακοῦ γὰρ ἀνδρὸς δῶρ' ὄνησιν οὐκ ἔχει (618).

quis ... dolus?: the chorus has hitherto had only vague misgivings about M.'s purpose (849 ff.).

883–4. vixque ... : 'even now that the horror has taken place I can scarcely believe it could happen'. Leo unnecessarily and against the manuscripts gave the words **quis ... modus?** to the messenger: this kind of prompting for details by the auditor is regular. *modus* is

probably 'manner' rather than 'limit', though the latter would also
be naturally answered by the messenger's next words.

885–6. The burning of the palace is not reported in Eur., though
considered as a possibility by M. (see above 147 n.), but this detail
is found in Ovid, *M.* vii. 395, *Ibis* 601–2, and was no doubt a spec-
tacular feature of his *Medea*. Other writers too record it: Diod. Sic.
iv. 54, Hyg. *fab.* 25, Val. Fl. i. 226, Apul. *Met.* i. 10.

887. urbi timetur: the impers. construction, and the dative with
timere, are common, e.g. Lucan, vii. 138 'urbi Magnoque timetur'.

890. ipsa ... occupat: 'it seizes even our defence against it', i.e. water,
which the fire lays hold of before (the full force of *occupat*) it can
itself be quenched.

891–2. The manuscripts vary in assigning these lines to the Nurse or
the messenger. While it is the latter who urges M. to flee in Eur.
(1121–3), the injunction comes more naturally from the Nurse, who
may be supposed to have returned by now, with or without the
children: see Leo I. 83, and the discussion by B. Gentili in *Maia* vi
(1953), 43 ff. (He assigns these lines to the chorus, but they are con-
sistently hostile to M. and would not now wish her to escape punishment, though they had wanted to be rid of her at 870 ff.)

    sede Pelopea: Corinth, where Pelops' father Tantalus was king
(745 n.): so Mycenae (ruled by his descendant Agamemnon) is
'Pelopian', Ovid, *M.* vi. 414, Virg. *Aen.* ii. 193, and Pelops gave his
name to the whole of southern Greece, Peloponnesus—which might
also be the meaning here (cf. *HF* 1164–5).

893–977. M.'s last long monologue, which ends with the murder of one
child. Once more she is in the dark tortured world of her own mind,
and as her resolution hardens to kill her own children she is torn
apart by her feelings as a mother and by the thought of the triumph
she will enjoy in this supreme revenge on Jason. As madness begins
to cloud her reason she sees a mob of Furies approaching her, and
with them the dismembered ghost of her brother Absyrtus (958 ff.);
she kills one child, hears the sounds of an approaching crowd, and
departs to climb on to the roof of her house.

    The wild state of M.'s feelings and the quick swerving of her
thoughts into opposite directions, as different moods follow each
other, are matched by the abruptness and incoherence of the language,
which gives a vivid impression of words tumbling out confusedly
in the effort to express her thoughts. In this respect the speech
compares favourably with similar self-debates in the plays: e.g. at
Tro 642 ff. Andromache has to choose between the death of her son
and the desecration of Hector's ashes, but the formal balanced
rhetoric of her soliloquy hardly suits the agony of her feelings. In
M.'s speech declamatory techniques are certainly present, but for once
they do not take charge. For similar shifts of mood see 137 ff. and n.

893. egone . . . : 'repudiating' question: 398 n.

894. ad hoc: to enjoy this news.

novas: 'strange' 743 n. *spectare* is regularly used of watching a play or spectacle: M. visualizes the horrible scene she has contrived.

895. anime: Eur. *M.* 1242–3 ἀλλ' εἶ' ὁπλίζου, καρδία. τί μέλλομεν / τὰ δεινὰ κἀναγκαῖα μὴ πράσσειν κακά; above, 41 n. M. addresses her soul three times in this speech (here, 937, 976) and again 988. Here the address continues to 904—hence the masculines *furiose, violentus*.

896. quota: 'how small'. *quotus* always has this meaning in the tragedies: also Ovid, *M.* ix. 69, *Am.* ii. 12. 10.

897. furiose: Bentley's emendation of *furiosa* is very likely, in view of *violentus* 904: cf. *dolor/furiose* 139–40.

898. caelebs: 'widowed', a regular meaning, e.g. *Phae* 1215.

899. haut: cf. 942, 1014: a very common form in the manuscripts of the plays (see O–P–C).

temet: 228 n.

901. A general reflection continuing the thought of the previous line, but the words **purae manus** suggest also the gifts taken to Creusa by the children.

904. hauri: 'draw' (like water from a well) all the old violence from the storehouse of her breast. The following lines recall her words at 48–50, contrasting her earlier crimes with what she must do now. *admittere* is often used of doing wrong without an expressed word for the crime: Tib. i. 6. 56, Hor. *Ep.* i. 16. 53, Cic. *Mil.* 34.

905. hoc age: 562 n.

faxo sciant: 'I shall make them realize' (the Corinthians in general). This is the only occurrence in the tragedies of this archaic future of *facio*, which is quite common in Plautus and Terence and survived in later poetry, often expressing vehemence or threats: Virg. *Aen.* ix. 154–5 'haud sibi cum Danais rem faxo . . . esse ferant', xii. 316, Ovid, *M.* xii. 594–5 'faxo triplici quid cuspide possim / sentiat, iii. 271. These examples also show the survival of the paratactic subjunctive with *faxo*, like *sciant* here. (For a discussion of *faxo* and related forms see Fr. Thomas in *Rev. Phil.* xxx (1956), 204 ff.)

906. vulgaris notae: 'the common brand': cf. *Ben.* iii. 9. 1 'quaedam [beneficia] non sunt ex hac vulgari nota sed maiora', above, 693 'fraude vulgari'.

907. quae . . . scelera: sc. *isti*: lit. 'the crimes I lent to him', i.e. 'committed to serve him'. M. had, as it were, put her misdeeds at the disposal of Jason. *commodare* sometimes has this meaning of running a risk or staking one's life for the sake of something else: Tac. *A.* xv. 53 'inanem ad spem Antoniam nomen et periculum commodavisse', *Ag.* 32. 1 'licet dominationi alienae sanguinem commodent' (a likely emendation).

prolusit: 'practised, rehearsed' for the real task now. Cf. *de ira* ii. 2. 5 where Sen. says that emotions like those we experience when reading or seeing a show are not genuine feelings but 'principia proludentia adfectibus', *NQ* iii. 28. 3 'non laedi terrae debent sed abscondi. denique cum per ista prolusum est, crescunt maria'.

908. rudes: 'unpractised'.

909. puellaris: cf. 49 'haec virgo feci'.

910. Her prediction at 171 *fiam* is now fulfilled.

crevit ingenium malis: difficult to translate. Is *ingenium* 'wit, inventive skill', with *malis* meaning 'crimes'; or more generally 'nature, essential character', and *malis* 'sufferings'? The first interpretation suits the following list of her misdeeds, but *ingenium* may not be restricted to her capacity for evil.

911 ff. M. gloats unrestrainedly (note the repeated **iuvat**) over the murder of Absyrtus, the theft of the fleece, and the killing of Pelias.

arcano . . . sacro: 'his treasured relic': the fleece had for Aeetes the aura of a holy object and was kept in a grove of Ares (Ap. Rhod. ii. 404–5).

911–12 provide a notable sequence of two consecutive third-foot anapaests, *răpŭisse, sĕcŭisse*: the anapaest is the rarest third foot in Senecan iambics, and is found elsewhere in this play only at 676, 897, 949. (912 is also unique in having synaloepha following the word which contains the third foot anapaest—*sĕcŭissẹ ẹt*: Strzelecki, 78.)

914. materiam: 'fresh matter', the raw material for further crime: *Phae* 685–6 'scelerique tanto visus ego solus tibi / materia facilis?'

M. has urged her *animus* to action: now she addresses her *dolor* (again at 944), *ira* (916, 953), *furor* (930). These urgent apostrophes are the very stuff of Senecan monologues, the apostrophe being a device of rhetoric popular among the Latin poets of the Silver Age, and carried by Lucan to a tiresome extreme in his epic. Virgilian usage is more restrained and sensitive: see Austin on *Aen.* i. 555, and, generally, E. Hampel, *De apostrophae apud poetas Romanos usu*, Diss. Jena, 1908. Quintilian has some interesting remarks on apostrophe: ix. 2. 38–9, ix. 3. 24–6.

915. non: 365 n.: in the tragedies *non* very frequently negates an adj., e.g. *Tro* 82 'non indociles', *Phae* 274, 'non miti'.

rudem: 908 n.

916 ff. In similar vein Atreus reveals his plotting soul: 'nescio quid animo maius et solito amplius / supraque fines moris humani tumet / instatque pigris manibus—haud quid sit scio, / sed grande quiddam est. ita sit. hoc, anime, occupa' *Thy* 267–70.

917. hosti: the rift with Jason is complete (also *hostis* 920): in 27 *hostes* was more general.

nesciŏ: 350 n.

920. paelice: 462 n.

921. quidquid . . . : the thought abruptly strikes her that Jason's and her children are in a sense now Creusa's: n. on 549 ff. (If *Creusa peperit* seems too strained we might consider *Creusa, peperi* (Garrod, *CQ* v (1911), 217).) Note the lack of an adversative connection, and the change from first person to second person self-address (*properavi/ tuum*), as in 126 ff.

923. ultimum: 'extreme, crowning': it is used with *poena* and *supplicium* of capital punishment.

924–5. liberi . . . poenas date: at last the explicit statement of her resolve, from which she at once recoils in 926 ff.: cf. Eur. *M.* 792–3 τέκνα γὰρ κατακτενῶ / τἄμ'—but there M. emphatically claims the children as still hers.

926 ff. This section of M.'s soliloquy, in which she is most in the grip of conflicting emotions, should be compared with her speech in Eur. *Med.* 1021–80 (esp. 1040–64), and there are two other notable versions: a fragment from Neophron's *Medea* (Stobaeus, *Flor.* xx. 34, quoted in D. L. Page's edition of Euripides' *Medea*, xxxiii, who also discusses its relationship to Eur.), and Corneille's *Médée* 1335 ff., who follows Sen. fairly closely. An interesting comparative study can be made of all four passages in which Sen. is not disgraced. See too Procne's conflicting feelings as mother and wronged wife before killing her son, Ovid, *M.* vi. 619 ff.—a passage already noted as the possible model for the simile in 863–5.

926. gelu: the chill of fear or horror: *Tro* 624 'torpetque vinctus frigido sanguis gelu'.

928. tota: probably *totā* with *mater*.

929. egone ut . . . : again an angry 'repudiating' question: 398 n., 893.

930. melius: sc. *loquere* or the like, as at 139–40 'melius, a melius, dolor / furiose, loquere'.

932. quoque: 'even'. For the thought *quod scelus . . .* cf. *Thy* 1100 'quid liberi meruere?' (Atreus) 'quod fuerant tui'.

933–4. For the alliteration see 362 n.

934. non sunt mei: i.e. no longer mine: 921 n.

936. fateor . . . : 'yes—and so was my brother' (yet he was killed).

937. titubas: 'falter, waver': elsewhere in the tragedies the verb is applied to physical movement, but it is quite commonly used of hesitation in thought or speech.

938. variamque: (and **incertam** 939) sc. *me*.
    ira, amor: cf. 866 ff.

939 ff. The simile is like Ovid's description of Althaea's mental turmoil before destroying her son: 'utque carina / quam ventus ventoque rapit contrarius aestus / vim geminam sentit paretque incerta duobus, / Thestias haud aliter dubiis adfectibus errat' (*M.* viii. 470–3); and

Clytaemnestra's self-analysis: 'fluctibus variis agor, / ut cum hinc profundum ventus, hinc aestus rapit, / incerta dubitat unda cui cedat malo' (*Ag* 138–40). Here Sen. first suggests the analogue with the ambiguous word *aestus* (surge of sea/emotion), and then develops the simile in detail. For *anceps* of the sea cf. Mela, ii. 115 '(fretum) angustum et anceps alterno cursu'.

942. dubiumque: 554 n.

943–4. pietatem, pietas, pietati: M.'s mother-love temporarily absorbs her thoughts (cf. Jason's assertion of his *pietas* towards his children, 438, 545)—but even here Sen. cannot resist the play on case-endings (polyptoton: 233 n.).

945. The children were sent off at 848, and are supposed to have returned by now.

946. solamen: see 538–9 and n. The phrase *unicum solamen* occurs also at *Tro* 703–4, *Phae* 267.

947 ff. In the next few lines the wild oscillation of her feelings reaches a climax, and her language is incoherent and elliptical. Even so the sense is difficult to grasp, and many have suspected corruption in the lines. 'Let the father have you unharmed, provided the mother does too.—But exile and wandering threaten me: soon, soon will they be dragged roughly from my embrace, weeping, groaning.—Let them be lost to their father's kisses as their mother has lost them . . .' If 'patri' *E* is read in 950 (giving a similar verbal pattern to 24–5) *osculis* goes very awkwardly with the preceding words, and Gronovius' 'o scelus' should perhaps be accepted. But sense and the rhythm of the line suggest that it should be taken with the following words, and **osculis patris** will be a vivid expression for 'loving father'. Leo rather desperately remarked (I. 25): 'locum commendamus eis qui emendare vel, quod magis optamus, defendere eum valeant'.

949. The words portray a very violent action, as at *Ag* 187 'nec rapere puduit e sinu avulsam viri'.

952–3. repetit . . . Erinys: originally in early Greek literature the Erinyes (Sen. prefers the singular) were avenging spirits who hounded those particularly who were guilty of crimes against kin (n. on 13 ff.); but here as elsewhere in the tragedies (*HO* 609 ff., *Oct* 161 ff.) Erinys is more generally a wild spirit of discord. In any case they afflict men with madness or delusion: Hom. *Od.* xv. 233–4. Their Latin counterparts were the *Furiae* (below, 958, 966), though Sen. apparently distinguishes them here.

Most editors accept Gronovius' *invitam* for *invisam* of all manuscripts. If the hand is M.'s this certainly makes better sense; but perhaps it is the Erinys' hand, in which case read *invisa manu* (A. Ker, *CQ* xii (1962), 50).

ira . . . sequor: cf. Ovid, *Her.* xii. 209 'quo feret ira, sequar'.

954 ff. turba Tantalidos: 'the brood of Tantalus' daughter', i.e.

Niobe, who boasted of the number of her children compared with Leto's; to punish her Apollo and Artemis then killed them all: Hom. *Il.* xxiv. 602 ff., Apollod. iii. 5. 6, Ovid, *M.* vi. 148 ff., *HO* 1849 ff. The number of her children varied in different accounts (see Frazer's Loeb note to the Apollod. passage), and Sen. follows a popular version which gave her seven sons and seven daughters.

956. sterilis . . . : 'too barren was I for my vengeance—yet the two I bore are enough to atone for my brother and my father'.

958 ff. M.'s deranged fancy sees the host of Furies approaching her (n. on 952-3), and with them the mangled ghost of her brother. Dido on the verge of madness is similarly described: 'Eumenidum veluti demens videt agmina Pentheus' (*Aen.* iv. 469). There is some evidence in vase-paintings for Fury-figures associated with M.'s story. On a fourth-century Italiote bell-crater in Naples is depicted the death of Creusa observed by a winged figure like a Fury (a drawing of it is in Séchan, *Études sur la tragédie grecque*, fig. 118); and on the celebrated volute-crater, also fourth-century, from Apulia (illustrated in M. Bieber, *Denkmäler zum Theaterwesen*, p. 106) the multiple scenes include M.'s escape-chariot driven by the figure Οἶστρος ('Frenzy'), holding torches. (Both paintings are discussed by D. L. Page in his *Medea*, lix–lxiii.)

960 ff. For the Furies' conventional torches and snake-scourges (or snake-hair) see above 14 ff., *HF* 86 ff. 'adsint . . . Eumenides, ignem flammeae spargant comae, / viperea saevae verbera incutiant manus, Virg. *Aen.* vi. 570 ff. 'continuo sontis ultrix accincta flagello / Tisiphone quatit insultans, torvosque sinistra / intentans anguis vocat agmina saeva sororum', vii. 447 ff.

961. sonat: 'hisses'.

962-3. trabe: 'brand': cf. *HF* 102-3 'Megaera . . . vastam rogo flagrante corripiat trabem'. The Furies were called Allecto, Megaera, and Tisiphone.

964. incerta: probably 'faltering', taken closely with *dispersis membris*, but it might mean 'dimly seen'.

965. sed omnes.: Bothe's punctuation has been generally adopted: Sen. is fond of this qualifying or limiting use of *sed* (above, 576, *Oed* 951, 'morere, sed citra patrem', *Phoe* 106-7 'ensem parenti trade, sed notum nece / ensem paterna', 109-10 'natus hunc habeat meus, / sed uterque, *HO* 1484-5 'ut ingens Herculem accipiat rogus, / sed ante mortem'). The idiom is a common one: K–S ii. 77. *omnes* is probably acc. with *poenas* understood: 'I shall pay the penalty—yes, a full one'. Similar is Apul. *Met.* iv. 31 'vindictam tuae parenti, sed plenam tribue'. (C. E. Stuart (Cambridge notebooks) suggested that it is nominative, and that M. includes Jason and the children with herself in atoning for her crime against Absyrtus.)

    fige: addressed to Megaera.   **luminibus:** 'my eyes'.

967. ultrices deas: 13 n. In Ap. Rhod. Erinys witnesses the murder of
Absyrtus: ὀξὺ δὲ πανδαμάτωρ λοξῷ ἴδεν οἷον ἔρεξαν / ὄμματι νηλειεῖς
ὀλοφώιον ἔργον Ἐρινύς (iv. 475–6).

970–1. She now kills one child (cf. *corpus* 975) as an offering to Absyrtus'
ghost.

    manes tuos: *manes* was originally a collective term for the spirits
of the dead, and seems to be first used of individuals in Cic. *Pis.* 16
(if the reading is right: see Nisbet ad loc.). They could exact
vengeance and were often the subject of placatory inscriptions: cf.
Livy iii. 58. 11 'manesque Verginiae . . . per tot domos ad petendas
poenas vagati, nullo relicto sonte tandem quieverunt' (with Ogilvie's
note).

    ista: 'this' (cf. *Thy* 627, *Phoe* 169)—a sense which *iste* began to
acquire in the Augustan period and which became common in Silver
Latin.

972. petunt: 'they . . .': she does not have to specify her enemies—
though she might not have expected Jason to lead them. Her surmise
is proved true by his words at 978 ff. Jason's arrival is differently
motivated in Euripides' play, where he is concerned mainly to
protect his children from being involved in the Corinthians' revenge
on Medea (see his speech at 1293 ff.). Sen. may be following Ovid's
Medea here, if *Met.* vii. 397 'ultaque se male mater Iasonis effugit
arma' is a clue to such a scene in that play.

974. incohata: the ominous menace of the word is obvious.

976. hoc age: 562 n.

977. perdenda: 'squandered'. *perdere* is often used in Sen. and Lucan
in the particular sense of a wasted or fruitless action: *Ag* 519 'perdenda
mors est?', *Thy* 1097–8 'perdideram scelus / nisi sic doleres'; Duff on
Cons. Helv. iii. 2.

    approba . . . : 'prove to the people the power of your hand'.

978–1027. Jason appears with armed followers to wreak vengeance on
M. From the house-top she taunts him madly, and, in spite of his
anguished appeals, kills the second child, and is then carried away
in a winged serpent-chariot.

978. regum: 873 n.

980. armiferi: voc. plur. with *fortis cohors* in apposition. For the interlocking word-order of which Sen. is quite fond (*HF* 552, *Tro* 63, *Ag*
800), see Virg. *G.* iv. 168 'ignavum fucos pecus', 246 'dirum tineae
genus' (and more complex examples in the *Eclogues*), Hor. *C.* i. 20. 5
'clare Maecenas eques'. The mannerism was probably derived from
Hellenistic Greek poetry: see the interesting discussion by G. Williams, *Tradition and Originality in Roman Poetry*, Oxford, 1968, 726 ff.
On the compound *armiferi* see 685 n.: it is hard to decide between
armiferi and *armigeri* (the manuscripts are similarly divided at *Phae*
909).

981. vertite: for *evertite* (mainly poetic): cf. Virg. *Aen.* ii. 625 'ex imo verti Neptunia Troia'.

982 ff. Probably M. does not see Jason until 992—and Jason has seen her by 995. She now exults in the thought that her present revenge compensates for all she and the Colchians had lost by her services to Jason: see 466 ff. and notes.

984. virginitas: more explicit than *pudor* 238, 488: cf. Ovid, *Her.* xii. 111 'virginitas facta est peregrini praeda latronis'.
　　redit: i.e. *rediit*, 248 n.

985. placida: 'propitious, gracious'. *placidus* sometimes has this sense applicable to a divinity: Virg. *Aen.* iii. 266, iv. 578, Ovid, *F.* iv. 161.

987. perage . . . : 'finish off (your revenge) while your hands are at it'. But *faciunt* seems flat, and *fervent* is strongly suggested by *HO* 435 'scelus occupandum est: perage dum fervet manus' (Cornelissen, *Mnemos.* ii. 5 (1877), 187).

988–90. The final appearance of a softer feeling which is instantly banished.

992. ecce: at sight of Jason.

993. nil . . . : 'I count nothing done as yet', because Jason had not witnessed the first child's death. **facti** is the regular genitive with *nil*, like *sceleris* with *quidquid* in 994.

994. perit: (i.e. *periit*, 248 n.) 'is wasted', like *perdere*, 977 n., for which *perire* supplies the passive.

996. ignes: from the still-burning palace, and so M.'s own fire (*suis* 997).

998. funus: 'pyre': though it is hard to find another example of *funus* used for *rogus*, this seems better than to translate *congere funus* more tamely as 'prepare the obsequies'.

999. iusta . . . functis: 'the ceremonies due to the dead'. *functis* for the more common *defunctis*: *Oed* 579, Stat. *Th.* iv. 511.

1003. non . . . fides: seems to contradict both the facts and his earlier words 'non timor vicit fidem / sed trepida pietas' 437–8, but he now urges anything that might make an impression on her and he would justify himself again by inescapable outside pressures.

1006. hac: into the body of the second child: cf. 550.
　　ferrum exigam: 126 n.

1007–8. virginum . . . matres: for the sarcastic plurals see 279 n.

1009–11. i.e. if my vengeance required only one life it would not have been worth claiming it: but even two are not enough. (Cf. 956–7: two merely satisfy the claims of M.'s father and brother.)
　　ut: 'even if'.

1012. matre: we have to translate 'my womb': M. uses the word which expresses the greatest horror she now has—to be a mother by Jason. (Leo deleted 1012–13 as an interpolation suggested by *HO* 345–6.)

1015. Either 'and at least give my sufferings a respite' or '. . . spare my sufferings the suspense' (*dona = condona*): in either case the meaning is 'get it over with'.

supplicis for *suppliciis*: 481 n.

1016 ff. Savouring to the full the one day granted her by Creon (285 ff., 399–400), she must here slowly and deliberately raise her knife against the second child, and this action wrings from Jason the agonized cry 'kill *me* instead' (for *memet* see 228 n.). M. retorts that that would be an act of pity and completes the murder of the child.

ne propera: *ne* with the imperative is common in Plautus and Terence and in later poetry, and Sen. uses the construction frequently in the tragedies. It is rare in prose, though Sen. himself has *ne repugnate* at *Const. Sap.* 19. 4. For details see L–H–S ii. 340.

1019. bene est . . . : for the tone cf. 'bene est, tenetur' 550 and note.

1020. litarem: the children are a sacrificial offering to M.'s *dolor*.

tumida: 'swollen' from weeping, 'welling up' with tears: a strong word, used of diseased eyes by Celsus (ii. 6).

1021. ingrate: 465 n.

1022 ff. sic fugere soleo: M.'s serpent-chariot was familiar to many writers: Apollod. 1. 9. 28, Hor. *Epode* iii. 14, Ovid, *M.* vii. 218 ff., 350, Hyg. *fab.* 27, and probably Pacuvius fr. 397R, and it appears on vase-paintings going back at least to the fourth century (Page, *Medea*, xxvii). In Eur. she escapes in a chariot sent by the Sun (1321–2), and serpents are not mentioned (staging difficulties?); Sen. on the other hand does not mention the source of the chariot, though it is presumably from the Sun (from whom she had requested a chariot for a different purpose at 32 ff.). Our play is the only one in the Senecan corpus which if staged would require stage machinery, with the possible exception of *HO* 1940 ff.—if that is by Sen.

1024. recipe . . . : she throws down the bodies to Jason in a final act of disdain: he can dispose of what is left of his own sons.

1025. M. does not name her destination as she does in Eur. (Athens).

1026. If 'sublimi aetheri' *E* is accepted it is a local dative with *vade* (like Virgil's 'it caelo clamor' *Aen.* xi. 192). But a genitive seems required (cf. *HF* 958 'in alta mundi spatia sublimis ferar') and, with *aetheris*, *sublimi* is the genitive of the second-declension form (not elsewhere used by Sen.). With Farnaby's (*sublimi*) *aethere* the phrase is a local ablative. Wagenvoort's *sublimis poli* is worth considering, *aetheris* being an intrusive gloss (*Mnemos.* iv. 6 (1953), 228: he compares the readings at *HF* 821–2).

1027. qua veheris: governed by *testare*: 'bear witness that wherever you go . . .'. Jason's last anguished cry is that no god could now endure Medea's presence.

nullos esse deos is not a characteristic complaint in Greek tragedy, even in Euripides: rather the sufferer asks 'How can the gods allow these things to happen?' Cf., however, trag. adesp. 465.1N τολμῶ κατειπεῖν μήποτ' οὐκ εἰσὶν θεοί, Eur. fr. 292.7N εἰ θεοί τι δρῶσιν αἰσχρόν, οὐκ εἰσὶν θεοί.

On this ending T. S. Eliot remarked: 'In the verbal *coup de théâtre* no one has ever excelled him. The final cry of Jason to Medea departing in her car is unique; I can think of no other play which reserves such a shock for the last word . . .' ('Seneca in Elizabethan Translation' in *Selected Essays*, 1948, 73).

INDEX NOMINUM

Absyrtus, 44–5, 131 ff., 452–3, 473, 893–977 (introd.), 967
Acastus, 133, 257
Accius (*Medea*), 1 (introd.)
Admetus, 662–3
Aeetes, 28 ff., 131 ff.
Aeson, 83, 133
Ajax, 660–1
Alcestis, 662–3
Alcides, 634
Alcman, 56–115 (introd.)
Alpheus, 81
Amalthea, 64 ff., 313
Amazons, 214, 215
Anaxagoras, 792 ff.
Ancaeus (son of Lycurgus), 643–4
Ancaeus (son of Neptune), 618
Apollo, 86 ff., 700
Arabians, 711
Arcturus, 313, 314 ff.
Argo, 3, 238 ff., 335 ff., 349
Argonauts, 233
Aristarchus of Samos, 401
Astraea, 440
Athos, Mt., 720 ff.
Aulis, 622
Ausonium mare, 355 ff.
Ausonius, 56–115 (introd.)

Bacchus, 84, 85, 110
Baetis, 726
Bears (stars), 314 ff., 404, 697
Bellona, 806 ff.
Bentley, 572–4, 897; *see also* 'text'
Black Sea, *see* Pontus
Boötes, 313, 314 ff.
Bothe, 746–7

Calais, 231
Calliope, 625
Calvus, 56–115 (introd.)
Camenae, 625
Cassandra, 660–1
Castor, 88–9
Catullus, 824

Caucasus, 43
Chaos, 9
Charybdis, 408
Chimaera, 828
Claudian, 56–115 (introd.), 113
Colchians, 483
Colchis, 43, 44–5
Columbus, 379
Corinth, 105, 745, 891–2
Corneille, 32 ff., 150 ff., 166, 926 ff.
Creon, 179–300 (introd.), 194, 252 ff.
Creusa, 17, 23 ff., 37–40, 56–115 (introd.), 75, 93–101 (introd.)

Danaids, 744 ff., 748–9
Danuvius, 724
Deianira, 639 ff.
Diana, 86 ff., 700
Dictynna, 795
Diomedes (grammarian), 301
Dionysus, 384
Dis, 638
Draco, 694 ff.

Eliot, T. S., 1027
Enceladus, 410
Ennius (*Medea*), 1 (introd.)
Erasmus, 56–115 (introd.)
Erinyes, 13 ff., 952–3, 967
Eryx, 707
Euripides (*Medea*), 1 (introd.), 56–115 (introd.), 150 ff., 179–300 (introd.), 218 ff., 257, 431–559 (introd.), 438, 466 ff., 490, 538–9, 541 ff., 549 ff., 572–4, 670–739 (introd.), 817, 846–7, 885–6, 924–5, 926 ff., 972
Euxine, *see* Pontus

Fury, Furies, 13 ff., 16 ff., 37–40, 893–977 (introd.), 952–3, 958 ff., 962–3

Geremia da Montagnone, 195
Glauce, 17

Glover, 32 ff.
Gronovius, 23 ff., 517, 572–4, 707, 710–11, 715, 746–7, 952–3; *see also* 'text'

Haemonius, 720 ff.
Haemus, 590
Harpies, 781–2
Hecate, 6–7, 670–739 (introd.), 728 ff. (introd.), 750–1
　Diana aspect, 815
　dogs, 840
　parentage, 814
　variety of names, 740–842 (introd.), 787, 795
Hercules, 634 ff. (introd.), 639 ff. (introd.), 701–2, 783–4
Hercynia silva, 713
Herrmann, 572–4
Herrick, 56–115 (introd.)
Hesperia, 727
Hesperus, 71 ff.
Hister, 724, 763
Hyades, 312
Hydaspes, 725
Hydra, 701–2
Hylas, 634 ff. (introd.), 646 ff.
Hymen(aeus), 1, 56–115 (introd.), 67–70, 69, 70, 110
Hyrcanius, 713

Idmon, 652 ff.
India, 484
Iolcos, 457
Isthmus of Corinth, 35, 36
Ixion, 744 ff.

Jason, 1 (introd.), 7–8, 19 ff., 23 ff., 37–40, 56–115 (introd.), 75, 82–9, 257, 431–559 (introd.), 547, 557 ff., 1003
Jonson, Ben, 56–115 (introd.)
Juno, 1, 21, 59 ff.
Jupiter, 1, 59 ff.

Kids (stars), 313

Leo, 37–40, 99 ff., 123, 194, 306 ff., 433–4, 467–8, 477, 652 ff., 670–739 (introd.), 768, 883–4, 891–2, 1012; *see also* 'text'

Leto, 700, 954 ff.
Libya, 682 ff.
Longepierre, 32 ff.
Lyaeus, 110
Lynceus, 231–3

Malea, 149
Medea, appeal to Hecate, 752 ff.
　argument with Jason, 431–559 (introd.), 530
　banishment, 144 ff., 179–300 (introd.)
　children, 23 ff., 37–40 (introd.), 282 ff., 541 ff.
　conflicting emotions, 926 ff.
　description, 752
　exultation, 982 ff.
　final monologue, 893–977 (introd.)
　incantation, 740–842 (introd.)
　pleading, 501 ff.
　reconciliation, 557 ff.
　revenge, 1 (introd.), 297–8, 549 ff., 924–5
　robe (gift), 579
Medusa, 831 ff.
Meleager, 644–6
Minyae, 233
Mopsus, 652 ff.
Morris, William, 355 ff.
Mulciber, 824–5

Nauplius, 658–9
Neophron (*Medea*), 926 ff.
Neptune, 2, 3, 4–5, 597–8
Nessus, 639 ff.
Niobe, 954 ff.
Nysa, 384

Oertel, Abraham, 379
Oeta, 639
Olenus, 313
Ophiuchus, 698–9
Orpheus, 228–9, 348, 355 ff., 357, 625, 632
Ovid (*Medea*), 1 (introd.), 56–115 (introd.), 123, 179–300 (introd.), 466 ff., 670–739 (introd.), 720 ff., 752 ff., 885–6, 972

Pallas, 2
Pangaeus, Mt., 721

Pax, 62–3, 64 ff., 66
Peleus, 657
Pelias, 133, 201, 257, 664 ff.
Pelorus, 350 ff.
Periclymenus, 635
Perseis, 814
Phaëthon, 32 ff., 599–602, 826–7
Phasis, 44–5, 102 ff., 211 ff.
Pherae, 662–3
Philodemus, 56–115 (introd.)
Phineus, 781–2
Phrixus, 471
Pieria, 357
Pindus, 384
Pirene, 745
Pleiades, 93 ff., 96–8
Plutos, 64 ff.
Pollux, 88–9
Pontus, 43, 44–5, 213
Prometheus, 821 ff.
    blood of, 708–9

Sappho, 56–115 (introd.)
Scylla, 350 ff.
Scythae, 483
Seneca, 382 ff., 484, 726
Sidonius, 56–115 (introd.)
Sirens, 355 ff.
Sisyphus, 105, 744 ff., 746–7

Sparta, 77 ff.
Spenser, 56–115 (introd.), 64 ff.
Statius, 56–115 (introd.)
Studley, 56–115 (introd.), 178, 465,
    634, 740
Stymphalus, 783–4
Suebi, -ae, 713
Symplegades, 341 ff., 610

Tantalus, 744 ff.
Taurus, 682 ff.
Taygetus, 77 ff.
Tempe, 457
Tethys, 377
Thales, 96–8, 697
Thermodon, 215
Thessaly, 335, 670–739 (introd.)
Thule, 379
Ticidas, 56–115 (introd.)
Tiphys, 2, 3, 301 ff., 318 ff., 617
Typhoeus (Typhon), 410, 773–4
Tyre, 99 ff.

Venus, 62–3
Virgil, 351
Vulcanus, 824–5

Wandering Rocks, 341 ff., 610

Zetes, 231

INDEX VERBORUM

admittere, 904
alligare, 96–8
alma, 876
alumna, 158
amores, 867
amputare, 530
anceps, 939 ff.
angulus, 249
animi, 175
Arctica, 314 ff.
Arctous, 683
Argi, 658–9
aries, 471
armiferi, 980
astra, 344
attrectare, 719
audax, 301–79 (introd.)
aurum, 572–4
auspex, 68
auspicatus, 285

barbarus, 127 ff., 612
bene est, 550
bimaris, 35
bubo, 733

candida, 329
cantare, 730
caput, 465
cardo, 177
cessare, 406
cithara, 357
clepere, 156
Colchicus, 225
commodare, 907
complicare, 680
crimen, 236–8
cruenta, 722
cruores, 810
cum, 356
currus, 599–602

dare, 528
dextra, 248
dies, 28 ff.

dirae artes, 576
dominator, 4–5
domus, 766
dubius, 554 ff.

entheus, 382 ff.
et, 134–5, 525
ex(s)-, 49
excidere, 561
excutere, 112
explicare, 678
ex(s)ertare, 687

falx, 722
fausta, 12
favere, 58
fax, 67
faxo, 905
femina, 61
-fer, 685
ferox, 186
ferrum, 728
fetus, 822
fides, 248, 434 ff.
flagitia, 236–8
flos, 226
frenare, 3
fugitiva, 114
functi, 999
funus, 998.

gener, 421
genius, 1
geminus, 641
-ger, 685

habenae, 346–7
haut, 899
hiatus, 352
hoc age, 562

iacere, 802–3
iamdudum, 191
ignis, 591
immane quantum, 671

immanitas, 407
inauditus, 199 ff.
incerta, 964
incessere, 236–8
induere, 43
infaustus, 12
ingenium, 910
ingerere, 132
inhospitalis, 43
innumerare, 636
inquit, 690
iste, 970–1
ite nunc, 650–1
iubere, 189
iuga, 32 ff.

labare, 769
laeva manus, 680
largire, 288
latex, 810
laxare, 420
letifica, 577–8
lina, 320
lorum, 875
lues, 183–4
lustrare, 753
lymphatus, 386

mactare, 644–6
machinatrix, 266
maenas, 382 ff.
mala, 910
Manes, 10, 970–1
marcidus, 69
memoria, 268
-met, 228
metus, 467–8
minuere, 175
mitis, 66
modus, 883–4
moliri, 181
mulcere, 356

navita, 326
nebulosus, 583
ne, 1016 ff.
nec, 592 ff.
nidificus, 714
nitidus, 402
non, 915
noti, 322

novus, 743

oblitterare, 557
obscenus, 732

paelex, 462
parvus, 457
Pelasgus, 127 ff.
Pelia, 201
perdere, 977
peregrinus, 114
perire, 994
perurere, 547
pietas, 438, 545 ff., 943–4
piger, 314 ff., 736
placare, 507
placidus, 985
plaga, 724
praeses, 248
pudor, 236 ff., 236–8

quin, 506
quippe, 256 ff.
quire, 124
quota, 896

ramus, 805
recursare, 385
referre, 152–3
religare, 612
remetiri, 28 ff.
repudium, 52 ff.
roscidus, 101

sacra thalami, 299
sacro . . . sancta, 605
sacrum, 680
sanguis, 775–8
sanies, 732
sceptrifer, 59 ff.
semina flammae, 834
sequi, 404
serere, 26, 281
siccus, 404
silentes, 740
sipara, 328
Sirena, 360
si vivo, 41
soceri, 106
sollemnis, 112
solvere, 114

sonare, 785–6
spatia, 28 ff.
spectare, 894
squamifer, 685
status, 879
strix, 733
suci, 712
supparus, 328

taeda, 67, 581
tardus, 314 ff.
Tartari ripae, 742
tecta, 577–8
tempus erat, 111
tenera, 722
tenere, 550, 840
timere, 887
titubare, 937
tonans, 59 ff.
torpere, 348
tortus, 718
totus, 52

trifida, 687
tueri, 262–3

ultimus, 847–8, 923

ve- (*vae-*), 123
vel, 272 ff.
vertere, 981
victimae, 37–40
virginitas, 984
virgo, 49
vis, 843
viscera, 37–40
vitta, 802–3
vivax, 826–7

ἀδύνατα, 372–4, 401 ff.
ἄξενος, 43
ἔνθεος, 382 ff.
ἐπιθαλάμιον, 56–115 (introd.)
εὔξεινος, 43
νύμφη, 386
ὑμέναιος, 56–115 (introd.)

INDEX RERUM

ablative, extent of time, 291
  instrumental, 35
alliteration, 362
ambiguity, 293, 847–8
anachronism, 109, 113, 364 ff., 489,
  562, 796
anaphora, 71 ff.
anger, 382 ff.
antithesis, 52 ff.
apostrophe, 914
asyndeton, 20 ff., 45 ff., 365, 449 ff.,
  921

Bacchante, 382 ff., 849–78 (introd.)

chariot, 1022 ff.
chiasmus, 722
chorus, 56–115 (introd.), 75 ff., 114,
  301–79 (introd.), 579–669 (introd.),
  656–63, 849–78 (introd.)
colonization, Greek, 369
complaints, characteristic in Greek
  tragedy, 1027
connective particles, 592 ff., 824
contentment of stay-at-home, 333
controversiae, 179–300 (introd.)
cornucopia, 64 ff.

dative, agent, 437
  end of motion, 37–40
dead, shades of, 740 (see also *Manes*)
dittography, 306 ff.
dogs (of Hecate), 840
dowry, 489
dye, 99 ff.

emotion, Seneca's ideas on, 907
epigram, 163
epithalamium, 56–115 (introd.), 67–
  70, 71 ff., 75 ff., 107 ff.

Fescenninus, Fescennina iocatio, 56–115
  (introd.), 107 ff., 113
Fortune, 220
  in Stoic doctrine, 176

genitive, quality, 20 ff.
  predicative, 137–8
German tribes, 713
Golden Age, 329 ff.
Golden Fleece, 485
Greek word-form, 35, 44–5, 201, 360,
  410

hymn, 71 ff.
hypallage, 230, 607

imperative, 'middle', 51, 507
  with *ne*, 1016 ff.
impersonal, 460 ff., 887
inverse *cum* clause, 356

knees, touched in supplication, 247

laments, 451 ff.

magic, *see* witchcraft
messenger, function of, 879–92 (introd.)
metre:
  anapaests, 1 (introd.), 740–842
    (introd.); anapaestic dimeters,
    301–79 (introd.); third-foot
    anapaest, 911–12; fifth-foot
    anapaest, 126
  consonantal *i*, 491
  contraction, 248, 481, 743, 1015
  dactylic hexameters, 56–115 (in-
    trod.), 110–15 (introd.), 113;
    dactylic fifth foot, 266
  glyconic, 56–115 (introd.)
  iambics, 1 (introd.), 740–842 (in-
    trod.); iambic dimeters, 849–78
    (introd.); iambic trimeter and
    dimeter couplets, 740–842 (in-
    trod.); fifth-foot iambic, 512,
    708–9
  minor asclepiad, 56–115 (introd.)
  proceleusmatic, 488, 670
  proceleusmatic final word, 266
  sapphic, 579–669 (introd.), 636,
    656–63 (introd.)

metre (*cont.*):
  shortening of final *o*, 350, 518
  synaphea, 301–79 (introd.)
  tribrach, 52 ff., 200, 447, 450
  trochaic tetrameter, 740–842 (introd.)
moon, 96–8, 788 ff.
  eclipse, 792 ff.

nature, laws of, 401 ff.
navigation, invention of, 301–79 (introd.), 579–669 (introd.)
nurse, 116–78 (introd.), 150 ff.

owl, 733
oxymoron, 261, 333

palace, burning of, 149, 885–6
papyri (magic), 670–739 (introd.)
parodos, 56–115 (introd.)
participle, 'middle', 351
perfect, 'gnomic', 152–3
polyptoton, 233, 943–4
prayers, word-order of, 285 ff.
pronuba, *-ae*, 16 ff., 37–40, 56–115 (introd.)
prophetic presents, 622, 644–6
proverb, 159, 195, 882

recitation of tragedies, 382 ff.
repetition of words, 644–6, 646 ff., 911 ff.
rhetoric, 1 (introd.), 19 ff., 41, 52 ff., 127 ff., 137 ff., 150 ff., 157, 159, 179–300 (introd.), 218 ff., 236 ff., 301–79 (introd.), 341 ff., 372–4
rhetorical question, 452–3
rivers, 80 ff., 81, 372–4

sacrifice, 59 ff.
sail, 320 ff.
Saturnalia, 109
self-apostrophe, 41, 895
sententia, 426–8, 433–4
simile, 939 ff.
sinners, lists of, 744 ff.

soliloquy, 1 (introd.)
stichomythia, 290 ff.
Stoic hero, 634 ff.
Stoic primitivism, 301–79 (introd.)
Stoic *rex*, 520
subjunctive, conditional, 434 ff.
  paratactic, 905
  potential, 356
  repudiating, 398–9
sun, 4–5, 28 ff.
symmetry, 503

three, ritual number, 771–2
text, 2, 19 ff., 22–3, 35, 99 ff., 136, 142, 171, 194, 226, 230, 249, 267, 306 ff., 314 ff., 344, 366–7, 389, 459–60, 467–8, 477, 485, 512, 513, 516, 517, 570, 577–8, 605, 652 ff., 656–63, 680, 710–11, 713, 715, 718, 742, 746–7, 766, 841–2, 883–4, 891–2, 897, 921, 947 ff., 952–3, 980, 987, 1012, 1026
torches, 27, 37–40, 56–115 (introd.), 67
topsail, 327–8
tripod, 86 ff.

universe, divided by lot, 597–8
  views of, 401

variatio, 267
verse-division, 157, 171
vocative attraction, 605

wedding-procession, 27
wedding-song, 56–115 (introd.)
wife, wronged, 1 (introd.), 579 ff.
witchcraft, 6–7, 577–8, 670–739 (introd.), 674, 728 ff., 750–1, 752, 762, 771–2, 785–6, 787, 792 ff., 800–1, 802–3
word-order, emphatic, 879, 882
  interlocking, 980
word-play, 472–3

zeugma, 278–9